Bridging the Divide

Religious Dialogue and Universal Ethics

Bridging
the
Divide

Religious Dialogue and
Universal Ethics

Papers for The InterAction Council

Foreword by Helmut Schmidt
Edited by Thomas S. Axworthy

School of Policy Studies, Queen's University
McGill-Queen's University Press
Montreal & Kingston · London · Ithaca

SCHOOL OF
Policy Studies

Publications Unit
Policy Studies Building
138 Union Street
Kingston, ON, Canada
K7L 3N6
www.queensu.ca/sps/

Library and Archives Canada Cataloguing in Publication

Bridging the divide : religious dialogue and universal ethics / foreword by Helmut Schmidt ; edited by Thomas S. Axworthy.

Papers for the InterAction Council.
Includes bibliographical references.
ISBN 978-1-55339-220-0 (bound).—ISBN 978-1-55339-219-4 (pbk.)

1. Peace—Religious aspects. 2. Religion and politics. 3. Religion and ethics.
I. Axworthy, Tom, 1947-   II. InterAction Council III. Queen's University. School of Policy Studies

BL65.P4B75 2008   201'.7273   C2008-902707-8

CONTENTS

PART THREE
POLITICS AND RELIGION: SPEAKING TRUTH TO POWER OR POWER TO TRUTH?

PART FOUR
CONCLUSIONS OF THE INTERACTION COUNCIL

ACKNOWLEDGEMENTS

The publication of *Bridging the Divide: Religious Dialogue and Universal Ethics* in The Global Agenda: Papers for the InterAction Council Series, Volume One, was greatly assisted by a grant from the OPEC Fund for International Development. We wish to thank the OPEC Fund for their considerable support.

The School of Policy Studies at Queen's University in Ontario, Canada, also made a generous grant to this project, timely enough so that we were able to commence expeditiously. We wish to thank especially Arthur Sweetman, Executive Director of the School of Policy Studies, for his interest and support.

Most of all we wish to thank the many authors who contributed to the volume by agreeing to publish the papers they had originally presented at various meetings of the InterAction Council. These authors subsequently worked diligently to answer my many questions about the meaning of their texts, or the sources of their quotations. Since English is not the first language of many of the authors, I especially appreciate their good-natured efforts to meet my many editorial demands.

To Helmut Schmidt, Oscar Arias, and Malcolm Fraser, members of the Council who contributed their own essays, we owe a special debt of gratitude. Helmut Schmidt in particular did double duty by also contributing a foreword. Ingvar Carlsson, current co-chair of the Council, not only convened three recent meetings in Jordan, Germany, and Austria, all dedicated to the religious theme, but also actively encouraged the idea of publishing the results of these labours so that a wider audience might benefit from insights hitherto provided only to the Council members themselves.

Mark Howes, Ellen Barton, and Valerie Jarus of the School of Policy Studies' Publications Unit at Queen's University were responsible for the book's design, factual accuracy, and generally excellent copyediting. Julie Burch of the Centre for the Study of Democracy helped to oversee the Centre's involvement in the project.

Keiko Atsumi and the dedicated Secretariat of the Council, which includes my friend Tanya Zaritzky of Canada, organized the expert roundtables and the annual meetings of the Council itself, and it is from this great effort that the intellectual content of the book is drawn. Many papers of equal value could have been included, since the work of the Council on religious matters goes back to 1987. The government of Japan has been a major backer of the InterAction Council since its inception by Takeo Fukuda, and this volume as well as the rest of the planned series will be only a minor down payment on the debt the Council gratefully acknowledges to the people of Japan.

I have been enriched by the meetings of the Council since 1996 when Pierre Trudeau invited me to join the experts' group in Vienna, which was beginning to work on the concept of a Universal Declaration of Human Responsibilities. This invitation resulted in my renewing a relationship with Helmut Schmidt, a special friend of Trudeau's since the 1970s. Helmut Schmidt, former chancellor of Germany, most actively took the lead in committing the Council to doing what it could to prevent a clash between religious civilizations. Anyone who knows him cannot help but be inspired by his intellect, his grasp of history, and his continuing desire to make a better world.

Malcolm Fraser, former prime minister of Australia, was co-chair of the Council for most of the sessions I have attended. His great knowledge of law, his commitment to humanitarian organizations such as CARE, and his honesty in demanding better of the Australian government, headed by his own party, are living examples of how one should speak truth to power. Through the Council, too, I met Hans Küng, one of the great theologians and ethical leaders of our time. Nothing has stimulated me more intellectually than working with Hans Küng on the Universal Declaration of Human Responsibilities.

As in so many aspects of my career, I also owe a deep debt to Pierre Trudeau. He first invited me to contribute to the work of the Council and, interestingly, the "father" of the Canadian Charter of Human Rights and Freedoms was inspired at this late stage in his career by the concept of human responsibility. Through Trudeau, I came to know the work of the InterAction Council, and this has been one of the most rewarding experiences of my academic life. Because of my debt to him, and due to his long involvement with the InterAction Council, this volume is dedicated to his memory.

Thomas S. Axworthy
Chair, Centre for the Study of Democracy
Queen's University

FOREWORD

Twenty-six years ago, the InterAction Council held its first meeting: the former Japanese prime minister Takeo Fukuda conceived of the idea of a council of former leaders to make a continuing contribution to analyses of world problems. He described the twentieth century as "the century of glory and remorse." I was glad to join him in his initiative, and since that time the InterAction Council has commissioned papers from world experts in law, ethics, energy, international finance, defence, and foreign policy. From these commissions, our Council has undertaken active exchanges and dialogues with the authors of the papers. On an annual basis, therefore, the InterAction Council has united thinkers with practitioners, resulting in a number of published policy communiqués.

I am delighted that the Council has decided to publish highlights and excerpts from this body of work in a multivolume series that will place, before a wider audience, the Council's deliberations in many policy fields. Prime Minister Fukuda always stressed the importance of "heart-to-heart communication," and through this series, the Council will continue to work toward his goal of making "contributions to threatening problems."

Bridging the Divide: Religious Dialogue and Universal Ethics, the first volume in this series, addresses one of the most important themes that the Council has taken up: the role of religions in our world, and the necessity of universal ethical standards. In my essay "On a Politician's Ethics" in this volume, I recount how a devout Muslim, Anwar Al Sadat, first inspired me to consider the moral laws common to the great religions. My friend Al Sadat was killed because he obeyed "the law of peace."

Takeo Fukuda was also seized with the potential unity that religions could achieve through dialogue and the equally large potential for extremism and division that faith sometimes spawns. Together, in 1987, we convened a meeting in

Rome between religious leaders and members of the Council that identified the ethical standards shared by all major religions. At the time, religion was regarded as a non-factor in world politics. We Europeans certainly knew the historical impact that religion has had on politics—the Thirty Years' War in the seventeenth century between Roman Catholics and Protestants devastated Germany for generations. But in the 1980s, our secular age was prone to forget the lessons of history. A decade later, al-Qaida burst into our consciousness, and the terrible events of September 11 certainly reminded us that a clash of religious civilizations could be more real and more visceral in impact than any academic theory.

Fukuda's concept was that within the luxury of contemplation afforded by time, a group of former leaders would be free to reflect on their experience, and they would be able to look beyond the immediacy of current issues to focus on the long-term structural factors driving the global agenda. This expectation was certainly realized when the Council, in its early years, began to examine the religious schisms that, in a decade's time, would preoccupy decision makers and theologians alike.

In 1996–97, the Council built on the earlier work of the Rome Statement by codifying the assumption of a common ethical base in a Universal Declaration of Human Responsibilities. Here, the driving force was Hans Küng, already renowned as a theologian and initiator of the Global Ethics Project. Two of Küng's papers for the Council are contained in the volume, and the communiqués from the 1996– 97 meetings, which include the Universal Declaration, are reproduced in Part Four.

President of Costa Rica Oscar Arias declared in a 1997 essay published in this volume that "it is time to talk about human obligations." Prime Minister Malcolm Fraser of Australia, for many years the chair of the Council, took up Arias's challenge and convened several meetings of the Council that focused on responsibilities—our obligations under international law, our duties toward the deprived, and our obligations not to forget justice as we confront terror. His essay "Human Rights and Human Responsibilities in the Age of Terrorism," contained in this volume, is only one of Malcolm Fraser's many contributions on this theme.

In 2006 in Amman, Jordan, the Council examined the complicated relations between the Islamic world and the West. Last year, to mark the twenty-fifth anniversary of the Council, former prime minister of Sweden Ingvar Carlsson convened an expert group meeting in Tübingen, Germany, on how to restore world religions as a force for peace, justice, and ethics. The Council as a whole took up this challenge at the annual meeting in Vienna, Austria, in May 2007. Several papers from these three recent sessions are contained in this volume. Whatever the authors' faith, as Part One demonstrates, they all agree that religion plays a powerful role in the identity of the individual. Religious decisions involve every dimension of human experience: personal ethics, values, faith, and fundamental beliefs. Religious leaders must protect the integrity of their religion's core values and combat religious extremism and the politicians who encourage it.

But we make a mistake by looking only at the potential of religions to divide. Part Two of the volume, on the application of religiously based ethics, shows that religious leaders have a significant role to play in harnessing the power of people to face global problems. One does not have to be religious to be ethical, yet, as this volume argues, ethical standards are largely derived from our religious traditions.

In Part Three, Oscar Arias, Malcolm Fraser, and myself, as members of the Council, write about how ethics informed our past actions and how ethics should inform and inspire today's generation of leaders. For me, the final authority remains my own conscience. Immanuel Kant described the conscience as "the awareness of an inner court of justice in man." Whether a person is a Christian, a Muslim, a Jew, a Buddhist, an agnostic, or a free thinker, every human being has a conscience. Whether we follow or ignore our conscience is the question that we each face every day of our lives. This volume may help us make the right decision.

Helmut E. Schmidt
Former Chancellor of the Federal Republic of Germany

CONTRIBUTORS

KAMAL ABOULMAGD, Professor of Law, Cairo University, Vice President of the National Council for Human Rights, Egypt

THOMAS S. AXWORTHY, Chair, Centre for the Study of Democracy, Queen's University, Kingston, Ontario, Canada and associate member of the InterAction Council

METTANANDO BHIKKHU, Special Advisor on Buddhist Affairs to the Secretary-General, World Conference of Religions for Peace (WCRP), Thailand, and WCRP representative to the United Nations Economic and Social Commission for Asia and the Pacific

MALCOLM FRASER, Former Prime Minister of Australia

ACHARYA SHRIVATSA GOSWAMI, Acharya at Sri Radharamana Mandir and Director, Sri Caitanya Prema Samsthana, Vrindavan, India

DAMIANOS HEGUMEN, Archbishop of Sinai, Saint Catherine's Monastery

HANS KÜNG, President, Global Ethic Foundation and Professor Emeritus, Tübingen University, Germany

JONATHAN MAGONET, Rabbi and Professor, Leo Baeck College, United Kingdom

KOSHIN OHTANI, former president of Japan Buddhist Federation, and leader of Jodo Shinshu Buddhists in Japan

OSCAR ARIAS SANCHEZ, President of Costa Rica

STEPHAN SCHLENSOG, Secretary-General, Global Ethic Foundation, Tübingen, Germany

HELMUT SCHMIDT, Former Chancellor of Germany

ABODOLKARIM SOROUSH, Senior Research Fellow, International Institute for the Study of Islam in the Modern World, The Netherlands, and Academy of Philosophy, Iran

SEIKEN SUGIURA, Member, House of Representatives, Former Minister of Justice, Japan

TU WEIMING, The Harvard-Yenching Professor of Chinese History and Philosophy and of Confucian Studies, Harvard University, and Dean and Chair Professor of the Institute for Advanced Humanistic Studies, Peking University, USA/China

OSAMU YOSHIDA, Toyo University, Japan

Part One

THE WORLD'S RELIGIONS: UNITY IN DIVERSITY?

There is no "one" Christianity, "one" Islam, "one" Buddhism or Hinduism. Each major religion has a diversity of schools within, even as each major religion differs in conceptions of the divine. This diversity within religions is reflected in this volume: Abodolkarim Soroush and Kamal Aboulmagd, for example, explain the Shia and Sunni traditions of Islam. But the concentration of the various essays is directed toward an appreciation of the commonalities among religions. Hans Küng makes the point that the three monotheistic or Abrahamic religions, usually seen as being in opposition to each other, are, in fact, in *relationship* to one another. "In all religious, philosophical, and ideological traditions," he states, "there are some simple ethical imperatives" of humanity. He identifies two fundamental principles. First of all there is the Golden Rule, formulated by Confucius centuries before Christ and known in all the great traditions: "What you do not wish done to yourself, do not do to others." The second core principle, which builds on the Golden Rule, is the imperative of humanity: "Every human being, whether young or old, man or woman . . . Christian, Jew, or Muslim, should be treated humanely." Based on this common ethical premise, which is reflected in each of the ten papers on differing religious traditions, the authors approach this interfaith dialogue as an opportunity to learn as well as to teach. As TU Weiming observes, dialogue "is neither a tactic of persuasion nor a strategy of conversion, but a way of generating mutual understanding" through shared common values. If there is one dominant conclusion in this section of the book, it is that knowledge about others' religions and cultures must be encouraged and broad, sweeping generalizations discouraged.

THE THREE ABRAHAMIC RELIGIONS: HISTORICAL UPHEAVALS, PRESENT CHALLENGES

Hans Küng

INTRODUCTION

We face the threat of a *general suspicion*—this time not of Jews but of Muslims. It is as if they were all incited up by their religion and were all potentially violent. Conversely, all Christians are taught by their religion to be non-violent, peaceful, and loving—that would be a fine thing!

Of course there are many problems, especially in Europe with its big Muslim minorities, but let's be fair: We citizens of a democratic constitutional state in the name of human dignity reject forced marriages, the oppression of women, honour killings, and other archaic inhumanities—and most Muslims join us in doing so. They suffer from the fact that sweeping condemnations are made of Muslims and Islam, without differentiation. They do not recognize themselves in our picture of Islam, because they want to be loyal citizens of the Islamic religion.

Let's be fair: Those who make Islam responsible for kidnappings, suicide attacks, car bombings, and beheadings carried out by a few blind extremists ought at the same time to condemn Christianity and Judaism for the barbarous maltreatment of prisoners, the air strikes and tank attacks (tens of thousands of civilians have been murdered in Iraq alone) carried out by the US Army, and for the terrorism of the Israeli army occupation in Palestine. After five years of war, those who

This paper was presented at the InterAction Council High-Level Expert Group Meeting on "World Religions as a Factor in World Politics," held May 7–8, 2007, in Tübingen, Germany.

Bridging the Divide: Religious Dialogue and Universal Ethics, ed. T.S. Axworthy. Montreal and Kingston: McGill-Queen's University Press, Queen's Policy Studies Series.

pretend that the battle for oil and hegemony in the Middle East and elsewhere is a "battle for democracy" and a "war against terror" are trying to deceive the world—without success. And the majority of Americans realize that.

In the third Global Ethic Lecture in Tübingen in 2003, the UN Secretary-General Kofi Annan emphasized, "No religion or ethical system should ever be condemned because of the moral lapses of some of its adherents. If I, as a Christian, for instance, do not wish my faith to be judged by the actions of the Crusaders or the Inquisition, I should be very careful to judge anyone else's faith by the actions that a few terrorists may commit in its name."

So I am asking you: Should we go on with a tit-for-tat reckoning that leads only deeper into misery? No, another basic attitude toward violence and war is called for. And people everywhere want it, unless—in the Arab countries and sometimes also in the United States—they are being led astray by power-obsessed and blind governments and their minds are being dulled by ideologues and demagogues in the media.

Violence has been practised in the sign of the crescent, but also in the sign of the cross. Medieval and contemporary crusaders have perverted the sign of reconciliation, the cross, into a sign of war against Muslims and Jews (Spain). Both Christianity and Islam have expanded their spheres of influence aggressively throughout history and have defended their power with violence. In their respective spheres they have propagated an ideology not of peace, but of war. So the problem is a complicated one.

We are all in danger of being inundated by gigantic floods of information and thus losing our bearings. And one can sometimes hear even scholars of religion expressing the opinion that in their own discipline it is hardly possible to see the forest for the trees. So some of them—for example, in the sociology of religion—concentrate on microstudies and are no longer prepared to think in wider contexts, or they are no longer capable of it. Here, I believe, new categories are necessary to embrace the changes.

So I shall attempt to offer you a certain basic orientation of the three Abrahamic religions: Judaism, Christianity, and Islam. To get straight to the point: I want to address three complexes of questions: The Abiding Centre and Foundation – what must unconditionally be preserved; Epoch-Making Upheavals – what can change; and Present-Day Challenges – the tasks that press in on us.

THE ABIDING CENTRE AND FOUNDATION

This is a very practical question: What should be preserved, what should be unconditionally preserved, in each of our religions? In all three prophetic religions there are extreme positions. Some say "Nothing, just this, should be preserved," while others say "Everything, really everything, should be preserved."

Completely secularized Christians say that *nothing* should be preserved. They often do not believe either in God or in a Son of God, and they may be agnostics or atheists. They ignore the church and dispense with preaching and sacraments. At best they treasure the cultural heritage of Christianity: the European cathedrals and Johann Sebastian Bach, the aesthetics of the Orthodox liturgy and also, paradoxically, the Pope—the pope as a pillar of the established order, though of course they reject his sexual morality and authoritarianism.

Completely secularized Jews also say that nothing should be preserved. They think nothing of the God of Abraham and the patriarchs; they do not believe in God's promises; they ignore synagogue prayers and rites; and they ridicule the ultra-Orthodox. Many secular Jews have found a modern substitution for a Judaism evacuated of religion: the State of Israel and an appeal to the Holocaust. This substitute religion creates a Jewish identity and solidarity for secularized Jews, but at the same time it seems to justify state terrorism against Arabs, which is contemptuous of human rights.

And completely secularized Muslims say that nothing should be preserved. They do not believe in one God; they do not read the Qur'an; Muhammad is not a prophet for them; they roundly reject the Sharia; and the five pillars of Islam play no role for them. At best, Islam—emptied, of course, of its religious content—is to be used as an instrument for political Islamism, Arabism, and nationalism.

You certainly understand now that as a counter-reaction to "preserve nothing," the opposite cry can be heard: "Preserve everything." *Everything* is to remain as it is and allegedly always was.

Not a stone of the great edifice of Catholic dogma may be torn down; the whole structure would totter, trumpet Roman integralists (and traditionalists).

Not a word of the Halacha may be neglected; the will of the Lord (Adonai) stands behind every word, protest ultra-Orthodox Jews.

Not a word of the Qur'an may be ignored; each syllable is the word of God, insist many Islamist Muslims.

You see: here conflicts are preprogrammed everywhere, not just *between* the three religions but, above all, *within* them, wherever these positions are advocated militantly or aggressively. Often the extreme positions goad each other on.

To be sure, the reality is not quite so gloomy. For in most countries, unless they are loaded with political, economic, and social problems, the extreme positions do not form the majority. There are always a considerable number of Jews, Christians, and Muslims—of different magnitudes of course depending on the country and the time—who though perhaps indifferent, lazy, or ignorant in their religion, by no means want to give up everything in their faith and life. Nor are they prepared to keep everything: Many Catholics do not swallow all the dogmas and moral teachings of Rome and many Protestants do not take every statement in the Bible literally; many Jews do not observe the Halacha in all things; and many Muslims do not strictly observe all the commandments of the Sharia.

Be that as it may, if we focus not on later historical forms and manifestations but on the foundation documents, the original testimonies—I mean the holy scriptures of each religion—if we look at the Hebrew Bible, the New Testament, and the Qur'an, there can be no doubt that what must *abide* in each religion is not simply identical with what *exists* at any given time, and that what makes up the nucleus, the substance, the essence of this religion can be defined by its holy scriptures. So the question here is quite a practical one: What should be the abidingly valid and constantly binding element in each of our own religions? It should be clear that not everything need be preserved, but what must be preserved is the *substance of faith*, the centre and foundation of the religion concerned, its holy scripture—its faith! John XXIII formulated this question in his famous opening speech to the Second Vatican Council, in which I participated as theological adviser, together with my dear colleague Joseph Ratzinger, now Pope Benedict XVI, as the two teenage theologians! But you may ask me some more concrete questions, and I give you very brief and basic answers.

1. You may ask me: What must be preserved in Christianity if it is not to lose its soul? My answer: No matter what historical, literary, or sociological Biblical criticism may analyze, interpret, or reduce, in light of the Christian foundation documents of faith that have become normative and influential in history, in light of the New Testament (seen in the context of the Hebrew Bible), the central content of faith is Jesus Christ, as the Messiah and Son of the one God of Abraham who is also at work today through the same Spirit of God. There can be no Christian faith, no Christian religion, without the confession that *Jesus is the Messiah, the Lord, the Son of God!* The name Jesus Christ denotes the dynamic centre of the New Testament (which is by no means to be understood in a static way).

2. And you ask me, What must be preserved in Judaism if it is not to lose its essence? My answer: No matter what historical, literary, or sociological criticism may analyze, interpret, or reduce, in light of the foundation documents of faith that have become normative and historically influential, in light of the Hebrew Bible,

the central content of faith is the one God and the one people of Israel. There can be no Israelite faith, no Hebrew Bible, no Jewish religion without the confession: *Yahweh (Adonai) is the God of Israel, and Israel is his people!*

3. Finally, you ask me, What must be preserved in Islam if it is still to remain Islam in the literal sense of "submission to God"?

My answer: No matter how wearisome was the process of collecting, ordering, and editing the different *surahs* (chapters) of the Qur'an, for all believing Muslims it is clear that the Qur'an is God's word and book. And even if Muslims see a difference between the Mecca *surahs* and those of Medina and take the background of the revelations into account for interpretation, the central message of the Qur'an is completely clear: *There is no God but God, and Muhammad is his Prophet.*

It is the special relationship of the people of Israel to their God that is the essence of Judaism. It is the special relationship of Jesus Christ to his God and Father that is the starting point of Christianity. And it is the special relationship of the Qur'an to God that is the nucleus of Islam, which constitutes it and around which it crystallizes. And despite the goings back and forth in the history of the Islamic people, this will remain the basic notion of the Islamic religion that will never be given up.

The distinctive feature of the three monotheistic religions that is to be preserved is something that they have in common and at the same time something that distinguishes them (see Figure 1). What do Judaism, Christianity, and Islam have in common? Faith in the one and only God of Abraham, the gracious and merciful Creator, Preserver, and Judge of all human beings; a view of world history and individual life that is not cyclical but oriented toward an end; the importance of prophetic figures; a normative scripture; and common ethical standards. And what distinguishes them?

For Judaism – Israel as God's people and land (essential for Israel).

For Christianity – Jesus Christ as God's Messiah and Son.

For Islam – the Qur'an as God's word and book.

The constant centre of the three religions is grounded in

- *originality* from earliest times,
- *continuity* through the centuries, and
- *identity* despite differences in languages, peoples, cultures, and nations.

However, this centre, this foundation, this substance of faith has never existed in abstract isolation, but in history: it has time and again been reinterpreted and realized in practice in the changing demands of time. Toynbee: challenge and

FIGURE 1. The Distinctive Features of the Three Monotheistic Religions

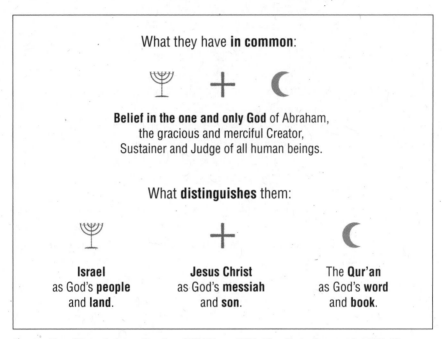

What they have **in common**:

Belief in the one and only God of Abraham,
the gracious and merciful Creator,
Sustainer and Judge of all human beings.

What **distinguishes** them:

Israel	**Jesus Christ**	The **Qur'an**
as God's **people**	as God's **messiah**	as God's **word**
and **land**.	and **son**.	and **book**.

Source: Hans Küng, *Judaism* (London: SCM Press, 1992; New York: Crossroad, 1992); Hans Küng, *Christianity: Essence, History, and Future* (London: SCM Press, 1995; New York: Continuum, 1995); and Hans Küng, *Islam: Past, Present and Future* (London: Oneworld Publications, 2007; Cairo: American University in Cairo Press, 2007).

response! For theologians, historians, and others it is important to combine a systematic-theological approach with a historical-chronological description, without which the former cannot be given a convincing foundation.

EPOCH-MAKING UPHEAVALS

Again and again new epoch-making constellations of the time—in society generally and in the faith community (in the proclamation of the faith and reflection on the faith)—have come up in the history of the three religions that have reinterpreted and concretized this one and the same centre. In Judaism, Christianity, and Islam this history is extraordinarily dramatic: In response to ever new and greater challenges in world history, the community of faith, small at first but then—particularly in the case of Christianity and Islam—growing quickly, has undergone a whole series of religious changes, indeed, in the longer term *revolutionary paradigm shifts*. This concept I learned from a historian of sciences, Thomas S. Kuhn, who in 1962 published *The Structure of Scientific Revolutions*. What changed in the Copernican revolution? The sun, the moon, and the stars remained the same, but *we* changed: our way of seeing, our world view, our paradigm—the entire constellation of beliefs, values, techniques, and so on shared by a given community changed. I apply the paradigm theory to the history first of the church then of Judaism and Islam. What changed, for example, in the Protestant Reformation? God, Christ, and the Spirit for Christians remained the same, but the view of believers changed: the paradigm, the models, changed.

The historical analysis of the paradigms of a religion, those macroparadigms or epoch-making overall constellations, serves to orient knowledge. Paradigm analysis makes it possible to work out the great historical structures and transformations by concentrating on both the fundamental *constants* and the decisive *variables* at the same time. In this way, it is possible to describe those breaks in world history and the epoch-making basic models of a particular religion that emerged from them.

So against the background of such a considerable history, a historical-systematic analysis of the epoch-making overall constellations of each of these religions must be attempted. In my book *Christianity: Essence, History, and Future* (1995), I worked out the macroparadigms in the history of the Christian faith (see Figure 2):

    I: the Jewish apocalyptic paradigm of earliest Christianity;
    II: the ecumenical Hellenistic paradigm of Christian antiquity;
    III: the medieval Roman Catholic paradigm;
    IV: the Protestant paradigm of the Reformation;
    V: the paradigm of modernity oriented on reason and progress; and
    VI: the ecumenical paradigm of postmodernity(?).

First insight: No religion appears as a static entity in which allegedly everything always was as it is now. Rather, every religion appears as a living and developing reality that has undergone different epoch-making overall constellations. Here a first decisive insight is that in religions, older paradigms can last down to the present, as shown by the vertical lines in Figure 2. In contrast, in the natural sciences older paradigms (for example, that of Ptolemy) can be empirically verified or falsified with the help of mathematics and experiment: decisions in favour of the new paradigm (that of Copernicus) can in the longer term be compelled by evidence. But you see in the sphere of religion (and art), things are different: in questions of faith, morals, and rites (for example, between Rome and the Eastern Church or between Rome and Luther) nothing can be decided by mathematics or experiment. And so in the religions old paradigms by no means necessarily

FIGURE 2. Paradigms Shifts in Christianity

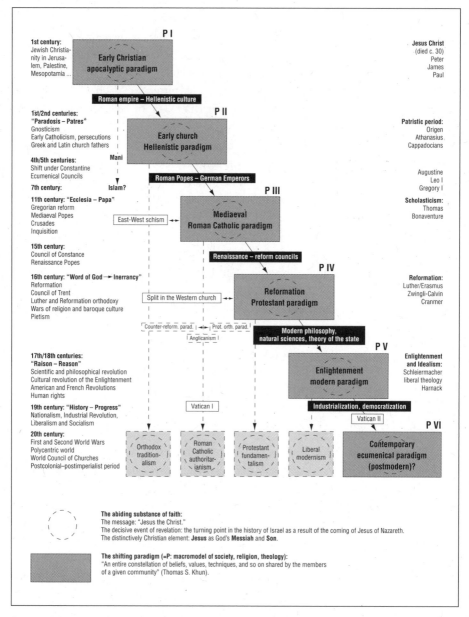

Source: Hans Küng, *Christianity: Essence, History, and Future* (London: SCM Press, 1995; New York: Continuum, 1995).

disappear. Rather, they can *continue to exist* for centuries alongside new paradigms: the new (the Reformation and modernity) alongside the old (the early church and the Middle Ages).

Second insight: The persistence and rivalry of different paradigms is of utmost importance in assessing the situation of religions. This is a second important insight. Why? Because in the present day, people of the same religion live in different paradigms. Their faith is shaped by particular historical conditions that for them are basic and ongoing. Thus, there are still Catholics today who are living spiritually in the thirteenth century (contemporaneously with Thomas Aquinas, the medieval popes, and an absolutist church order). There are some representatives of Eastern Orthodoxy who have remained spiritually in the fourth and fifth centuries (contemporaneously with the Greek church fathers). And for some Protestants, the pre-Copernican constellation of the sixteenth century (with the Reformers before Copernicus, before Darwin) is still normative.

Likewise, I worked out the macroparadigms in the history of Judaism (see Figure 3):

    I: the tribal paradigm before the formation of the state;
   II: the paradigm of the kingdom – the monarchical period;
  III: the paradigm of theocracy – postexilic Judaism;
  IV: the medieval paradigm – the rabbis and the synagogue;
   V: the modern paradigm – assimilation; and
  VI: the ecumenical paradigm of postmodernity(?).

The persistence of different paradigms is confirmed when we look at Judaism and Islam. For example, some ultra-Orthodox Jews see their ideal in medieval Judaism and reject the modern state of Israel. Conversely, many Zionists strive for a state that encompasses the frontiers of the empire of David and Solomon, even though that empire lasted only a few decades. Similarly, some Arabs still dream of the great Arab empire and long for the union of the Arab peoples in a single nation (Pan-Arabism). Others prefer to see what binds the peoples together not in Arabism but in Islam (Pan-Islamism).

In my book *Islam: Past, Present and Future* (2007), I describe the macroparadigms in the history of the Muslim faith (see Figure 4):

    I: the paradigm of the original Islamic community;
   II: the paradigm of the Arab empire;
  III: the classic paradigm of Islam as a world religion;

FIGURE 3. Paradigm Shifts in Judaism

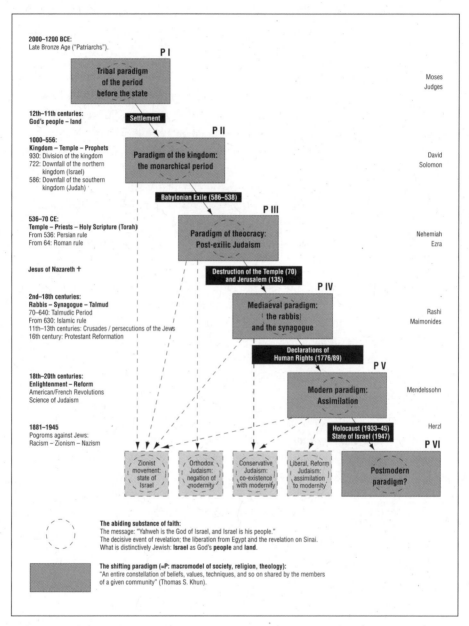

The following text appears within the figure:

2000–1200 BCE:
Late Bronze Age ("Patriarchs").

P I
Tribal paradigm
of the period
before the state

Moses
Judges

12th–11th centuries:
God's people – land

Settlement

1000–556:
Kingdom – Temple – Prophets
930: Division of the kingdom
722: Downfall of the northern
kingdom (Israel)
586: Downfall of the southern
kingdom (Judah)

P II
Paradigm of the kingdom:
the monarchical period

David
Solomon

Babylonian Exile (586–538)

536–70 CE:
Temple – Priests – Holy Scripture (Torah)
From 536: Persian rule
From 64: Roman rule

P III
Paradigm of theocracy:
Post-exilic Judaism

Nehemiah
Ezra

Jesus of Nazareth +

Destruction of the Temple (70)
and Jerusalem (135)

2nd–18th centuries:
Rabbis – Synagogue – Talmud
70–640: Talmudic Period
From 630: Islamic rule
11th–13th centuries: Crusades / persecutions of the Jews
16th century: Protestant Reformation

P IV
Mediaeval paradigm:
the rabbis
and the synagogue

Rashi
Maimonides

Declarations of
Human Rights (1776/89)

P V

18th–20th centuries:
Enlightenment – Reform
American/French Revolutions
Science of Judaism

Modern paradigm:
Assimilation

Mendelssohn

1881–1945
Pogroms against Jews:
Racism – Zionism – Nazism

Holocaust (1933–45)
State of Israel (1947)

Herzl

P VI

Zionist
movement:
state of
Israel

Orthodox
Judaism:
negation of
modernity

Conservative
Judaism:
co-existence
with modernity

Liberal, Reform
Judaism:
assimilation
to modernity

Postmodern
paradigm?

The abiding substance of faith:
The message: "Yahweh is the God of Israel, and Israel is his people."
The decisive event of revelation: the liberation from Egypt and the revelation on Sinai.
What is distinctively Jewish: **Israel** as God's **people** and **land**.

The shifting paradigm (=P: macromodel of society, religion, theology):
"An entire constellation of beliefs, values, techniques, and so on shared by the members
of a given community" (Thomas S. Khun).

Source: Hans Küng, *Judaism* (London: SCM Press, 1992; New York: Crossroad, 1992).

FIGURE 4. Paradigm Shifts in Islam

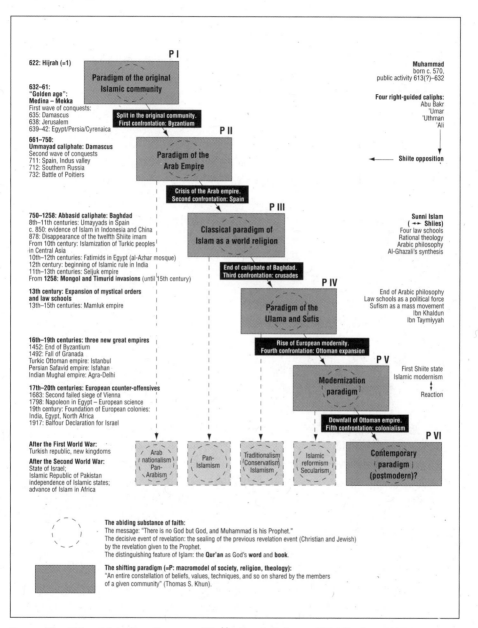

Source: Hans Küng, *Islam: Past, Present and Future* (London: Oneworld Publications, 2007; Cairo: American University in Cairo Press, 2007).

IV: the paradigm of the *ulama* and Sufis;

V: the Islamic paradigm of modernization; and

VI: the ecumenical paradigm of postmodernity(?).

Third insight: It is precisely this lasting quality, this persistence and rivalry of former religious paradigms today, that is one of the main causes of conflicts within the religions and between the religions—the main cause of the different trends and parties, the tensions, disputes, and wars. The third important insight that emerges is that for Judaism, Christianity, and Islam the central question proves to be this: How does this religion react to its own Middle Ages (seen at least in Christianity and Islam the "great time"), and how does it react to modernity, where one sees all three religions forced onto the defensive? After the Reformation, Christianity had to undergo another paradigm shift, that of the Enlightenment. Judaism experienced the Enlightenment first, after Napoleon and the French Revolution and, as a consequence, at least in Reform Judaism, it also experienced a religious reformation. Islam, however, has not undergone any religious reformation and so to the present day has quite special problems with modernity and its core components: freedom of conscience and religion, human rights, tolerance, and democracy.

PRESENT-DAY CHALLENGES

You may have experienced this yourselves: Many Jews, Christians, and Muslims who affirm the modern paradigm get along better with one another than with fellow believers who live in other paradigms. Similarly, a Roman Catholicism imprisoned in the Middle Ages can ally itself better, in questions of sexual morality for example, with the medieval element in Islam and in Judaism (as at the UN population conference in Cairo in 1994).

Fourth insight: Those who want reconciliation and peace will not be able to avoid a critical and self-critical paradigm analysis. Only thus is it possible to answer questions like these: Where in the history of Christianity (and of course in the history of the other religions) are the constants and where the variables, where is continuity and where discontinuity, where is agreement and where resistance? What must be preserved above all is the essence, the foundation, the nucleus of a religion—the constants given by its origin. Belief in the Christian spirit is constant; the law of celibacy is variable. What needs to be preserved is everything that is essential in light of the beginning: the kernel but not the shell, the foundation but not the structure. All the different variables can be given up (or developed) if that proves necessary.

Thus in the face of all the religious confusion, particularly in the age of globalization, a paradigm analysis helps guide us toward a global orientation. Beyond question, we find ourselves in a tricky closing phase in the reshaping of international relations, in the relationship between the West and Islam, and also in the relationships between the three Abrahamic religions—Judaism, Christianity, and Islam. The options have become clear: either we choose rivalry of religions, clash of civilizations, war of the nations—*or dialogue of civilizations and peace between nations as a presupposition for achieving peace between nations*. In the face of the deadly threat to all humankind, instead of building new dams of hatred, revenge, and enmity, we should be tearing down the walls of prejudice stone by stone and thus building bridges of dialogue, particularly toward Islam.

THE THREE RELIGIONS CONTRIBUTE TO A GLOBAL ETHIC

It is vitally important for this bridge-building that different though the three religions are, and different again the various paradigms that have shifted over the centuries, at the ethical level there are constants that make such bridge-building possible.

We as human beings evolved from the animal kingdom, and thus we had to learn to behave humanely and not inhumanely. But despite the use reason, which we have developed, because of innate drives the beast in us has remained a reality. And so time and again human beings have had to strive to be humane and not inhumane. Thus in all religious, philosophical, and ideological traditions there are some simple ethical imperatives that remain of the utmost importance to the present day:

- You shall not kill—or torture, injure, rape. Or in positive terms: Have respect for life. This is a commitment to a culture of *non-violence* and *respect for life*.
- You shall not steal—or exploit, bribe, corrupt. Or in positive terms: Deal honestly and fairly. This is a commitment to a culture of *solidarity* and a *just economic order*.
- You shall not lie—or deceive, forge, manipulate. Or in positive terms: Speak and act truthfully. This is a commitment to a culture of *tolerance* and a life of *truthfulness*.
- You shall not commit sexual immorality—or humiliate, abuse, or devalue your partner. Or in positive terms: Respect and love one another. This is a commitment to a culture of *equal rights* and *partnership between men and women*.

These four ethical imperatives, which are found in the writings of Patanjali, the founder of Yoga, as in the Buddhist canon, the Hebrew Bible, the New Testament, and the Qur'an, are based on two fundamental ethical principles.

- First of all there is the *Golden Rule*, framed many centuries before Christ by Confucius and known in all the great religious and philosophical traditions, though in practice it is by no means a matter of course: What you do not wish done to yourself, do not do to others. Elementary though this rule is, it is helpful for making decisions in difficult situations.
- The Golden Rule is supported by the *rule of humanity*, which is not at all tautological: Every human being—whether young or old, man or woman, disabled or non-disabled; Christian, Jew, or Muslim—should be treated humanely and not inhumanely. Humanity, the *humanum*, is indivisible.

From all this it becomes clear that a common human ethic or global ethic is not meant to be an ethical system like that of Aristotle, Aquinas, or Kant; but some elementary ethical values, criteria, and attitudes are to form the personal moral conviction of the human person and society. Of course, this ethic goes against the facts: its imperative for humanity will not be fulfilled a priori, but must be called to mind and realized time and again. As Kofi Annan said in his Global Ethic Lecture in Tübingen in 2003: "But if it is wrong to condemn a particular faith or set of values because of the actions or statements of some of its adherents, it must also be wrong to abandon the idea that certain values are universal just because some human beings do not appear to accept them." Let me conclude with the very words with which the former Secretary-General of the United Nations ended his speech:

Do we still have universal values?
Yes, we do, but we should not take them for granted.
They need to be carefully thought through.
They need to be defended.
They need to be strengthened.
And we need to find within ourselves the will to live by the values we proclaim—
in our private lives, in our local and national societies, and in the world.

THE *ANALECTS* OF CONFUCIUS

TU Weiming

The *Analects* is, I believe, the distillation of what must have been a series of rich, varied, spontaneous, timely, dynamic, memorable, and thought-provoking interchanges between Confucius (551–479 BCE) and his disciples over the stretch of several decades. It may have taken two generations for Confucius' most intimate and knowledgeable followers to compile the "book." It seems that they did not intend it to be a finished product but a work open and receptive to new contributions; however, it is obvious that they were cautious and judicious in choosing each entry. The reason for this strategy is not difficult to imagine. Presumably the purpose of the compilation was to keep alive memories of their Master, the paradigmatic personality whom they missed, adored, respected, and loved. To complete such a task, they could have chronicled the Master's most important activities, jointly authored an appreciative biography, or systematically recorded his core ideas. Instead, they opted for a highly personal style, recording authentically how he talked, acted, thought and, most vividly, responded to specific questions. It worked brilliantly.

As a classic, the *Analects* is open ended. It lends itself to new additions as well as to divergent glosses, different commentaries, and novel interpretations. Its text, by nature, is receptive to an ever-expanding network of contributors. It seems to be a vast public space with ample room to accommodate a variety of insights

This paper was presented at the InterAction Council High-Level Expert Group Meeting on "World Religions as a Factor in World Politics," held May 7–8, 2007, in Tübingen, Germany.

attributable to the Master. There are at least three versions recorded in historical bibliographies. This fluidity, however, led some scholars to regard the sayings attributed to Confucius with suspicion. Since a vast number of statements beginning with "the Master said" are scattered in many pre-Qin (third century BCE) texts, critical scholars were wary about the reliability of any of them. The cautious ones, under the influence of the school "Doubting Antiquity," even questioned the authenticity of the *Analects*. The impression that all of the Master's recorded statements are derivative and that we cannot be sure that any of them truly reflect his thought was pervasive among Sinologists. As Confucius was silenced, at least in scholarly circles, the search for the original Confucius became a Sinological preoccupation.

This situation dramatically changed with the Guodian discoveries in 1992. For the first time, archeologists and textual scholars were presented with bamboo strips predating the fourth century BCE containing the writings of Confucius' first-generation disciples and, most surprisingly, records of the Master's comments on the classics. The reliability of the *Analects* was greatly enhanced. Some of the other teachings attributed to Confucius, such as those in the *Book of Rites*, also seemed to ring true as the authentic voice of the Master. The contour of the transmission of Confucian teaching from the Master via his immediate disciples to the generation of his grandson, the presumed author of the *Doctrine of the Mean*, became apparent, and the climate of opinion in which the *Analects* was compiled is no longer a mystery. We are far from being absolutely sure about the images of Confucius emerging from the perceptions of his followers, but we are relatively certain that we are not dealing with invented recollections.

The current version of the *Analects*, enriched by centuries of scholarship, is layered with linguistic, philological, literary, and textual traditions, allowing for numerous understandings and misunderstandings, uses and abuses. Undeniably, the *Analects* is a fluid text that encourages divergent, even radically different, readings. Nevertheless, ways of approaching the *Analects* are not unlimited. The notion that there are as many legitimate interpretations as there are interpreters is, at best, an exaggeration. In fact, only a few significant commentaries have survived the centuries of commentarial traditions. Although there is plurality in interpretive strategies, relativism does not work either in theory or in practice.

Like the Gospels and the Socratic dialogues, the *Analects* is a source of inspiration for those who cherish the experience of seeing and hearing the Master's teachings directly. As several scholars have pointed out, Chapter X offers a subtle and nuanced depiction of Confucius' manner of dressing, walking, approaching superiors, meeting strangers, and receiving friends. Indeed, his facial expressions, his body language, and above all his ritual performance are vividly portrayed. The contextualized daily routine discloses his appropriateness in specific situations. In the eyes of his students, what he did evoked an aesthetic of elegance. He comes alive in lived concreteness rather than in abstract universalism. Even with the lapse of more than twenty-five centuries, an attuned ear can still hear his inner voice and sense his presence. Confucius' vibrant personality, indeed his humanness, is vividly revealed.

As digested conversations and condensed discourses, the dialogical mode pervades the *Analects*. Yet on the surface, two-way communication seems totally absent. Confucius, as the teacher, simply provides answers. Students look up to him for guidance, insight, and wisdom. The Confucian style of teaching, unlike the Socratic method, underscores experiential understanding and silent appreciation. There is little room for negotiation. Thus we rarely find a student challenging the Master's presuppositions. Even in the case of Zilu, who showed displeasure at the Master's decision to visit a disreputable noble woman, Confucius gave no explanation except to state that he did nothing wrong (6:28).[1] Perhaps students were so much in awe of Confucius' presence that they just listened attentively for guidance. The example of Yan Hui is pertinent here. "The Master said, 'I can talk all day to Yan Hui—he never raises any objection, he looks stupid. Yet, observe him when he is on his own: his actions fully reflect what he learned. Oh no, Hui is not stupid!'" (2:9). Yan Hui, widely acknowledged as Confucius' most esteemed student, was full of admiration for Confucius as a teacher:

> Yan Hui said with a sigh, "The more I contemplate it, the higher it is; the deeper I dig into it, the more it resists; I saw it in front of me, and then suddenly it was behind me. Step by step our Master really knows how to entrap people. He stimulates me with literature, he restrains me with ritual. Even if I wanted to stop, I could not. Just as all my resources are exhausted, the goal is towering right above me; I long to embrace it, but cannot find the way." (9:11)

Underlying these statements is the assumption that teaching by example, rather than by words, enables students to find their own path of self-realization. Contention is discouraged, for "clever words" are seldom a sign of goodness (1:3). "What is the use of eloquence? An agile tongue creates many enemies" (5:5). Indeed, "glib talk," like "affectation and obsequiousness," should be avoided (5:25). The art of listening, essential for personal knowledge, must be cultivated as a precondition for elegance in verbal expression.

Learning (*xue*), which features prominently in the *Analects*, involves practice as well as cognition. It is a spiritual exercise. One learns not only with heart-and-mind (*xin*) but also with the body (*shen*). Zengzi's reflection on his self-cultivation is pertinent here: "I examine myself three times a day. When dealing on behalf of others, have I been trustworthy? In intercourse with my friends, have I been faithful? Have I practised what I was taught?" (1:4). Learning so conceived entails transforming the body as well as enlightening the mind. As the practice of the "six arts" (ritual, music, archery, horsemanship, calligraphy, and arithmetic) clearly indicates, both physical and mental disciplines are required and learning and thinking (*si*) ought to complement each other (2:15).

Implicit in this style of education is the existence of a fiduciary community, a community of trust. The fellowship of the like-minded that Confucius formed with his disciples was a voluntary association dedicated to improving the human condition through education. Modern historians interpret the traditional description of Confucius as the "First Teacher" (*xianshi*) in terms of his social role; namely, he was the first scholar to establish private schools in China. While government-sponsored institutes of learning had existed centuries before, Confucius was the innovator of self-financed schooling. There is a single reference to a modest payment (tuition) in the *Analects* (7:7), but the students who gathered around Confucius, like Jesus' disciples, were not children but adult truth-seekers, passionately engaged in the quest for the meaning of life. They were attracted by his great vision and profound sense of mission. His radiant and yet unassuming personality must have been a source of inspiration: "To store up knowledge in silence, to remain forever hungry for learning, to teach others without tiring—all this comes to me naturally" (7:2).

Confucius may not have had a set curriculum, but the *Analects* offers sufficient evidence to support the claim that his educational purpose was no less than learning to be human. It is not surprising that, under the influence of the "foremost teacher," the primary aim of education in East Asia is character building. What does this mean? Neo-Confucian thinkers interpreted it to mean "learning for the sake of the self," "learning of the body and the heart-and-mind," "learning of the heart-and-mind and human nature," "learning of human nature and destiny," "learning of the sages," and "learning of the gentleman" (*junzi*, which can also be translated nobleman, superior man, or profound person).

Confucius made many references to the idea of the gentleman. At first glance, learning to be a gentleman does not seem to be particularly arduous: "A gentleman eats without stuffing his belly; chooses a dwelling without demanding comfort; is diligent in his office and prudent in his speech; seeks the company of the virtuous in order to straighten his own ways. Of such a man, one may truly say that he is fond of learning" (1:14). But Confucius made it clear that a gentleman is a responsible person; the defining characteristic is a state of being as much as a manner of acting. "A gentleman should be slow to speak and prompt to act" (4:24), preach only what he practises (2:13), seek virtue and justice (4:11), and always take the side of rightness in his dealings with the world (4:10).

However, Confucius cautioned, "a gentleman who lacks gravity has no authority and his learning will remain shallow. A gentleman puts loyalty and faithfulness foremost; he does not befriend his moral inferiors. When he commits a fault, he is not afraid to amend his ways." Learning for the sake of improving the self is relevant here (14:24). A gentleman broadens his learning through literature and restrains himself with ritual (12:15). He is at ease without being arrogant (13:26). He can bring out the good that is in people (12:16). It is easy to work for him but difficult to please him, for though he never demands anything that is beyond our capacity, he will not be pleased if we do not follow the Way (13:25). When Zilu asked: "What must a man be like before he deserves to be called a Gentleman?" The Master said, "One who is, on the one hand, earnest and keen and, on the other, genial deserves to be called a Gentleman—earnest and keen amongst friends and genial amongst brothers" (13:28).

Edward Shils notes that Confucius may have been the originator of the modern idea of "civility." The Confucian gentleman is civilized and civil. Although Confucius, an accomplished archer and an expert at handling horses, was fond of hunting and fishing, he deliberately chose to cultivate fine arts as expressions of the ideal personality that he so cherished. As a sportsman, he preferred archery: "A gentleman avoids competition. Still, if he must compete let it be at archery. There, as he bows and exchanges civilities both before the contest and over drinks afterward, he remains a gentleman, even in competition" (3:7). As a tireless traveller, Confucius demonstrated a great deal of courage in his arduous and hazardous adventures, but under normal circumstances he was always "warm, kind, respectful, temperate, and differential" (1:10).

Confucius lived in a period of political disorder and social disintegration. The elaborate ritual tradition or feudal system (*fengjian*) refined by the Duke of Zhou, one of the most influential statesmen, had become dysfunctional. Internecine warfare flared up between rival states. Several hermits tempted Confucius to withdraw from the world to enjoy a tranquil life in communion with nature. The Master, though respectful of such an existential preference, determined to pursue his own course of action: "I cannot associate with birds and beasts. Am I not a member of this human race? Who, then, is there for me to associate with? If the world were following the Way, I would not have to reform it" (18:6). It is not surprising that among the historical religions (Judaism, Buddhism, Jainism, Daoism, Christianity, and Islam), Confucianism is unique in refusing to distinguish between the sacred and the secular.

Strictly speaking, Herbert Fingarette's seminal book in which he argues that Confucius regarded the secular as sacred is misdirected.[2] Granted, Confucius did not posit a spiritual sanctuary (church, temple, synagogue, monastery, or ashram) as a sacred place for contemplation, meditation, prayer, and worship. Nor did he envisage a holy land or the other shore as ultimately real and radically different from our life-world here and now. By committing himself to transforming the human condition from within, he was inevitably intertwined with the political affairs of the time. However, it is misleading to propose that Confucius' true vocation was politics rather than teaching.

In the eyes of his disciples, the Master was occasionally preoccupied with matters of governance and apprehensive about his lack of access to political authority. He was definitely confident in his ability to bring about a new ritual order, had he been employed by a ruler to do so (13:10; 17:5). He had a clear sense of how a gentleman, as a scholar-official, ought to behave and was contemptuous of his contemporary politicians:

> Zigong asked: "How does one deserve to be called a gentleman?"
> The Master said: "He who behaves with honor and, being sent on a mission to the four corners of the world, does not bring disgrace to his lord, deserves to be called a gentleman."
> "And next to that, if I may ask?"
> "His relatives praise his filial piety and the people of his village praise the way he respects the elders."
> "And next to that, if I may ask?"
> "His word can be trusted: Whatever he undertakes, he brings to completion. In this, he may merely show the obstinacy of a vulgar man; still, he should probably be qualified as a gentleman of lower category."
> "In this respect, how would you rate our present politicians?"
> "Alas! These puny creatures are not even worth mentioning!" (13:20)

Even if we were to contend that Confucius' real calling was not teaching but politics, we would have to acknowledge that since he viewed politics as an extension of personal ethics, to him the cultivation of personal morality was a precondition for participation in politics. Politics, in this sense, does not mean the capacity to manipulate power, authority, or influence. Nor does it mean the use of tactics and strategies to gain power. Rather, it is just and efficient governance achieved through the art of moral leadership: "The rule of virtue can be compared to the Pole Star, which commands the homage of the multitude of stars without leaving its place" (2:1). Government that emulates this ideal requires neither force nor coercion:

"The moral power of the gentleman is wind; the moral power of the common man is grass. Under the wind, the grass must bend" (5:8). The natural sway of the grass under a gentle wind is an image not of coercive power but of a ritual dance in which the government and people are attuned to the same rhythm. In this context, although government service is the most effective means of articulating moral leadership, it is not the only arena that matters. A salient feature of the Confucian style of governance is the political significance of family ethics: "Someone said to Confucius: 'Master, why don't you join the government?' The Master said: 'In the *Documents* it is said: Only cultivate filial piety and be kind to your brothers and you will be contributing to the body politic. This is also a form of political action; one need not necessarily join the government'" (2: 21).

Furthermore, Confucius' theory and practice of humane government was so fundamentally different from the politicking of those "puny creatures" that he simply did not want to demean himself by playing their games. His purpose in conducting political activity was to ensure that the Way would prevail. His preferred method was to address the fundamental issues of the body politic as a precondition of governance and management. He believed that if these fundamental issues were relegated to the background, there would be no politics worth the name. What is politics then? Using a homonym, he defined politics (*zheng*) as "rectification" (*zheng*), which means that politics is primarily about leadership. If leaders do not rectify themselves as public servants, the quality of government will be eroded and the performance of governance will be compromised, even if we have adequate institutions.

His celebrated theory of the "rectification of names" is deceptively simple: "Duke Jing of Qi asked Confucius about government. Confucius replied: 'Let the lord be a lord; the subject be a subject; the father be a father; the son be a son.' The Duke said: 'Excellent! If indeed the lord is not a lord, the subject is not a subject, the father is not a father, the son is not a son, I could be sure of nothing anymore—not even of my daily food'" (12:11). Implicit in this assertion is the belief that although sufficient food, sufficient weapons, and the trust of the people are vitally important for the peace and prosperity of the state, trust of the people is the most essential.

Lest we think that Confucius' moralization of politics is an untenable ideal, a measure of realism guided his approach to the power structure of his time. In short, he did not have any illusions about the *Realpolitik*. He continuously assessed the overall situation and tried strenuously to seize opportunities for political appointments. He was well prepared to deal with the complexity of the political circumstances and hoped that, with the help of his able students, he could take an active part in improving the livelihood of the people. It was not an accident that among his students, there was great expertise in managing the state: ritual, music, finance, diplomacy, and military affairs. However, he would never sacrifice his principles for expediency, and he always adhered to his commitment that the well-being of the people was the principal justification for humane government (*renzheng*).

It seems apparent that Confucius was a failed politician; despite his initial courteous and respectful receptions at the courts of powerful lords, he did not secure a position to exercise his influence and was eventually forced to leave. His abortive attempts to steer rulers away from cabals who were mainly interested in wealth and power seem to indicate that he was not particularly adept at political intrigue. He may have been a tragic hero in the eyes of sympathetic historians who believed, as he did himself, that he could have partly restored the political order of the glorious Zhou dynasty had he been given an opportunity to demonstrate his statecraft (17:5). Nevertheless, to characterize his self-understanding only in present-day political terms is misleading. For one thing, his perception of politics as rectification involves knowledge, culture, morality, and taste. It is a vision of community laden with epistemological, ethical, and aesthetic implications.

As previously mentioned, Confucius believed that dutifully discharging one's familial obligations is bona fide political engagement. In his view, the political process begins at home. It is inseparable from one's way of living. Implicit in this style of Confucian praxis is the creation of a discourse community through self-understanding and mutual learning. Confucian disciples were grown-up men, who, fully aware of their capacity to positively engage in worldly affairs, decided to join a common course to improve the human condition. Their group solidarity was not imposed upon them by the Master according to a preconceived pedagogical model. Nor was it forged, like the Moists, by a firm resolve to perform a clearly defined political and ethical function. Rather, they gathered around Confucius in order to develop their own potential as knowledgeable, cultured, ethical, and tasteful contributors to the public good. This constructive mode enabled them to practise their own paths of self-cultivation through reciprocal respect and mutual appreciation. Confucius encouraged them not to become utensils defined in terms of their functional utility (2:12), but all-round *junzi* (gentlemen, noblemen, or authoritative and profound persons) capable of political action at different levels and under all circumstances.

The pattern of interaction between Confucius and his disciples and the joint venture they embarked upon was unprecedented in Chinese history and unique among major historical religions. Confucius was not the founder of the scholarly tradition that he identified with and urged his students to adhere to. It was not out of modesty that he described himself as a "transmitter" rather than an "inventor" (7:1). Nor was he the highest manifestation of the human virtue that his students were taught to aspire to. Again, it was not out of modesty that he declined to be characterized as "sage" or "humane" (*ren*; 7:34). Yet, his self-effacing personal portrayal did not at all diminish his awesome presence among his students. His source of inspiration came from a richly textured form of life that was concretely situated in a specific time and place, and yet the content embodied in it was a shared commonality that is universally significant.

Since Confucius regarded himself as the guardian of the Way of human survival and flourishing, he appealed to the sages and worthies who were architects of the cumulative tradition rather than to a transcendent reality beyond human comprehension or a natural evolution outside of human participation. The Duke of Zhou, who was instrumental in sustaining the political order of the Zhou dynasty by constructing an elaborate system of rites and music, was for Confucius a paradigmatic personality. Confucius' lifelong dream was to revive Duke Zhou's grand design and usher in a new era of world peace based on the ethics of self-cultivation, sympathy, justice, and responsibility. Despite the Duke's magnificent accomplishments, he was, like Confucius, a transmitter rather than an inventor, for he had inherited the great enterprise from the sage-kings: Yao, Shun, Yu, Tang, Wen, and Wu. Confucius' historical consciousness was shaped by his awareness of the cultural norm that could still be maintained and by an intense sense of mission that he was "chosen" to perform such a task.

As he wandered from state to state in search of a ruler who would offer him an opportunity to realize his dream, he formed, perhaps inadvertently, a discourse community, a group of like-minded students. In retrospect, although he was never entrusted with a territory in which to put into practice his idea of model government, the social reality that he constructed turned out to be profoundly meaningful. Through collaborative effort, he and his disciples created a fellowship that was open, flexible, communicative, interactive, inclusive, and mutually beneficial. He engaged his students, but not as a philosopher who methodically led them to see the essence of things step by step. There is nothing in the *Analects* that resembles the elaborate reasoning in the Socratic dialogue. Indeed, Confucius distrusted mere verbal persuasiveness, despised glibness, and resented clever expressions. Although he highly valued eloquence in diplomacy, lucidity in thought, and articulateness in literature, in teaching he preferred silent appreciation, as in the case of Yan Hui, to effective argumentation. The latter reminded him of the trickery in legal disputes, even litigiousness. In civil cases, he favoured negotiation, mediation, or out-of-court settlement, rather than formalistic, arbitrary, and coercive mechanisms of control.

The ideal society Confucius envisioned and the discourse community he created through exemplary teaching was a voluntary association. The primary purpose of such an association was to facilitate the self-realization of each member. The polity based on such a social vision involves a reflectivity among the political and intellectual elite and an effective procedure by which humane government is set in motion. Unsurprisingly, Confucius insisted that the ruler through vigilant self-cultivation would ensure that the supervisory power of officialdom embodied a two-way process: responsible self-consciousness on the one hand and conscientious implementation of policies that impinge on the livelihood of the people on the other. Grave matters of the state, such as agriculture, famine relief, and material affairs, must be conducted with utter seriousness bearing, first of all, the welfare of the people in mind. Contrary to Hegel's misconception, sovereignty rests with the people rather than with the ruler. Indeed, sovereignty is bestowed upon the people by the Mandate of Heaven. The ruler entrusted with the Heavenly charge is duty-bound to act morally, that is, responsively and responsibly in relation to the demands of the people.

People, so conceived, are neither ignorant nor helpless. The great tradition preceding Confucius stipulated that the cultivation of virtue (*de*) legitimizes the ruler's role as "father and mother" of the multitude. As Mencius, following Confucius' lead, insisted, if the ruler fails to discharge his duty ("the ruler should act like a ruler"), his ministers should remonstrate with him. If he fails to heed their complaints, they should resign in protest. Under extraordinary circumstances, regicide is permissible. According to the principle of the rectification of names, the irresponsible ruler is no more than a mere loner without power, authority, and legitimacy. He can be banished or killed for the sake of the people. The people are like a body of water; they can support the boat, and they can also capsize it. "Heaven sees as the people see and Heaven hears as the people hear," is not an abstract notion but an option that is practical and, not infrequently, practised.

Confucius' determination to transform politics through moral strength, cultural values, social cohesiveness, and historical consciousness, often misunderstood as naïve enthusiasm for the primacy of the political order, was predicated on the perception that the ultimate purpose of politics is human flourishing. Surely, politics is intertwined with power, influence, and authority, but, as already mentioned, the purpose of politics is ethics through education. The maintenance of security and the sustenance of livelihood are not ends in themselves but conditions for human flourishing. The Confucian instruction that "from the ruler to the commoner all should regard self-cultivation as the root" is intended to provide the basis for a fiduciary community, not to inculcate a mechanism of social control. To use Emile Durkheim's terminology, Confucius, through mutual understanding and corporate self-consciousness, brought about an organic solidarity. Among Confucius' disciples there were literati, farmers, artisans, soldiers, merchants, and practitioners of a variety of other occupations. The division of labour enriched Confucian fellowship by its diversity of backgrounds and plurality of life orientations.

The implicit democratic spirit inspired H. G. Creel, a Chicago professor and dean of Sinology in the 1950s, to characterize Confucius as a liberal democrat and a rational humanist at that. It is an exaggeration, if not anachronistic, to label Confucius in such terms. The idea of a liberal democrat was probably not even a rejected possibility in the Confucian world of ideas. However, it is important to note that what Confucius envisioned as the proper way of human interaction transcends modern political categories no matter how broadly they are conceived. In the fragmentation of spheres of interest and the disaggregated scheme of professional disciplines, the idea of "organic" rather than "mechanic" unity, like universal brotherhood, appears to be merely an imagined possibility. Modern academic theoreticians, under the influence of specialization and professionalization, have difficulties recognizing that a sense of wholeness is a perennial human quest. The camaraderie that Confucius and his disciples realized was no more than the concretization of a common human aspiration.

Confucius' charisma lay in his magnetic power to draw a divergent group of energetic men to share his vision and mission to transform the world from within by tapping the mental and physical resources of each one of them through the art of self-cultivation. Confucian self-cultivation, far more complex than the personal quest for inner spirituality, is multidimensional. It involves not only the body and mind but also the total environment of one's existence. Confucius' own depiction of his spiritual journey is a case in point: "At fifteen, I set my heart upon learning. At thirty, I took my stand. At forty, I had no delusions. At fifty, I knew the Mandate of Heaven. At sixty, my ear was attuned. At seventy, I could follow the desires of my heart without transgressing any rule" (2:4). This pithy autobiographic note has inspired numerous interpretations. Obviously, Confucius lived up to his self-understanding that he was primarily a learner: "In a hamlet of ten houses, you will certainly find people as loyal and faithful as I, but you will not find one man who loves learning as much as I do" (5:28).

Throughout his life Confucius persistently tried to improve himself. He fully acknowledged that sagehood or moral perfection was beyond his reach, and so he learned without flagging and taught without growing weary (7:34). Indeed, he sought every opportunity to learn: "Put me in the company of any two people at random—they will invariably have something to teach me. I can take their qualities as a model and their defects as a warning" (7:22). He frankly admitted that he had to acquire the cumulative wisdom of the past to make himself wise: "I was not born of knowledge, but, being fond of antiquity, I am quick to seek it" (7:20). Furthermore, he was deeply concerned that he might lapse in his self-cultivation: "Failure to cultivate moral power, failure to explore what I have learned, incapacity to stand by what I know to be right, incapacity to reform what is not good—these are my worries" (7:3). In short, he was the sort of learner "who, in his enthusiasm, forgets to eat, in his joy forgets to worry, and who ignores the approach of old age" (7:19).

The content of Confucian learning is rich and varied. In the *Analects*, some of Confucius' disciples are said to excel in virtue, eloquence, government, and culture (11:3). These are apparently not subjects of Confucian teaching but dimensions of human flourishing that are particularly valued in Confucian education. Presumably, Confucius wished that all his students were virtuous, cultured, eloquent, and committed to public service, but only the most outstanding among them demonstrated exceptional attainments in any one attribute. As a rule, Confucius emphasized four things in his teaching: literature, conduct, loyalty, and trust (7:25). Correct behaviour is important in Confucian pedagogy, but the emphasis is on attitude and belief. Behavioural exactness that is not buttressed by right attitude and belief is only corruptible formalism. Although how one looks, listens, talks, and acts in all circumstances is important to the proper way of self-cultivation (16:10), it is only through "firmness, resolution, simplicity, [and] silence" (13:27) that we can hope to realize our full humanity. Indeed, "courtesy, tolerance, trust, diligence, [and] generosity," (17:6) the five practices that can put humanity in the service of social intercourse, are attitudinal as well as behavioural.

In a broader context, Confucian education is not confined to ethical instruction alone. As a comprehensive and integrated program of learning to be fully human, it covers the whole range of what we refer to as liberal arts education today. The Six Classics symbolize an all-embracing humanistic vision, a vision that encompasses the poetic, musical, political, social, historical, and metaphysical aspects of human existence. In the *Analects*, Confucius instructed his son as well his students to begin their study with *Poetry* and *Rites* in order to learn the basic language and practice of the Confucian Way. He made references to the three sage-kings, Yao, Shun, and Yu, in the *Documents* to show his admiration for their humane governance. He also mentioned that his continuous reading of the *Changes* helped to liberate him from committing major mistakes in life. Furthermore, his personal experience with music and his tacit appreciation of the Mandate of Heaven enabled him to convey a sense of human flourishing rooted in the art of listening and respect for the transcendent.

Thus, underlying Confucian education is the firm conviction that human beings are multivalent and multidimensional. The reductionist mode of thinking is not only simplistic but also misleading. We are not merely rational animals, tool users, or linguistic beings; we are aesthetic, social, ethical, and spiritual. We can fully realize ourselves only if we care for our body, heart, mind, soul, and spirit. As we move from the centre of our existence to ever-expanding and increasingly complex relationships, we embody home, community, nation, world, earth, and the cosmos in our sensitivity and consciousness. This is why true humanity is relational and dialogical as well as psychological and spiritual. Education must take as its point of departure the concrete, living person here and now, a person embedded in primordial ties, especially the affective bond between parent and child.

By implication, such ties as race, language, gender, status, age, and faith are also relevant from a modernist perspective. In a way, each of us is fated to be that unique person, situated in a particular time and space, who has never existed before and will never appear again. Indeed, we are as different as our faces. Yet, Confucians also believe that the commonality and communicability of our heart-and-mind is such that our nature, in essence, is the same and that we can share our perception of sight, sound, emotion, will, sense, taste, and experience. This confluence of difference and similarity enables us to become who we ought to be not by severing the primordial ties that make us unique persons, but by transforming those ties into vehicles for self-realization. That is the reason that, as learners, our lives are enriched by encountering a variety of people who share a great deal of information, knowledge, and wisdom together. Furthermore, our feelings, desires, motivations, and aspirations are personal but not necessarily private. We often reveal our intensely personal concerns to relatives, friends, colleagues, associates, and even strangers. Their sympathetic understanding of our inner worlds is profoundly meaningful to us.

Human life is multidimensional. Any attempt to reduce the variety of lived experience to merely the physical, mental, or spiritual is counterproductive. Human beings are by nature psychological, economical, social, political, historical, aesthetic, linguistic, cultural, and metaphysical animals. The full realization of human potential is never one-sided. Confucius believed that the enabling environment for human flourishing is "harmony without uniformity" (13:23). The respect for difference is vitally important for the development of a wholesome community.

The Confucian ethic implicit in this line of thinking is an ethic of ultimate ends, pure motivation, situational appropriateness, political engagement, social responsibility, and joy. It covers the whole range of our lived world. It presupposes a complex form of life. The core value in the *Analects* is *ren*, which is variously rendered as benevolence, goodness, human-heartedness, and love. I find Wing-tsit Chan's straightforward translation as "humanity" most suggestive and compelling. For Confucius, humanity is the cardinal virtue that embraces all other virtues, such as rightness, civility, loyalty, trust, wisdom, considerateness, and filial piety. Humanity is also the comprehensive virtue that can be enriched by all manifestations of human excellence. For years, scholars of Confucian studies have assumed that *ren* is inevitably social, for etymologically the character combines the ideograph of the human and the sign for two. In a seminal essay, eminent Sinologist Peter Boodberg argues that the proper way of deciphering *ren* is "co-humanity."[3]

In the *Analects*, humanity is sometimes associated with and sometimes differentiated from wisdom (*zhi*) and ritual propriety (*li*, civility). It seems to suggest an inner quality defining the truth and reality of a concrete, living person. This may have been the reason that Confucius characterized authentic learning as "learning for the sake of the self"; only through self-reliance, self-cultivation, and self-realization can we become fully human. Since in the Confucian tradition a person is a centre of relationships, people are both personal and social. In the bamboo strips unearthed in Guodian, the character *ren* (humanity) is depicted by two graphs: body (*shen*) on top, and mind-and-heart (*xin*) below. It vividly symbolizes that the meaning of humanity is not only social but profoundly personal.

Economic globalization is characterized by instrumental rationality, science, technology (especially information and communication technologies), technocratic management, professionalism, materialism, liberalization, legitimization of desires, and individual choice. The "economic man" is a rational animal conscious of his self-interest, motivated by the desire to increase his wealth, power, and influence, and committed to maximizing his profit in the free market adjudicated by law. He embodies a host of modernistic values, such as freedom, rationality, rights consciousness, work ethic, knowledge, technical competence, cognitive intelligence, legality, and motivation. Yet other essential values requisite for social solidarity are either relegated to the background or totally ignored, notably justice, sympathy, responsibility, civility, and ethical intelligence.

In a world characterized by materialistic and egocentric tendencies, the thirst for spiritual gratification often takes the form of fundamental extremism and exclusive particularism. Confucian humanism, as expressed in the *Analects*, is a balanced and open approach to the purpose of life. It offers a spiritual exercise essential for self-knowledge. Its primordial wisdom is a source of inspiration forever meaningful to human self-understanding.

NOTES

[1] Quotations from the *Analects* are from Simon Leys, trans., *The Analects of Confucius* (New York: W. W. Norton & Company, 1997), and D. C. Lau, trans., *Confucius—The Analects* (London: Penguin Classics, 1979).

[2] Herbert Fingarette, *Confucius: The Secular Sacred* (New York: Harper & Row, 1972).

[3] Peter Boodberg, "The Semasiology of Some Primary Confucian Concepts," *Philosophy East and West* 2, no. 4 (1953): 317-332.

OVERCOMING IGNORANCE, GREED, AND HATRED WITH INSIGHT, INTERDEPENDENCE, AND PEACE: A BUDDHIST PERSPECTIVE

Koshin Ohtani

I wish to begin by expressing my deep appreciation for this opportunity to share my thoughts with the InterAction Council. I am here as the result of being recommended by the Japan Buddhist Federation, the largest association of traditional Buddhist schools in Japanese Buddhism.

Buddhism originated over 2,500 years ago in North India with the teachings of Gautama Buddha, and was transmitted northeastward from Central Asia to China and southeastward from South Asia to Southeast Asia, developing in various ways as it took root in different cultures and societies. Buddhism was introduced into Japan in the sixth century, toward the end of that eastward transmission, and constitutes one of Buddhism's distinctive developments. Among the Japanese schools, Jodo Shinshu (with which I am affiliated) is unique in that there are no monks and nuns who adhere to the monastic precepts and engage in rigorous training.

I shall try my best to address issues that are common to all Buddhists.

HISTORY AND PRESENT SITUATION OF BUDDHISM

In the world of Buddhism today, we can distinguish between two main regions: places where Buddhism has existed for over two thousand years, and places

---

This paper was presented at the 25th Annual Plenary Session of the InterAction Council, held May 21–23, 2007, in Vienna, Austria.

Bridging the Divide: Religious Dialogue and Universal Ethics, ed. T.S. Axworthy.
Montreal and Kingston: McGill-Queen's University Press, Queen's Policy Studies Series.
© 2008 The School of Policy Studies, Queen's University at Kingston. All rights reserved.

where Buddhism has arrived in modern times. In Asian countries with a long history of Buddhism, the religion is intertwined with indigenous beliefs and customs, deeply influences the thinking of the people, and coexists peacefully with other religions. With the exception of what we might call religious "professionals"—monks and nuns who strive for enlightenment by renouncing the world—most lay Buddhists are concerned with finding happiness in this life and in the afterlife. In Asia, Buddhism has helped to support this search for happiness by providing a foundation for an ethical and moral life. Buddhism was transmitted in modern times to Europe and North America, where Buddhist groups have been created by refugees and immigrants and by those with a personal interest in Buddhist spiritual practices.

Although Buddhism over the course of its long history has not always been peaceful, military clashes have been few in number and attributed to foreign invasions. I believe that this culture of non-violence can be largely attributed to a teaching based on controlling desire. However, Buddhism has been criticized for what has been viewed as its passive call for peace and its tolerance of social injustice. It is true that because the aim of Buddhism is understood to be individual enlightenment or salvation, many Buddhist institutions have not been actively involved in social issues or in movements for social change.

In contrast to this traditional approach, in recent years we have seen a new movement called "engaged Buddhism," notably in South and Southeast Asia. The work carried out by Dr. A.T. Ariyaratne, who has long been involved with the InterAction Council, is one of the earliest and best known examples of engaged Buddhism.

The aim of Buddhism is to become a Buddha. The spiritual path calls us to control our desires and attain the wisdom rooted in truth—to realize the spiritual insight that approximates that of the Buddha. There are, of course, various teachings concerning the means as well as the time required for attaining that aim. For example, one path involves leaving the secular world to live a monastic life, following the precepts and engaging in rigorous training. Another path centres on sitting mediation, while still another calls for reciting mantras or the names of the Buddhas. And there is also a path, which I personally follow, that calls us to entrust our lives to Amida or Amitabha Buddha (the celestial Buddha of Infinite Light) and awaken to his salvific power.

Despite differences in beliefs and practices, the various Buddhist paths subscribe to basic ethical teachings: do not kill, do not steal, do not engage in sexual misconduct, and do not lie. These teachings have much in common with the ethical guidelines of other religions. I believe, therefore, that many Buddhists would be in agreement with much of what is found in the Universal Declaration of Human

Responsibilities, which was prepared by the InterAction Council for adoption by the United Nations.

THE THREE POISONS

In Buddhism the most basic obstacles to enlightenment are the Three Poisons: greed, hatred, and ignorance. I believe that the teachings concerning the Three Poisons can be helpful in examining many of the troubling issues we are facing in today's world.

Ignorance

Ignorance refers to our failure to understand the truth of Dependent Origination, according to which all phenomena occur as a result of various conditions that come together. This truth of interdependent origination does not render absolute the distinctions between good and bad, friend and enemy. Instead, such distinctions are regarded as relative and provisional, an insight that helps to moderate conflicts.

If we can change some of the causes and conditions, the effects can also be changed. Our human existence is contingent upon the interconnected web of life that encompasses flora and fauna, water and air. The tragic events of the world and personal suffering take place within this complex set of interconnected relationships. While suffering cannot be completely eliminated, it can be reduced, and each of us shoulders part of that responsibility.

Since the aim of Buddhism is to overcome delusion and realize enlightenment, those who have yet to realize enlightenment all become the recipients of salvation and compassion. They are certainly not the objects of punishment. Buddhism does not make absolute distinctions between the saved and the unsaved. Instead, it seeks to find a common ground where we can share one another's sorrows as well as joys.

As we think about the conflicts in the world today, should we not consider the suffering and the sorrow of those involved before judging matters in terms of good and evil, right and wrong, profit and loss? From a Buddhist perspective, such worldly judgments are all relative in nature! The leaders of the world, therefore, are asked to carefully inspect the tragic consequences of armed conflicts.

Greed

Greed has two dimensions, the first related to the individual and the second related to the economy and environment. The desire to live is intrinsic to all creatures. For human beings, economic expansion seems inevitable, for we seek a quality of life that is safe and enjoyable, and a lifestyle that allows us to realize our potential. However, this does not mean that we are permitted to sacrifice the lives of others, deplete natural resources, and destroy the environment. Globalization has its merits as a theory, but in practice it tends to benefit stronger countries and organizations at the expense of weaker ones.

Human beings and stronger nations should not consume whatever they want, for all living creatures must support and help each other. Further, we must maintain the earth system, which includes air and water, in a state of balance and harmony. Failure to do so will have catastrophic consequences for all of us. When we realize that many of the world's conflicts today are economic in nature, we ought to be seeking wealth that does not come at the expense of others.

This issue goes to the very foundation of Buddhism. However, in East Asian countries where economic development and industrialization have become prominent, particularly in China, Korea, and Japan, I regret that Buddhism has had little influence on social issues and movements for change, with the exception of the social activism of the nuns in Taiwan. I believe that Buddhists have a responsibility to lead the efforts toward an ecologically supportive way of life.

Hatred is the Greatest Obstruction to Peace

Hatred is one of the greatest obstructions to the attainment of peace. We find the following statement among the words of Gautama Buddha, the founder of Buddhism:

> In this world, if we respond to hatred with hatred, hatred will never cease. Only by relinquishing hatred will hatred cease. This is an eternal truth. (Dhammapada, verse 5)

I believe that these words, among all the words in Buddhism, are a treasure that can be appreciated by all people. Of course, eliminating hatred is not easily accomplished, but it is far better to think about how we can reduce hatred than to return hatred with hatred.

The Buddha also stated:

> All beings are fearful of violence, for life is dear to all. Thus, knowing this and feeling for others as for yourself, you must not kill, and you must not cause others to kill. (Dhammapada, verse 130)

The Buddha further admonished as follows:

> Life is joyous for the person who is satisfied with what one has, listens to truth, and sees truth. It is also joyous not to be angry and hateful toward people of the

world and to exercise self-control toward all living creatures. It is also joyous to overcome greed and desire toward matters of the world and to transcend various desires. And it is of utmost joy to conquer the vanity of ego-centred thought of "me, me." (Vinaya 1–3; Udana 10)

The Buddhist teaching is non-violent. If there were fundamentalism within Buddhism, it would not lead to military conflict. When Buddhists become involved in armed conflict, either they have interpreted the teachings according to selfish needs, or they have forgotten or hidden the true message of Buddhism. Misinterpretation has been a continuous problem in the transmission and popularization of Buddhism. The tension between self-interest and Buddhist teachings can come to a head especially when people who identify as Buddhists also identify strongly with a specific ethnic group or nation. When military conflicts develop, they find themselves torn between the teachings of Buddhism and their ethnic or national loyalties. It is regrettable that such conflicts have taken place in South and Southeast Asia in recent years.

Generally speaking, religion itself carries inherent dangers. Religion speaks deeply to the human situation, to existential as well as communal concerns, and it is therefore natural that religious teachings hold a strong sway over believers. But just as medicines that cure diseases can cause serious harm if prescribed incorrectly, religious belief can have devastating consequences when there are errors in judgment. We must be careful not to be self-righteous or exclusive. I believe that the future challenge for religious people is to affirm their own faith and, at the same time, accept and affirm people of other religions.

Conclusion

The teachings of Buddhism clearly oppose violence. Although Buddhists in the past have found it difficult to practise non-violence when ethnic and national loyalties were involved, Buddhists today can and should make a renewed effort to resolve conflicts and prevent warfare. Buddhism does not rigidly determine "good and evil" or "right and wrong," which is helpful in dialogue and negotiation. Moreover, the Buddhist insight that all living things are interdependent should lead us to alter the conditions that cause social injustice and environmental damage. We should not utilize religion to escalate conflicts. We should not increase human greed. May we reflect on the simple truth of the Buddha's statement:

If we respond to hatred with hatred, hatred will never cease.

JUDAISM AS A FACTOR IN WORLD POLITICS

Rabbi Jonathan Magonet

I am greatly honoured to have been invited to speak in this important forum and conscious of the responsibility I carry. At the same time I fear that in order to do justice to the topic, I must weave a rather complex web of information and opinion. This is inevitable whenever religion and politics meet and mix, but particularly so in the case of Judaism precisely because it is the religious tradition of a particular people. I will therefore address the subject under three headings:

- the nature of Jewish identity in the past and present,
- three types of Jewish political existence, and
- the unique contribution of Judaism among the world religions.

THE NATURE OF JEWISH IDENTITY TODAY – BETWEEN A FAITH COMMUNITY AND A PEOPLE

The Hebrew Bible reflects a struggle over the period of a millennium by a particular people to comprehend and find a way of living with a revolutionary understanding of the nature and demands of God. This God was understood to be the single Creator of, and power within, the universe; this God was invisible and in no way to be represented by physical symbols. Yet this God had entered into a special relationship with their ancestor Abraham and, ultimately, with them—the

This paper was presented at the InterAction Council High-Level Expert Group Meeting on "World Religions as a Factor in World Politics," held May 7–8, 2007, in Tübingen, Germany.

Bridging the Divide: Religious Dialogue and Universal Ethics, ed. T.S. Axworthy.
Montreal and Kingston: McGill-Queen's University Press, Queen's Policy Studies Series.

descendants of Abraham, the people Israel. The basis of that relationship in one important formulation was that Abraham would educate his offspring to champion the values of "righteousness and justice" in the world (Gen 18:19). This relationship would be exemplified by the society they would build in the land promised to them. Moreover, through them all the families of the world would find "blessing," a Biblical term embracing fruitfulness, material prosperity, and security. This promise was borne out by the rescue of Abraham's descendants from slavery in Egypt, thus enshrining the concept of freedom from slavery within the Biblical religious system. It was enshrined in a covenant of mutual responsibility between God and the people of Israel, at Mount Sinai. It was sealed and confirmed by the triumphant entry into the land of Canaan. As a later rabbinic view would express it, if Israel had lived up to the conditions of the covenant with God, we would have needed only the Five Books of Moses and the Book of Joshua!

The subsequent Biblical materials describe the ups and downs of that experiment in creating a new society, the challenges it faced internally from human failures and follies, and the difficult interactions with both local neighbouring nations and the contemporary superpowers: Egypt to the south, and Assyria, Babylon, and their successors to the north. Key elements in this story include the creation of a successful state and, briefly, a minor empire of their own, and the division of that empire into a northern and southern kingdom, both of which became subject to conquest and the deportation of their leadership and large segments of the population. Only the southern kingdom, Judah, with its capital in Jerusalem, was restored after a period of exile in Babylon. In light of this experience, the Jewish people expanded and further refined their concept of God and religious values.

The second exile, under the Romans, continued the process of creating what we now know as the Jewish Diaspora, scattered communities of Jews throughout the world. Without the previous landmarks of their national religious identity—the Temple in Jerusalem, its priesthood, the land itself, and a monarchy—the Judaism that emerged, created by a scholarly elite of rabbis, emerged as a faith community, struggling to maintain its unique identity in widely differing circumstances. Living subsequently under both Christianity and Islam, the Jewish people found ways of responding to the very different spiritual challenges these situations raised, whether by forming isolated and often oppressed minority communities, or some kind of intellectual and spiritual symbiotic relationship with the majority society and culture when possible. The basic principle of *dina d'malkhuta dina*, "the law of the land is the law," enabled Jewish communities to conform and, indeed, to contribute to the surrounding societies, as long as the law of the host society did not undermine some ultimate Jewish values.

Among the consequences of this history were the removal of any missionary zeal from Judaism and a marked caution about welcoming newcomers. But as a corollary Judaism taught that any individual or group would be acceptable to God if they kept seven basic social laws: the "laws of the sons of Noah," mostly derived from the Ten Commandments. The first six laws were prohibitions, but the seventh was a political command to ensure that the society created the necessary institutions for promoting justice and the rule of law—Abraham's legacy.

This successful model of Jewish existence, this "paradigm" as Hans Küng terms it, was to change radically following the European Enlightenment and Emancipation. For the first time, Jews found themselves to be independent citizens of their respective emerging national societies. Their previous collective existence, enforced externally by the society in which they lived and supported internally by the cohesive nature of Jewish law, with sanctions enforced by rabbinic authorities, was replaced over time by individuals whose relationship with the Jewish collective became a matter of choice. Individuals could also choose between different religious groupings as a number of movements and trends emerged within the collective Jewish identity, ranging from Liberal or Reform Judaism through to Conservative and varying degrees of Orthodox Judaism, as well as a national movement, Zionism, which brought about the successful creation of the State of Israel.

Yet these trends account for only part of the Jewish response. It can be argued that the major Jewish post-emancipation experience was assimilation to the host society to the extent that this was possible. This desire to "normalize" the Jewish situation, though experienced as a private matter and as a personal break with the past, was nevertheless shared by many and influenced by traditional elements. For example, Jews as individuals identified themselves, often in large numbers, with a number of emerging intellectual and ideological trends, usually playing a leading role. While they understood this activity as a conscious rebellion against what they saw as the backwardness and constraints of the Judaism of their parents' generation, certain aspects of this trend can be seen as "secular" versions of the earlier religious value system. Thus the demand for social justice in prophetic teachings and rabbinic law, especially the messianic expectations of the former, found their expression in socialist and communist movements, particularly in the history leading up to the Russian revolution and the creation of the Soviet Union.[1] The traditional commitment to study as a central religious value of rabbinic Judaism was translated into intellectual attainments in the sciences, academia, and the professions. The role so often given to Jewish communities in the areas of commerce and international trade, supported by family networks and underpinned by a shared legal system, developed into major entrepreneurial activity.

The more that Jews adapted to the secular culture of their respective countries, the more separated the previous interweaving of peoplehood, religious belief, and practice became. To put it another way, today most Jews live within a complex and often confusing web of loyalties, identities, and allegiances formed not only by their sense of belonging to a specific people but also by their acculturation in the particular country in which they were raised and live. At the same time they are affected by the expectations of a religious tradition to which they have an ambiguous relationship, whose ritual activities are identified as cultural or family commitments. Perhaps as many as seventy percent of Jews today regard themselves as essentially secular or humanist.

Whereas for almost two millennia the question occupying Jews was the nature of their relationship collectively to God in their often difficult exile, the question that most engages Jews today is that of their individual identity.[2] This issue of identity has become even more significant in light of the *Shoah*, the Holocaust. The destruction of one-third of the Jewish people has strengthened the defiant resolve of some to ensure the continuity of Jewish existence, be it in secular or religious, cultural or nationalistic terms. But the *Shoah* carries a deeper price in terms of an ultimate insecurity, borne out by real and imagined levels of anti-Semitism, which must also lead to the intuitive awareness by some that to be Jewish is a dangerous luxury best left behind for the comfortable obscurity of assimilation in the outside world—insofar as this is possible.

The point I wish to make by this introduction is that Judaism encompasses a wide variety of people and institutions, and both religious and secular expressions, so that generalizations become difficult. Moreover, if Judaism is a term that governs the particular religion of the Jewish people, it is seldom Judaism as a religious phenomenon that makes an impact on world politics. Apart from issues surrounding the State of Israel, it is rather individuals of Jewish descent, irrespective of the degree of their particular religious engagement, who are identified as having a significant social, cultural, or political impact. Such a definition would apply to the great triumvirate of Freud, Marx, and Einstein. In fact, it is quite possible to assert that the identity of individual Jews who do make some sort of contribution to world politics is without conscious, specific Jewish content other than that which has become a common element within Western culture.

THREE TYPES OF JEWISH POLITICAL "EXISTENCE"

If we are to address the Jews as a collective political phenomenon, I would suggest that there are three categories that need to be explored:

- The Jewish Diaspora,
- The State of Israel, and
- The Jews of the Public Imagination.

The Jewish Diaspora

The first is the plurality of communities that make up today's Jewish Diaspora. These communities range from powerful, well-organized congregations and other institutional frameworks in the United States to far smaller communities in parts of West, Central, and Eastern Europe, the Commonwealth, and South America whose long-term viability is considerably in doubt. A book with the title *Vanishing Diaspora* predicts the demise of European Jewish societies, on the basis of demographic evidence of aging and shrinking communities, and the general estrangement from classical forms of Jewish religious life.[3] Nevertheless, there is a kind of resilience that should not be underestimated, coupled with the impact of, for example, the opening up of Europe, which fosters greater mobility and potential mutual strengthening of Jewish community life.[4] Such communities are largely restricted in their political impact to a fundamental role that they share with other religious congregations, namely, to provide one of the essential building blocks of civil society through their commitment to education, welfare, good neighbourliness and, in most cases, democratic values in terms of their governance and external relations.

The only Jewish community that can be seen to have a larger role, because of its size and impact, is that in the United States. Here the lobby system by different interest groups means that Jews are also engaged in the public arena with a range of agendas. However, it is important to distinguish between the Israel Lobby, whose focus is on influencing American foreign policy in the Middle East, and the various Jewish advocacy organizations and representative bodies that address domestic and local issues of Jewish and general concern, like civil rights, the separation of church and state, and social services.[5] The Israel Lobby, of course, is not exclusively Jewish but rather a coalition of groupings, with a significant component from the Christian religious right, whose diverse concerns range from the pragmatic to the apocalyptic. It is clearly an influential political voice, though the extent of its power will vary from administration to administration.[6]

The State of Israel

The Jewish political entity *par excellence*, and seemingly the obvious subject for this paper, is the State of Israel. Yet, paradoxically, since our topic is Judaism, the major religious issues, with the exception of the extent of the borders of the Holy Land and the debate about "land for peace," are internal to the nature and governance of the state. Because of the political setup of the state, and the deals that were cut from the beginning with the religious parties, the internal structure has favoured the growth and development of Orthodox institutions, the suppression of Reform and Conservative religious expressions, and what has been seen as a radical polarization between religious and secular Israeli life. It has also produced a common Israeli secular attitude that, while disliking the Orthodox world, its influence and demands, dismisses non-Orthodox movements as illegitimate compromises. Orthodoxy may be unacceptable, but it is at least in some way viewed as "authentic." This radical polarization, which presumably echoes other elements of the Israeli mindset, was derived from the secular origins of the state as a rebellion against what was seen as a weak Diaspora mentality, waiting for divine intervention to change Jewish destiny. Political Zionism was for the most part a conscious rejection of any theological position. The earliest and strongest opponents to the movement, though for different reasons, were those committed to Orthodox or Progressive religious positions.

Two things in recent decades have amended this commonly held picture. The first and most dramatic is the Six Day War, whose victory, including the recapture of Jerusalem, fed into a very simplistic but powerful religious equation. Though rarely articulated as such, it effectively asserts that God had taken six million from us in the *Shoah*, but compensated by giving us the State of Israel and restoring Jerusalem to Jewish control. Put at its most crudely, after the incalculable tragedy of the *Shoah*, where God's absence is inexplicable, God is back on our side! This extraordinary event affected a generation of Israeli and Diaspora Jews, leading, positively, to a greater commitment and public pride in Judaism. But the negative side has been a kind of emotional inflation that fed the political fantasy of "Greater Israel" and, for some, the religious dream of the imminent arrival of the Messiah and the end of days. (In political terms the American Evangelical Christian support for the State of Israel received an enormous boost from the same event, even though the underlying theology is radically different and, from a Jewish perspective, highly problematic.) Some forty years later, we are only now beginning to see the restoration of a degree of political pragmatism, less in thrall to right-wing religious imperatives.

The second factor that should be mentioned is the beginnings of a new kind of interaction between the religious and secular features of the state. There has always been a considerable degree of cross-fertilization, despite the secular-religious divide. Major elements of Jewish religious tradition and practice have been officially recognized by the state, such as the regulations regarding the *Shabbat*, the use of the Festival Calendar in determining public holidays and celebrations, and the teaching of the Hebrew Bible in schools as a national literary treasure.[7] In the absence of a separation of religion and state, all marriages have to be conducted under Orthodox religious auspices, although there is a thriving industry in weddings conducted in Cyprus. These and many other features have formed effectively the cultural underpinning of the national identity, both influencing and alienating people. However, events like the Yom Kippur War revealed the ultimate vulnerability of the state, despite its military power. This introduced a greater awareness of the continuity between Israeli and Diaspora experience, which had been consciously denied as part of the founding mythology of the State of Israel. Though one of the consequences of the Six Day War was the phenomenon of the Baal-Teshuvah movement, the return to strict Orthodox practice, there is emerging a more nuanced interest in the religious tradition as part of a postmodern individualistic culture that can tolerate the juxtaposition of a variety of different, even competing, sets of beliefs and values. Young Israelis who once made the trek to India in pursuit of spiritual direction might now be curious to visit Brooklyn.[8]

Within the more formally constituted religious movements, the existence of a Jewish state has exposed whole dimensions of earlier Jewish teachings and thought to the day-to-day issues of life in a complex society. A leading exponent of "Modern Orthodoxy," David Hartman, argues that "the moral and spiritual issues that surface in Israeli society challenge the basic foundations of Judaism and possibly provide new opportunities for the renaissance of Judaism. The quality of Jewish society that we build in Israel will be paradigmatic for the manner in which Judaism develops everywhere in the modern world."[9] The moral, spiritual, and political issues raised by the Occupation and the treatment of Palestinians, as well as internal issues of welfare and social justice, are hotly debated within the state. One important religious organization that raises such issues, and is prepared to demonstrate physical solidarity with Palestinians, is Rabbis for Human Rights, whose members belong to all denominations.[10] It can be argued that the virtual exclusion of religious voices from the various political attempts at formulating peace plans has itself encouraged the growth of religious rejection to any such programs or formulations. In light of this, the First Alexandria Declaration of the Religious Leaders of the Holy Land (January 21, 2002) represents another important area where people with religious authority within their own communities, inside and outside Israel, are undertaking new religio-political initiatives.

Although I have treated Israel and the Diaspora separately, they are bound together in complex and often contradictory ways, through family connections as well as different religious and political perspectives. The early Zionist ideology assumed that with the creation of a Jewish nation state, all Jews would immigrate and the Diaspora would wither away. Since that has not happened, there is instead the assumption, at least on a political level within Israel, that the Diaspora should be a largely uncritical supporters' club and a further source of potential immigration, financial, and political support. Conversely, within the Diaspora, Israel is a source of pride and to some extent an element in Jewish identity, but also a major, and sometimes problematic, factor in determining the social status of the Jewish community. While it was easy to support Israel publicly in earlier decades, the impact of the Occupation, the growing awareness of the tragic fate of the Palestinians, and the linkage of Israel with America have all diminished Israel's standing, particularly in Europe. While it is sometimes possible to equate anti-Zionism with anti-Semitism, Jews have to accept legitimate criticism of Israel's actions. Nevertheless, events that have major public disapproval, like the recent war in Southern Lebanon, lead to a rising number of anti-Semitic incidents. Diaspora Jews are often disturbed by the actions of Israel, but are sometimes silenced by the accusation that they have the luxury of distance and have no right to criticize decisions that are made by those on the "front line" of a long-term, ongoing conflict. Nevertheless, there are voices that protest and face the anger of the community; yet the community knows, despite its reservations, that there are times when it must show solidarity. However, the Diaspora does offer opportunities for bridge building, particularly in the area of interfaith dialogue with Muslims, though not enough is undertaken.

In the end it has to be stressed that Israel is a highly complex society, made up of first, second, and third generations of immigrants, from a myriad of different societies, each of which, despite attempts to create a melting pot, remains distinctive and exerts its own particular political pressure. The "never again" response to outside threats, a legacy of the *Shoah*, reinforced by the rhetoric and politics of the Arab and, increasingly, the Muslim world, meets the internal agendas of Israeli politics and the temptations that come with power to make an unholy political brew.

The Jews of the Public Imagination

In this section I want to address the phenomenon of anti-Semitism, though I am aware that it is an uncomfortable subject, and one to which Jews can sometimes overreact or even exploit for their own purposes. In some ways this is the most elusive and most disturbing part of my paper. Elusive, because fantasies about Jewish power and conspiracies abound, yet it is hard to pin down the direct political consequences of such a far-reaching phenomenon. Simply to list examples, such as Holocaust denial, is painful and perplexing.

One of the key documents is undoubtedly the *Protocols of the Elders of Zion*, long recognized as a forgery, but its repeated publication for anti-Jewish and anti-Israel purposes has been a major contributor to the hatred of Jews, even where none are present, and to conspiracy theories.[11] Its escalating reappearance worldwide came in the wake of 9/11, alongside the canard that no Jews died in the destruction of the Twin Towers, which was itself a Zionist or Zionist/American plot.[12] As in all such conspiracy theories, evidence of Jewish deaths is dismissed as Jewish counter-propaganda from "Jewish-controlled" media, thus confirming the original premise. It is understandable, if ultimately very frightening given the Israel-Palestine conflict, that the *Protocols* have been distributed widely throughout the Arab and Muslim world. But anti-Semitism also finds expression in a thirty-part minitelevision series in Egypt, *A Knight without a Horse*, and another Syrian-produced one, *Al-Shahat*, "The Diaspora," which includes a graphic portrayal of the medieval Christian blood libel that Jews use Christian blood to make *matzah*, cakes of unleavened bread, for Passover. Both shows have been screened throughout the Arab world, which means that the seeds of hate and potential actions against Jews are deeply rooted in the popular culture of a new generation.

At the political level, one need only cite the notorious speech of Prime Minister Mahathir Mohamad of Malaysia at the Tenth Islamic Summit Conference (October 16, 2003), where in his attempt to rally the Islamic world to a new self-respect and assertiveness he used the Jews as an example to be emulated and condemned at the same time.

> We are actually very strong: 1.3 billion people cannot be simply wiped out. The Europeans killed 6 million Jews out of 12 million. But today the Jews rule this world by proxy. They get others to fight and die for them. . . . They survived 2,000 years of pogroms not by hitting back, but by thinking. They invented and successfully promoted Socialism, Communism, human rights, and democracy so that persecuting them would appear to be wrong, so they may enjoy equal rights with others. With these they have now gained control of the most powerful countries and they, this tiny community, have become a world power. We cannot fight them through brawn alone. We must use our brains also.[13]

The speech received enormous coverage in the Jewish world, and a rebuke from President Bush. The standing ovation given by those in attendance, representing the leadership of the Muslim world, confirmed the worst fears of Jews about Islamic anti-Jewish sentiments, and undermined the efforts of those who have sought to develop Jewish-Muslim dialogue and mutual support. That the speech was primarily intended as a challenge to a perceived failure of Muslim society, with Jews used as a convenient stick, was largely, and understandably, overlooked. Here we see where the Jews of the public imagination become instrumentalized for political purposes on a global scale.

To such a mixture of irrational fears of the Jewish people and calls to action against them, it is hard to know how to respond. Jewish self-defence organizations understandably expose this phenomenon, which also escalates Jewish fears and reinforces precisely those attitudes, especially in Israel, that see the only response in military power and pre-emptive actions. It is hard to see a way out of this morass.

There is a further bitter irony in this whole conspiracy matter. In our quest for a post-emancipation identity made up of fragments from past religious, family, and cultural elements, we often take vicarious pride in the achievements of Jews who have "made it" in some way in the public consciousness. We point to what we see as a Jewish contribution to society at large, to great contemporary writers, to the movie moguls who created Hollywood, to the extraordinarily gifted songwriters who developed popular music, to entertainers of Jewish origin, particularly masters of humour, and to cultural icons from Derrida to Bob Dylan. There was even a time when we joked about the absence of Jewish sporting heroes, at least till the arrival of Olympic swimming champion Mark Spitz changed that as well. But such innocent, self-indulgent, and somehow reassuring confirmation of our continuing existence is the very stuff that confirms the worst suspicions and accusations of conspiracy purveyors and true believers. As the old joke would have it, just because you're paranoid, doesn't mean that they aren't out to get you!

THE UNIQUE CONTRIBUTION OF JUDAISM AMONG WORLD RELIGIONS TODAY

It is something of a relief to turn to the last part of my paper. I recall a debate in my Reform Jewish youth movement in Britain in the 1960s about the nature and purpose of Jewish existence. At one end of the spectrum, we were strongly influenced by ideas like those of the philosopher and theologian Emil Fackenheim, himself a survivor of concentration camps. He spoke of the need for an added commandment to the traditional number of 613 that Jews are to keep: to survive as a people and not grant Hitler a posthumous victory, though Fackenheim was quick to point out that this was not to be survival merely for its own sake but as an act of faith.[14] At the other end, a younger generation felt the need to ask a different question, epitomized by the title of a book by Dow Marmur, *Beyond Survival*.[15] Survival for its own sake seemed somehow decadent; rather, we wanted to find a meaning or purpose in our continued existence.

In retrospect, it was an extraordinary quest. Could Christians, Muslims, or adherents of other major faiths ever question the legitimacy of their own
self-perpetuation? Insofar as we found answers at the time, they were partly conventional, partly more radical. One aspect clearly involved strengthening Jewish
life, tradition, and values simply to have them available as a rich component of the
spiritual heritage of humanity. For many, the development of a dynamic new expression of Jewish existence in the State of Israel was to embody that purpose, a
view advocated by Fackenheim himself. A more radical expression lay in the quest
for a Jewish religious voice within a newly emerging Europe. This quest was expressed in the journal *European Judaism*, and reflected in new aspects of rabbinic
training at Leo Baeck College in London. For example, an exploration of the in-
terface between Judaism and psychotherapy, along with an ongoing counselling
program, was included in the five years of rabbinic studies, and the commitment
to interfaith dialogue, particularly with Christians and Muslims, became a new
spiritual imperative.

Regarding interfaith dialogue, one of the tragic fallouts of the Middle East conflict is the growing rift between Jews and Muslims. Without over-romanticizing
their past relationship in the "Golden Age of Spain," the two religions share a
considerable number of beliefs and values, the product of centuries of interaction,
including a faith rooted in and expressed through law, a revealed text with parallel
traditions of interpretation and commentary, and often a shared Hebrew/Arabic
spiritual vocabulary. Jews likewise share a lot with Christians as post-enlighten-
ment religions, products of historical-critical scholarship and more individualistic
thinking. Both faiths have in common the Hebrew Bible, and are joined and separated by the figure of Jesus of Nazareth, Jesus the Jew. Thus in an ideal world
Jews could play a mediating role between these two great spiritual stepchildren
that seem so determinedly to be on a collision course with one another. Though,
even if such a thing were possible, I fear that conspiracy theorists would undermine it.

One could list any number of features of Judaism that are unique. In particular,
the covenant relationship with God assumes a kind of partnership and, alongside
the demand for obedience to God's will, a respect for the individual human being
and an almost scandalous right to call God to account when things go wrong.
Though it seems odd to include a sense of humour as a religious value, nevertheless this is a characteristic of Judaism, a reflection of the ironic awareness of the
ultimate distance between God and human beings, between human ambitions and
actual achievements, between hope and reality. Though the existence of the State
of Israel has radically changed things, Jews still carry the lesson of how to exist as

a minority, how to retain a tradition and values despite persecution, and how to live with a deep existential insecurity without turning to fanaticism. In a world made up ever more of migrants and refugees, where the experience of being a stranger and a minority is growing, where questions and doubts about identity and loyalty have become increasingly the norm, Judaism offers a model and a kind of reassurance that it is possible to live and flourish in such circumstances.[16] Our very existence is seen by some as a threat; our very existence could provide a lifeline of hope for many.

I would like to conclude with a poem by the French Jewish poet Emmanuel Eydoux. There were many different incarnations of Jews in the last century, depending on their country of origin and circumstances: committed members of the communist revolution and later its victims; assimilated Americans, who nevertheless marched in disproportionate numbers with Martin Luther King for civil rights; and kibbutzniks in Israel trying to build a new socialist utopia. Each one might have identified with the sentiments of this poem, but for the word "Jew" they would have substituted that other identity. But today, it is the word "Jew" that has somehow come to represent the values expressed in the poem, even though how many of us might be willing to call ourselves Jews is uncertain. Nevertheless, this poem is a kind of manifesto for a Judaism that still has a role to play in world politics:

> To open eyes when others close them
> to hear when others do not wish to listen
> to look when others turn away
> to seek to understand when others give up
> to rouse oneself when others accept
> to continue the struggle even when one is not the strongest
> to cry out when others keep silent
> to be a Jew
> it is that
> it is first of all that
>
> and further
> to live when others are dead
> and to remember when others have forgotten.

NOTES

[1] For a fascinating and detailed account see Yuri Slezkine, *The Jewish Century* (Princeton and Oxford: Princeton University Press, 2004).

[2] One traditional classification of the nature of Judaism expresses it in terms of the interaction between three elements: God – Torah – Israel. If the major focus in the Biblical period was on understanding God, in the medieval period (with its rabbinic focus on interpreting and applying the content of revelation) the major element was Torah, whereas the modern period is more concerned with "Israel," the nature of Jewish peoplehood.

[3] Bernard Wasserstein, *Vanishing Diaspora: The Jews in Europe since 1945* (Cambridge, MA: Harvard University Press, 1996).

[4] Among the several important papers on contemporary Jewish life in Europe by Diana Pinto, see the recent "Are There Jewish Answers to Europe's Questions?" *European Judaism* 39, no. 2 (Autumn 2006): 47-57.

[5] For a well-documented study of the history and activities of these organizations, see Jerome A. Chanes, "Who Does What? Jewish Advocacy and Jewish 'Interest,'" in *Jews in American Politics*, ed. L. Sandy Maisel and Ira N. Forman (Lanham, MD: Rowman and Littlefield, 2004).

[6] For a recent controversial article on the Israel Lobby and the subsequent correspondence, see John Mearsheimer and Stephen Walt, "The Israel Lobby," *London Review of Books* 28, no. 6 (23 March 2006).

[7] For an analysis of the alienation of "secular" Israelis from such public "cultural" elements and the attempt to address this by a leading educationalist, see Eliezer Schweid, "The Festival as a Joint Cultural Expression of Religious and Secular Jews," in *Jewish Identity in Modern Israel: Proceedings on Secular Judaism and Democracy*, ed. Naftali Rothenberg and Eliezer Schweid, 78-97 (Jerusalem and New York: Urim Publications, 2002).

[8] For an exploration of new trends see Moshe Lavee, "The Eucalyptus Tree and the Talmud: The Return to a Jewish Literary Heritage as a Post-Zionist Jewish Identity," *European Judaism* 39, no. 2 (Autumn 2006): 106-28.

[9] Quoted in Jonathan Magonet, *The Explorer's Guide to Judaism* (London: Hodder and Stoughton, 1998), 268.

[10] For their website, see www.rhr.israel net/

[11] A recent study by David G. Goodman, "The Protocols of the Elders of Zion, Aum and Anti-Semitism in Japan," *Posen Papers in Contemporary Anti-Semitism 2* (Jerusalem: The Vidal Sassoon International Centre for the Study of Anti-Semitism/Hebrew University of Jerusalem, 2005), describes the impact of considerable numbers of books on the subject in the 1980s and 1990s in Japan as offering "an enabling ideology" for terrorism.

[12] A search in Google produces 473,000 items on the subject.

[13] The speech is recorded on the website of the Anti-Defamation League.

[14] Emil L. Fackenheim, "Jewish Values in the Post-Holocaust Future," *Judaism* 16, no. 3 (Summer 1967): 271-72.

[15] Dow Marmur, *Beyond Survival: Reflections on the Future of Judaism* (London: Darton Longman and Todd, 1982).

[16] For a study of the complexity of identity and its inherent insecurity in "liquid modernity," see Zygmunt Bauman, *Identity*, with Benedetto Vecchi (Cambridge: Polity Press, 2004).

HINDUISM: THE DALLIANCE OF RELIGION AND POLITICS

Acharya Shrivatsa Goswami

Greetings from India! the oldest and largest home to many major faiths of the world today. In this conflict-torn world, multifaith India captures the imagination. The President of the United States, on a visit to India on March 2, 2006, met with leaders of the major religious traditions. He opened his conversation with representatives of Hinduism, the fourth largest religious population in the world, with these words: "I want to listen and learn from you, how, in India, practically all major religions of the world have lived together for millennia."

Despite the predominately Hindu population, multifaith India is very much a dialogical country. India is proud of its history of keeping its borders open and welcoming those who want to make their home on the Indian continent. India is also willing to go beyond its shores to meet and interact with others. This Indian outreach has never been for the sake of expanding political boundaries. We are happy to share with the world Buddhist, Sufi, Ahmediya, and other religious traditions as a gift from dialogical India.

An ancient Hindu prayer, "Let noble thoughts come to us from all directions,"[1] must have had some power. A rich dalliance of races, religions, cultures, and languages is found in India.

This paper was presented at the 25th Annual Plenary Session of the InterAction Council, held May 21–23, 2007, in Vienna, Austria.

Bridging the Divide: Religious Dialogue and Universal Ethics, ed. T.S. Axworthy.
Montreal and Kingston: McGill-Queen's University Press, Queen's Policy Studies Series.
© 2008 The School of Policy Studies, Queen's University at Kingston. All rights reserved.

The different traditions appear to be in conflict, like the binary digits "one" and "zero"; yet neither the basic difference between one and zero, nor their seeming opposition, could stop their alliance. If India had not contributed "zero" to world culture and had not danced with "one," humanity would have been much poorer. After all, riches are counted in zeros!

In 1950, India declared itself a secular democratic republic, where religion does not interfere in the political process. In Indian politics, contrary to the *Oxford English Dictionary* definition, *secularism* means "respect for all religions." I am proud to say that despite the traumatic partition of India in the name of Islam, India is home to the second largest Muslim population in the world after Indonesia. Significantly, President Bush welcomed the Indian Prime Minister at the White House recently with the words, "You have the second largest Muslim population in the world, and yet no training camps for religio-political extremists?"

We might wonder, how so? The answer is that in a democratic and free country like India, the political, economic, technological, religious, and cultural dialogue is alive. And so I bring you special greetings from Vrindavan; this holiest of holy Hindu centres was a gift to my forefathers in the sixteenth century from the Muslim emperor, Akbar. It is the sacred abode of Lord Krishna, who is regarded as the Supreme Godhead of the Hindu pantheon, a determined warrior against evil, committed peacemaker, and greatest lover of humanity and nature.

Hinduism has developed metaphysical, logical, ethical, aesthetic, and spiritual grounds for sustaining dialogue. Logically speaking, difference and non-difference are facts of experience, and yet reality cannot be totally comprehended either in pure difference or in pure non-difference. Reality rests in *essential* non-difference, with *functional* differences. In political and religious terms, reality is not about only *me* or only *you*: it is about *us*. You and I make *we*: We stand on the common ground of humanity in essential non-difference in the midst of all the functional variety of race, language, religion, culture, and ideology. This logic leads us to the metaphysics of inclusive transcendence.

Feelings are a major factor governing human behaviour. Feelings depend upon a particular relationship between two persons, the subject and object of feeling. The dialectic of relationship presupposes at least two entities. Yet any relationship includes and transcends the duality and seemingly opposite nature of the individuals, for example, as in a relationship between a man and a woman. If we fear the partner and negate him or her, what will remain as pleasurable in human experience! On the contrary, when we acquaint ourselves with the "other," make an alliance with him or her and celebrate the essential "otherness" of the partner, then the dalliance between the two is enjoyable and enriching. If we do not recognize and care for the "other," the dalliance will turn out to be rape and exploitation, leading to misery and suffering.

Religious and political leaders have always been in relationship. A long time ago, in one such interaction, an emperor named Yudhisthira asked a holy man, "O Sage Narada! Please enlighten me about the values that will *eternally* sustain the human reality and environment, and elaborate upon the process of implementing those values." The sage replied, "There is nothing superior to human reality."[2] He then enumerated good qualities that sustain human existence: truth, non-violence, compassion, service, sexual morality, and so forth. These good human qualities, *dharma*, are the common ground of all religions, which Hans Küng and his colleagues have been speaking about in their deliberations. Incidentally, the word *Hindu* as the name of a particular religious tradition is missing from the Hindu texts until the nineteenth century. Hinduism traditionally has been called *Sanatana Manava Dharma*—the Eternal Value system sustaining humanity.

These values, the sage continued, characterize the individual, who is the constituent unit of any society. In the Hindu way, family is the core platform for any social, political, economic, or religious activity. An individual relating to other individuals forms this social institution called the family, which thrives on the process of loving relationships sustained by mutual care and service.

In the public domain of common values and the processes of working out those values, relationships and networking have to be strong, like a family. Unfortunately, mutual ignorance and suspicion have weakened the alliance between political and religious processes. The divorce between so-called civil society and religious institutions has not helped us much. Can we reverse this alienation?

Probably, yes. An example like the alliance between religious leaders and the former World Bank president, at the initiative of Prince Philip, Duke of Edinburgh, has given us a ray of hope. The resultant World Faith Development Dialogue is proving that when members of civil society are guided by "religious" or universally acceptable human values, and when they act responsibly, the resources and benefits in service to humanity are multiplied.

In 1947, India freed itself from the dominance of a foreign power through a peaceful process of political dialogue, which has become the universally preferred path to political freedom. Mahatma Gandhi, a Hindu believer who led this dialogue, explains the process:

> My motive has been purely religious. I could not be leading a religious life unless I identified myself with the whole of mankind, and this I could not do unless I took part in politics. The whole gamut of man's activities today constitutes an indivisible whole; you cannot divide social, political, and purely religious work into watertight

compartments. I do not know any religion apart from human activity. My devotion to truth has drawn me into the field of politics, and I can say without the slightest hesitation, and yet with all humility, that those who say that religion has nothing to do with politics do not know what religion means.[3]

Many people did not understand what Gandhi was saying, but Martin Luther King, Bishop Tutu, Ariyaratne, and many others did understand, and they adopted the Gandhian path of religious politics.

Sage Narada told the king that "a reasonable, equitable distribution of natural and material resources within the human family is imperative." Only then will the Hindu ideal of "earth as one family" be sustained. Hinduism professes and prescribes a dialogue, not a divorce, between humans and nature (including the animal kingdom), religion and politics, aesthetics and economics, and so on. But dialogue will happen only if religious and political leaders get over their mutual suspicion; we must see each other not as one trying to exploit the other, but as two lovers trying to serve and please humanity through a dalliance.

Lastly, spiritual discipline is necessary for any dialogue to succeed. The Hindu view of life is based upon the doctrine of *karma*, responsible human action that shapes our lives here and hereafter. The Divine Power, essentially a teacher, supports and guides us.

As Sri Caitanya Mahaprabhu, a politically aware religious leader of the sixteenth century, suggests and prays:

> Let us be smaller than a blade of grass
> Let us have more forbearance than a fruit-bearing tree
> Let us not be prisoner to our ego
> And let us respect and love the other.[4]

If that happens, there will be peace and prosperity.

For a Hindu, all interactions should end with the traditional peace blessing. This blessing is for us all, but specifically I invoke it for the InterAction Council, which is completing its silver anniversary and entering a golden era.

> Let there be peace in all directions,
> Peace in space,
> Peace in land and water,
> Peace in herbs and medicines,
> Peace in creatures,
> And finally let there be peace upon Peace.
> Then only will there be Peace undivided.[5]

Why peace upon peace? We cannot afford to make the perennial mistake of trying to get rid of ignorance through bigger ignorance, darkness through more darkness, violence through bigger violence. The process of peace *must* be peaceful. We have a ray of hope. Through a peaceful journey, we can come out of the dark tunnel and dance in full sunshine.

NOTES

[1] RgVeda I.89.i.

[2] Bhagavata Purana, Canto 7, Chapter 11.

[3] Quoted in Robert A. McDermott, ed., *Basic Writings of S. Radhakrishnan* (Delhi: Jaico Publishing House, 1981), 262.

[4] Edward C. Dimock, Jr. (trans. and commentator) and Tony K. Stewart, ed., *Caitanya Caritamrta of Krsnadasa Kaviraja: A Translation and Commentary* (Cambridge, MA: Harvard University Press, 1999), 994.

[5] Sukla-Yajur-Veda 36/17.

Japanese Shinto as a Factor in World Politics

Seiken Sugiura

The nature-worshipping, polytheistic, all-encompassing and tolerant Japanese Shinto has existed for millennia with the reverence for harmony at the core of its spirituality. But one grave mistake was made in the modern period. For seven decades, from 1868 to 1945, Shinto was used by the state. The lesson learned was that politics must never use religion, and religion must never allow itself to be used by politics.

Shinto as a faith developed spontaneously in Japan over the millennia of its history. It was nurtured by the characteristics of the island nation, blessed with bountiful products from land and sea, seasonal changes, and beautiful natural landscapes. The ancient Japanese people believed all natural and supernatural phenomena to be the doings of *kami* (gods or spirits). They held such spirits in reverence and prayed to them for blessings and protection, offering goods in appreciation or to placate the spirits.

Ancient Shinto is the indigenous religion of Japan. The nature-worshipping custom of Shinto developed into the observance of proper rituals to show respect and appreciation to the so-called eight million gods and deities. The divinities worshipped ranged from spirits in nature—such as the sun, moon, stars, wind, lightning, mountains, rivers, water, fire, and all living creatures—to ancestors, heroes, and human deities. They were the gods of heaven and earth.

This paper was presented at the 25th Annual Plenary Session of the InterAction Council, held May 21–23, 2007, in Vienna, Austria.

Shinto has no formal doctrine or scripture, and no founder, and as such some people may not consider it a religion. Nevertheless, Shinto shares a place among the world religions as a polytheistic faith characterized by an all-encompassing spirit of harmony and tolerance toward other religious beliefs. Shinto is closely tied to the daily lives of the Japanese, who frequent the shrines on special occasions such as New Year's Day, weddings, funerals, and festivals. In fact, Shinto beliefs and ways of thinking are deeply embedded in the subconscious fabric of modern Japanese society.

RELATIONSHIP WITH BUDDHISM

Into ancient Japanese society, with its countless gods and deities, Confucianism entered from the neighbouring continent in the third century and Buddhism in the sixth century. The influx of these religions had considerable impact on Shinto practices: it led to the building of shrines and the naming of "Shinto" to distinguish the indigenous traditions from the new faiths. Buddhist teaching spread rapidly in Japan and was readily accepted by the people, probably for its polytheistic trait in which anyone could attain the status of a Buddha through spiritual enlightenment. The imperial family under Prince Shotoku (574–622) joined Buddhism while continuing their adherence to Shinto, which eased the adoption of Buddhism in Japanese society.

Buddhism and Shinto coexisted and gradually merged over the centuries in Japan. By the feudal Edo period (1603–1868), there was at least one Shinto shrine or worshipping house in every village, altogether numbering more than 20,000 shrines throughout Japan. Buddhist temples were built in the same complex as Shinto shrines, and construction of joint Buddhist-Shinto worship buildings became popular. Today the number of shrines has increased to over 80,000, despite the merging and abolishing of municipalities following the Meiji Restoration. The Japanese Buddhists have now split into over one hundred sects, but their influence remains strong, as witnessed by over 75,000 temples that have been built throughout the country. These temple-shrines play a central role in the lives and events of communities.

CREATION OF A STATE RELIGION

The Meiji Restoration of 1868, when power was returned to the Emperor from the warrior class, introduced a new chapter to the Shinto religion. The Meiji government announced Shinto as the official state religion of Japan, and established a Ministry of Divinity to conduct religious rites of the state and to control all the shrines. A "Grand Teaching"—a national movement to disseminate the concept of the divinity of Japan's national origins and its Emperor—was promulgated. Priests were officially nominated by the state to thoroughly brainwash the people. The separation of Shinto and Buddhism was ordered, and although the law did not call for the abolition of Buddhism, many temples were in fact plundered and demolished, creating unprecedented scandals. The government controlled all the shrines in Japan under the divine mandate of the imperial family. These actions officially established Shinto as the state religion of the country.

The establishment of Shinto as a state religion was a natural consequence of the Meiji government's effort to restore imperial rule and unify the nation under a Shinto theocracy. It was also a way of counteracting the influence of the Western powers, symbolized by the arrival of "Black Ships" armed with the extremely powerful principles of Christianity. By singling out Shinto as the native religion, and separating it from the alien influences of Buddhism, the government sought to unify the county under Shinto with the Emperor at its apex.

As Shinto became the state religion, the polytheistic characteristics of tolerance and respect for harmony were greatly undermined. Following the forceful separation from Buddhism, Shinto was presented as a monotheistic religion centred on the Emperor as the one deity. In a way, the government leaders manipulated Shinto to befit their desire to create a monotheistic state religion, deeply conscious of Christianity, the religion of the Western powers.

DISASTROUS STATE SHINTO AND ITS TERMINATION

Incorporated into the political scheme, the impact of state Shinto on the course of Japan's history was extensive. The Meiji constitution proclaimed in 1890 clearly defined the Emperor as the head of state (Article 1) and of divine origin, sacred and inviolable (Article 3). In an era headed for the disastrous World War II, the Emperor was considered to be a human god and the country a divine state. The war was considered holy, and Japan considered itself invincible. An anti-foreign and exclusive ultra-nationalism became the philosophical rationale of the country. Shinto paved the way for this movement, encompassing the entire nation.

It cannot be denied that the Meiji constitution was also oriented toward modernization in many respects, including the introduction of the concepts of the division of administrative, legislative and judiciary powers, the rule of law, and the democratic system. The overall structure of the constitution attests to Japan's efforts to modernize in line with the world powers. However, the government also took advantage of the so-called sacred words of the Emperor to override the law. As a result, the legislative authority gradually became extremely distorted. An outstanding example was the enactment of the Imperial Rescript on Education. The Rescript, which was strongly influenced by the teachings of Confucius (by then quite Japanized), preached total loyalty and filial devotion to the Emperor as the head of the state and the direct descendant of god and, thus, a father to the Japanese people. These teachings had a significant impact in nurturing the later absolute obedience to militaristic education.

The Meiji constitution defined the Emperor as the military commander-in-chief (Article 11) with sole prerogative over all military matters (Article 12). These defects in the constitution, coupled with the premature development of democracy, allowed the Japanese military to engross power and get away with anything. Nationalistic and exclusivist sentiments gained momentum, no doubt legitimized by Shinto as the state religion. The ultimate outcome was Japan's defeat. The Allied occupation authorities issued an order on December 14, 1945, calling for the complete separation of state and religion, and the abolition of Shinto as the national religion. The shrines were returned to the ways of ancient Shinto.

RETURN TO ORIGINAL SHINTO IN THE POST-WAR ERA

In the aftermath of World War II, Japan adopted a new constitution that provided for freedom of religion and the separation of religion and the state. Shinto was thus restored to a position of equality with other religions, all falling under the jurisdiction of the Religious Corporation Law. The most prominent characteristic of this law is that absolutely no political interaction or intervention is permitted with regard to "religious" activities. As the strong monotheistic emphasis was dismantled and state patronage of Shinto shrines came to an end, Shinto regained its original attributes as a polytheistic folk religion.

No one definition exists for the gods of Shinto, but according to a prominent eighteenth-century Japanese scholar, Norinaga Motoori, Shinto deities represent all that is supernatural and wise. In my hometown of Kota in Aichi Prefecture, a shrine was built in honour of Chiang Kai-shek and named after his later designation as *Zhongzheng*, meaning "central uprightness." It was built by Japanese soldiers who had returned safely from China through the generosity of Chiang Kai-shek, who believed in the lofty ideal of returning virtue for enmity. He not only ensured their safe return, but also forfeited his right to demand war indemnities from the Japanese government. Every year on May 4, the anniversary of his death, a special memorial service is held at the shrine and surviving members of the deceased's family are invited from Taiwan. This is but one example of the return of Shinto to its ancient practice of showing reverence for deeds of superior quality.

FUTURE ISSUES

Two problematic issues can be pointed out for Shinto. One is that although Shinto has returned to its ancient form, its pre-war status as the state religion has left a strong impression in the minds of people both inside and outside Japan. The idea that Shinto is a state religion has not been completely eradicated. This misunderstanding, which is especially conspicuous among neighbouring countries, stems from a lack of knowledge about the history of Shinto. It is up to Shinto to dismantle this misunderstanding.

The other issue relates to the visits of government leaders to the Yasukuni Shrine. Constructed during the state religion days by the army, the Shrine is dedicated to the spirits of those who died fighting in wars on behalf of the Emperor. No soldier or commander who did not die in a war was enshrined. However, a grave mistake was made in the 1970s when convicted Class A war criminals were enshrined along with war heroes. The deification of war criminals, and Shrine visits by the prime minister and cabinet members, have provoked protests from China and Korea. It is extremely unfortunate that diplomatic controversy has developed over Yasukuni. The solution is in the hands of Yasukuni officials, as the government can no longer intervene in any religious activities whatsoever, worship included. Yasukuni officials must rectify the situation and restore original Shinto practices.

Incidentally, speaking of the war dead, what about the millions of Japanese civilians—women and children included—who lost their precious lives in the Second World War? What about foreigners who died in Japan? And what about Self-Defence Force officials who have lost their lives abroad while serving on a government order, such as participating in a peace-keeping operation? None of them are enshrined at Yasukuni. It seems to me that the state should respond to these questions but, more importantly, how will Shinto cope with this problem?

Lastly, a very positive proposal can be made for the role of Shinto today and in future. Shinto's original trait of valuing harmony rather than confrontation can and should be adopted by those Japanese engaged in international relations to encourage cooperation. Shinto's tolerance and acceptance of other faiths offers a model for peaceful coexistence. And the Shinto spirit of reverence for nature can also teach us a valuable lesson in this age of global climatic change caused largely by the destruction of nature by human beings.

BUDDHISM AS A FACTOR IN WORLD POLITICS: A THERAVADA EXPERIENCE

Mettanando Bhikkhu

First let me thank the InterAction Council for inviting me to address a topic that I find most interesting and relevant in this age of globalization.

Personally, I am a Thai Buddhist monk, but I did not pass through the traditional monastic training that begins in childhood. I was also educated in the West. My experience of spending eleven years in a Catholic school in Bangkok gave me a special opportunity to learn about Catholicism and Christianity. I have been a core member of the Wat Phra Dhammakaya temple and the Dhammakaya Foundation, a fundamentalist Buddhist group in Thailand, which has given me insight into the precepts and practices of nationalist Buddhists in my country. The Dhammakaya Foundation has become the largest Buddhist community in Southeast Asia actively engaged in politics and massive fundraising.

Before I begin, I have to confess that I once held the idealistic view that Buddhism was the only true answer and solution to all the problems in the world. Thankfully, my community experience, my academic research on HIV/AIDS and Buddhism in Thailand, and my service in the World Conference of Religions for Peace have enriched my life. These experiences have transformed me from a promoter of the Buddhist faith in exclusion to all others into a religious reformist.

This paper was presented at the InterAction Council High-Level Expert Group Meeting on "World Religions as a Factor in World Politics," held May 7–8, 2007, in Tübingen, Germany.

Bridging the Divide: Religious Dialogue and Universal Ethics, ed. T.S. Axworthy.
Montreal and Kingston: McGill-Queen's University Press, Queen's Policy Studies Series.

Orthodox Theravada Buddhists are often horrified by my talks and writings, but my views are shared by most reformists and liberal thinkers. Those who have followed my series of publications on the Internet can confirm my attitude toward the Buddhist religion in Thailand—that it is in deep crisis and in need of urgent reform. I still believe, however, that once it is properly reformed Buddhist teachings will serve as the main powerhouse for democracy, human rights, justice, education, the arts, health care reform, social development, and regional politics in Southeast Asia.

This short article is part of my ambitious attempt to explore the social impact of Buddhism in Theravada countries, where there are about 100 million Buddhists. I will limit my discussion to Theravada Buddhism, since Mahayana Buddhism is addressed in another chapter. Briefly, Theravada Buddhism and Mahayana Buddhism are distinguished by many differences in doctrine and practice, and by geographical area. Theravada Buddhism is seen as the orthodox, conservative form of Buddhism (Pali, believed to be the language of the Buddha, is used in Theravada scriptures and rituals). Theravada Buddhism is the dominant form of the religion in the Southeast Asian countries of Thailand, Laos, Sri Lanka, Cambodia, and Myanmar.

Southeast Asia is one of the fastest developing economic regions of the world, and religious diversity and conflict are ever present. I will discuss both the positive and negative aspects of the Theravada Buddhist worldview, and then offer an alternative interpretation of Buddhism that could bring security and harmony to the world.

BUDDHISM AND POLITICS

When I speak of politics, I am speaking about processes of decision making by a group of people, not power games or struggles for social status. Everyone is involved in politics, because no one can live in isolation. When a crisis breaks out in one region of the world, it affects other people around the globe. Without doubt, the topic of world politics is huge, complex, and diverse; it covers international relations, political theories, human rights, justice, the United Nations and its administration, non-governmental organizations, and problems facing the whole of humankind such as global warming.

Although the world has been made smaller in the past century with the advancement of technology and the advent of the Internet, the problems of the world have not been reduced. Rather, the problems facing us have become more complicated and seemingly too difficult for any particular country or group of countries to deal with. Adding to the complexity, people with religious agendas have been more actively involved with politics at grassroots, national, regional, and global levels. The relationship between religion and politics is by no means one-way. It is a bilateral engagement that is taking place at different levels and in different modes.

Buddhism has a special position in the world of spirituality. Many scholars, especially in the West, classify Buddhism as a school of oriental philosophy, because it has no concept of a Creator God. Buddha denied any association between his teachings and God, the Supreme Creator. He referred to himself as the "one who shows the way," as a beautiful friend to the world, and he never asked anyone to be converted to his religion or doctrine. In Buddhism not only are there no commandments to follow, the Buddha encouraged his students to believe not in him but in his teachings. Before he died, he declined to appoint a new leader for his community; instead, he nominated his own teaching as the guide.

This radical and liberal attitude, and the respect for individual dignity and freewill at the philosophical core of the Buddha's teachings, should have made Buddhism a most suitable spiritual institution to engage in dialogue with science, Western democracy, social reform, and human rights movements. Buddhist philosophy could be applied in the struggle to eliminate poverty and bring harmony to the world.

As it turned out, the Buddha's teachings were integrated into local cultures, and the religion absorbed aspects of native culture, tradition, supernaturalism, and feudalism from the countries it entered. Consequently, many Asian communities have their own version of Buddhist practices—an eclectic mix of Buddhist philosophy, animist traditions, and native culture. By the twelfth century, Buddhism was fully integrated into most civilizations in Asia, and the religion lost its vitality to spread beyond those countries. It was not until very recently, after the end of the Second World War and the Chinese occupation of Tibet, that Buddhism has been gaining more and more popularity in Western countries.

Buddhism does not have an established social institution that actively represents the faith in global politics. In contrast, many other world religions do have such institutions: for example, there is the Vatican, the official voice of Roman Catholicism; the World Council of Churches, which speaks for Protestant Christians; and the Organization of the Islamic Conference, which is working globally for the solidarity of Muslims. So far, the largest Buddhist organization that has served as an umbrella for world Buddhist communities is the World Fellowship of Buddhists, with its headquarters in Bangkok. However, the organization's policy is to stay away from all political conflicts; it has never taken part in any campaigns for world peace or human rights, or in international development projects of the United Nations and related organizations. Since its establishment in 1950, the World Fellowship of Buddhists has shown no interest in being an international NGO member of the United Nations or in participating in its activities. Of course, being quiet and keeping a distance from politics may be seen as a political agenda.

As a Buddhist, I cannot say that there is an official institution that represents the Buddhist faith. However, several Buddhist communities are engaged in national politics. In the present situation in Asia, Buddhism is a growing religion that influences politics in both active and inactive ways. Major Buddhist communities have their own political policies. Some of these communities are large with millions of followers, but extremely few are actively engaged in international politics.

THE BUDDHIST VIEW OF THE MATERIAL WORLD

The Buddhist worldview is distinct from that of the major Western religions of Judaism, Christianity, and Islam. Buddhism, as you may know, is a religion from India founded by the sage Siddhartha Gautama (Siddhattha Gotama in Pali[1]) around the fifth century BCE. Although the Buddha never said explicitly that he respects the rights of individuals, this attitude is clear in his position as "the one who shows the way"; he did not promote himself as a prophet or authority to command anyone. Buddhist canon reveals that the Buddha respected the will and opinion of his listeners. He never said that by denying him or his teachings a person would be born into hell or suffer eternal damnation.

The Buddha's teachings are based on the perception of a moral universe in which each individual has the innate potential to develop to perfection in morality and wisdom, through his or her own effort. Nevertheless, Buddhism is not a monolithic religion. Indeed, the religion of the Buddha is full of diversity, and even in one tradition there can be more than one school of interpretation and practice. In order to cultivate peace for individuals and society, it is necessary to know the unique worldview of Buddhism.

The Buddha describes the cosmos as a huge space, dynamic but uncreated. It is composed of thousands of world-systems, each with its own sun, moon, stars, and unseen worlds of angelic beings and demons. According to this description, the Earth is not the only planet inhabited by humankind, animals, and plants. This non-geocentric attitude is common to different schools of Buddhism. Each being is an individual who repeatedly is born and dies in the endless rounds of transmigration (*samsara*). From time to time, a being who has accumulated sufficient virtue and wisdom becomes enlightened and known as the Buddha. He then declares the same teaching and forms the same kind of community that the historical Buddha, Siddhartha Gautama, has done. At any point in time, the cosmos always has a number of Buddhas preaching in different parts of the vast universe. Some schools of Buddhism do not worship the historical Buddha as much at the cosmic ones. One school in particular, known as Pure Land Buddhism, worships the Buddha of Infinite Life (or Light), who created his own paradise in the western region of the heavens as the centre of Buddhist faith.

Every school of Buddhism agrees with the historical Buddha that an individual can finally be enlightened as a Buddha. Someone who is committed to reaching this highest state of enlightenment in his or her last existence is called a *bodhisattva*. The Mahayana Buddhist tradition, in particular, makes it almost compulsory that everyone take on this ambitious spiritual goal, whereas the conservative Theravada tradition holds that people can be different and have the right to determine their final liberation on their own terms.

According to the Buddha, there is no eternal damnation, regardless of how serious the crime one has committed. However, an individual may suffer an extremely long retribution for malicious acts in purgatories, which can also lead to a series of rebirths in woeful conditions in the afterlife. Nevertheless, after paying off the bad debt of the bad actions (*karma*), the person is subject to be born again in the human condition. Nirvana is the only eternal resting place, which is reached when all karmic debt of the being is completely paid off.

The Buddha refused to discuss the issue of the "prime cause," the "end days," and the existence of the self after nirvana, simply because these things are beyond the limits of human understanding. However, he affirmed that the *Dharma*—the universal principle, the ultimate foundation of the universe as defined in his teachings—is available for everyone to experience. Once liberation is attained, the mind is free to probe the mysteries of the universe. Since the Buddha's experience of enlightenment, in which he realized the *Dharma*, can be taught to and learned by others, Buddhism is not dependant on belief but on experience and proof through personal effort.

Everyone Is Basically Equal

The *Agganna Sutta: On Knowledge of Beginnings*,[2] one of major narratives in the Book of the Long Discourses of the Buddha (known as the *Digha Nikaya* of the Tipitaka) describes the transcendental origin of the human race, which later developed into the society and caste system of ancient India. The story is an allegory of a dialogue between the Buddha and two Brahmin postulants who were looking forward to being ordained into the order of Buddhist monks.

According to the Buddha, humans are descendants of genderless, self-luminous celestial beings who were trapped on earth by their temptation. Having lost their supernatural ability, they were subject to change and decay resulting from their greed and prejudice, and began to steal and fight among themselves. In order to prevent further chaos, they elected the first king, Maha-Sammata, a title that means "The People's Choice," to have the authority to keep justice and to penalize those who should be penalized. The relevance of this *sutra* (scriptural text) today is seen in the use of the word *sammata* in the Burmese language for the position of the elected president of a state.[3]

According to this story, members of the human race are all equal; men are not superior to women or vice versa. Moreover, the power of the king or government comes directly from the people. Prejudice based on the colour of the skin is not acceptable as it was a cause of decay and was seen as one of the earliest sins committed by the ancestors of the human race. Buddhist scholars have interpreted this story as an alternative to the famous Hindu Hymn of Creation, the Rig-Veda, where castes are respected as fundamental to the creation of the universe. Historically, this sutra paved the way for the early Buddhist community to solve problems through councils where each monk had an equal right to express ideas.

In Buddhist culture, the impact of this sutra remains strong. It is one of the most commonly quoted sources of scripture for the principles of democracy in Theravada Buddhist culture in reference to the equality of all people and the authority of the government. The Buddha never endorsed a utopia of Buddhists, but the sutra is clearly supportive of the equality of individuals and opposed to the division of humankind into castes or even nationalities. The message is this: We are all members of the same race from the beginning, and all of us deserve the respect and rights that are bestowed upon us as a part of Nature—"the interdependent wholeness of existence in which every being is connected to all other beings."[4] Buddhist countries should promote the sutra; it can serve as a strong ground for the development of democracy, human rights, and environmental campaigns.

DIVERSITY OF INTERPRETATIONS IN THERAVADA BUDDHISM

Teachers and experts in Theravada Buddhism have diverse opinions on the priority of precepts and practices to follow. Those who see Buddhism as a school of spiritual liberation oriented toward the radical attainment of nirvana, called the

Nibbanic system of Buddhism,[5] would limit the goal of their lives to the pursuit of spiritual liberation through the Eightfold Path, as part of the Four Noble Truths. Accordingly, they see that life is full of suffering, and the only way to make true progress in life is to detach themselves from everything, merit and demerit (karma) included, as their goal is not to be reborn in any condition.

However, the majority of Theravada Buddhists would argue that this goal might not be sufficient, as they see the Karmic Law as authoritative. In Kammatic Buddhism,[6] the goal is to accumulate the maximum merit for achievement in this life and in the lives to come. Merit is seen as the real spiritual treasure that can be taken into the afterlife, whereas demerit is the opposite. According to this group of Buddhists, the true meaning of life is the accumulation of merit for themselves. Most Buddhists who belong to this school of thought prefer to limit their merit-making to the community of Buddhist monks; the poor or the needy are not seen as the most fertile soil for merit-making.

Another group of Theravada Buddhists ground their faith in the coming of the Fifth Buddha, the Lord Metteyya, who is prophesized by Siddhartha Gautama (the fourth Buddha of this age) in the Book of the Long Discourses.[7] According to this sutra, the future Buddha will be enlightened after the world passes through a period of global catastrophe, which some Millennium Buddhists believe will happen 2,500 years from now.[8] Lord Metteyya will be the fifth and the last Buddha of the world who will preach the exact same doctrine as Siddhartha Gautama. His dispensation will last 80,000 years, and he will restore the world to its true balance.[9] For this group of Buddhists, the course of the world is predestined and cannot be changed. Individuals, however, may dedicate their lives to the search for a special panacea to rejuvenate their bodies so that they may live to meet the Lord Metteyya.

These three interpretations of Buddhism are all grounded in the Tipitaka, the Buddhist canonical literature of the Theravada tradition. All three groups accept the authority of the same scriptures, take refuge in the same Buddha, and agree on the same model of reality. Their differences lie in the priority given to different texts.

DOCTRINE OF KARMA AND ITS NEGATIVE IMPACT ON SOCIETY

When I was doing my research on Buddhism and HIV/AIDS in Thailand in 1992, it was the peak period of HIV transmission this country. Thailand was then called the "World Capital of AIDS," and so I was struck by the lack of interest in the epidemic among the Buddhist majority. At that time, I had an opportunity to address a large group of Buddhists who had been practising the religion for over ten years. I raised the question to the audience: What would you do if one day you found out that one of your neighbours had converted his house into a brothel?

Surprisingly, from over six hundred people I received only two answers. One said that he would engage in contemplation of the Three Characteristics of existence identified by the Buddha: impermanence (*anicca*), suffering (*dukkha*), and non-self (*anatta*), which would immediately release him from concern over the problem. The other answered that the problem displayed the Law of Karma in which every party involved was tied in karmic payback. Both answers shared a similar response to the social problem: no social awareness.[10] Apparently, the more they practised Buddhism, the more tolerant of social injustice they became. It was then that I began to realize that instead of offering a solution to social problems, the religion has been part of the problem.

Although Buddhism is a godless religion and the Buddha explicitly explained that his system of teaching is not based on belief in a Supreme Creator—the existence of God as a central tenet of belief has no place in the teaching of the Buddha—most Buddhists in Thailand and other Theravada countries believe that the Law of Karma is the Absolute Universal Mechanism that awards those who do good and punishes those who do evil.[11] The Law of Karma serves as an invisible hand of an impartial God that maintains justice in the world so that the Buddhist universe is moralized, always just and fair to everyone. In Thailand, the teaching of morality in schools and monasteries is grounded in the belief in the Law of Karma. Therefore, a good Buddhist is always afraid of committing any crime or sin. Even trivial mischief like smashing a mosquito, telling white lies, or using harsh language is frowned upon as sinful and unethical. Since the Buddha said that karma is the "intention," bad thoughts are also seen as sinful and can result in deplorable conditions.

The majority of Buddhists in Theravada countries are taught that karma is what the teaching of the Buddha is all about. They see the world through the lens of karmic law—what we are now is the result of what we have done in the past, and karma determines what we will be in the future. The logic of the Law of Karma is simply based on the belief that what goes around comes around. Karma dictates our present condition, and the future is conditioned by our actions today. Buddhists take it for granted that karma cannot perish, but will remain until a proper fruition of the karma comes into existence.

The Law of Karma is popular in Theravada Buddhism because it is seen as the grounds for merit-making. As mentioned previously, the community of monks is considered the most fertile field for merit-making—any good or bad that is bestowed on the monks will result in plenty of karma. This belief has generated a lot of donations to monks and Buddhist communities in Theravada countries. Apparently, monasteries that promote belief in the Law of Karma are usually large, well decorated, and opulent, and monastic members have a high standard of life.

However, the Law of Karma has its flipside. Since everything is just and fair, victims of social abuse of any kind—people with HIV/AIDS, the homeless, abused children, prostitutes—are seen not merely as suffering bad luck, but as receiving payback by karmic retribution for their actions either in this life or in former ones. Likewise, those in power, even if they are known to be corrupt and evil, must have done great merit in their former lives; their fortune and success are being paid back to them. People deserve whatever they have, since the Law of Karma is fair and this is the way things are in the universe. The only way that individuals might improve their lives is through merit-making, which is centred on patronizing monastic communities.

The karmic worldview has created an ultra-conservative attitude in Theravada countries, where the law of the land is deemed redundant because the cosmic Law of Karma is eternally just and fair. The words of monks command more attention than the injunctions of the law. The Buddhist majority lives in religious complacency, feeling that social problems have nothing to do with them. Individuals should do good, but only to accumulate merit for themselves; no one is responsible for others. This belief encourages Buddhists to limit their concerns to themselves. They do not focus on the needs of society, as the karmic consequence works only on an individual basis.

The belief in karmic law among the Buddhist majority is always on the side of the mighty and powerful in society, because their power and authority are not merely acquired from their efforts in this life but from previous merit. The rich and powerful must have been good people in their past lives, and so they deserve their privileged positions; hence, the status quo is highly secure in Buddhist countries. Since the amount of merit gained through donation to Buddhist monasteries is always great, corrupt politicians, mafia, criminals, and tyrants enjoy the publicity of their big merit-making ceremonies. It is surely a good way to redeem their sin. Not only does the ceremony free them from guilt, it also rubber stamps their status of authority and respect in society. As a result, corrupt politicians and tyrants, together with some monks and monasteries, are richer, while the public is poorer.

The belief in karma has provided a strong social foundation for government and rulers in Buddhist societies. A good example is Myanmar where over seventy percent of Burmese Buddhists firmly believe in karmic justice. The faith in karma has justified any authority in power, making the development of democracy and human rights an uphill battle.

For the development of civil society, Buddhists urgently need to renew the interpretation of the Law of Karma, so that everyone is not merely seen as an isolated individual: one's karma always affects others, with or without intention. All of us in this world are responsible for one another, and we are also a part of the cosmic manifestation of karma; without this understanding, the belief in the Law of Karma will remain the biggest hindrance in the development of justice, human rights, and civil society.

BUDDHIST NATIONALISM: A CAUSE OF SOCIAL STRIFE

Apart from the Law of Karma—the Buddhist doctrine par excellence that affects society as well as national and regional politics—when Buddhism is combined with nationalism, the hybrid is often social violence. This social trend, which is emerging in Thailand, is straining international relations between ASEAN (Association of Southeast Asian) countries.

Buddhism has a worldwide reputation as a religion of peaceful meditation and compassion, but this impression conflicts with the historical pattern of fear and social unrest that arises time and again when Buddhism is married with nationalism.[12] Thailand (Siam) in the seventeenth century during the reign of King Narai the Great is a good example of this sad stereotype. Although the reign of King Narai of Ayutthaya was seen as the golden age of Siam when the country enjoyed close relations with France and other European countries, it ended with a coup propelled by Phra Petracha, an army general, together with his son Khunloung Sorasak, who was in charge of Buddhist Affairs. The coup was clearly driven by religious nationalism, and we are seeing the same pattern emerging today. At that time, many Buddhist monks were hostile toward Catholic missionaries in Siam. The coup reinforced this suspicious attitude toward European ties and, consequently, the country remained isolated from the West for the next two hundred years.

A history of xenophobia in Buddhist peoples emerged again in Tibet in the nineteenth century, when Dalai Lama XIII launched his modernization policy and opened a school to teach European languages, as he felt that his country was undeveloped and in need of education and a modern system of government. Abbots from five major monasteries protested his project, and Tibet was left far behind in development. Many historians believe that this setback paved the way for the invasion of the Chinese.

A similar situation emerged in Burma in the early 1960s. Nationalist Buddhist monks led a series of demonstrations against the democratically elected government of U Nu, who was promoting freedom and equality among all religions. This policy resulted in social unrest and a military takeover by General Newin. For over forty years, Burma has been ruled under the same military regime.

The same demon was born again in Sri Lanka thirty years ago. Again Buddhist monks were at the forefront of a radical nationalist movement to alienate Christian, Hindu, and Muslim minorities. To discriminate against these minority groups without touching religious differences, the radical constitution of Sri Lanka endorsed Sinhalese—the language of the Buddhist majority—as the national language of the country. The ratification of the constitution prompted the rise of the terrorist organization Tamil Tiger. Since then, the once peaceful Sri Lanka has been entangled in a series of bomb attacks and assassinations. It has been estimated that the continuous violence has led to more than 67,000 deaths and millions more injured or displaced. A series of international attempts to introduce a truce between the government of Sri Lanka and the Tamil minority has disgruntled a large number of Buddhist monks, who are campaigning against the peace agreement. For over three decades it seems that there has been no end to the social unrest and civil war inflamed by religious nationalism.[13]

The decree of Thailand's military junta, who assumed control of the country in a coup on September 19, 2006, to draft a new constitution and put it to a referendum in August 2007 opened a Pandora's box. It resurrected the previously failed campaign of Thailand's Buddhist leaders to have Buddhism named the national religion of Thailand. They had been deeply disappointed by their defeat in the previous draft constitution of 1997. Major Buddhist temples and monastic universities in Bangkok renewed their campaign, vowing to gather no less than two million signatures. Books and anonymous publications were circulated in Buddhist communities that accused Muslims of conspiring to take over the country, inflaming hatred and nationalist fervour.[14]

As the referendum approached, there were mass demonstrations of increasing size and sentiment. On April 8, 2007, a group of five hundred monks under the leadership of the provincial ecclesiastical administration of Chonburi vowed to sacrifice their lives in protest if the new draft of the constitution failed to honour their request.[15] In June 2007, thousands of Buddhist monks and supporters marched around the parliament building and joined in a fast to exert pressure on the government.[16] However, later that month the Constitution Drafting Assembly rejected a special status for Buddhism,[17] and in August 2007, on the advice of the Queen, the monks halted their campaign.[18] Although the campaign failed yet again, nationalist Buddhist monks and laity remain determined to push politicians to amend the constitution in their favour.

Politicians and governments in Thailand have always been sensitive enough to non-Buddhist Thais not to respond to calls from Buddhist nationalists to enshrine Buddhism in the constitution. Nevertheless, the propaganda has had a deeply destabilizing effect on Thailand's already fragile intercultural relationships and served to fuel the increasingly omnipresent violence. This approach hardly reflects the compassion and acceptance of others that Buddhist teachings propound.

THE MANGALA SUTTA: TOWARD A PEACEFUL SOCIETY

One fact that has been accepted by scholars and Buddhists worldwide is that the Buddha never mentioned an ideal system of administration or utopia. Moreover, none of the traditional interpretations of Nibbanic, Kammatic, or Millennium Buddhism express much interest in social and global issues. Practicing Theravada Buddhists tend to be uninterested in social problems and non-religious conflict.

My interest therefore turns to one of the earliest Buddhist sutras, the Mangala Sutta, which may be translated "Aphorism on Good Omens." [19] I believe that this sutra could be used as another way of interpreting Buddhism that would contribute directly to the building up of peaceful society. [20] Traditionally, the Mangala Sutta is often recited as part of *paritta* chanting, in which sutras offering protection from evil and strengthening of mind are chanted by monks and nuns at auspicious celebrations and festivities. The term *mangala*, a Sanskrit word shared with Pali, refers to a traditional belief that a significant event is foretold by a sign. This aphorism may be an ethicized version of Indian superstition, a version that evolved when the early community of monks and nuns engaged with local culture. Nevertheless, the belief in omens or signs is common even in our modern life.

The sutra is a dialogue between the Buddha and a deity who comes to inquire about the nature of Good Omens, which has long been a subject of debate in heaven and on earth. The dialogue is given in twelve verses. In the first verse, the deity states his intention for the visit. The Buddha then expounds the thirty-eight Good Omens, which offer a holistic approach that helps us to understand Buddhist social ethics, the foundation of civil society. Each verse, except for the last, ends with the phrase, "This is the highest Good Omen."

The Mangala Sutta is probably the only systematic interpretation of Buddhist practices given in the Tipitaka. It shows the coherence of Buddhist precepts and practices for spiritual development. The good omens are not arbitrarily arranged;

SUMMARY OF THE MANGALA SUTTA

Verse 1

- the deity questions the Buddha

Verse 2

- not to associate with a fool
- to associate with the wise
- to honour those worthy of honour

Verse 3 ·

- to reside in a good environment
- to have done merit in the past
- to establish "self" in the right course

Verse 4

- to have great learning
- to be skilful in arts and handicrafts
- to master discipline
- to be well spoken

Verse 5

- to take care of parents
- to cherish children and spouse (family)
- to have a peaceful livelihood

Verse 6

- to be generous in giving
- to practise virtue
- to help one's relatives
- to be blameless in action

Verse 7

- to abstain from evil
- to abstain from intoxicants
- to be vigilant in duties

Verse 8

- to be respectful
- to be humble
- to be content
- to be grateful
- to listen to the *Dhamma*

Verse 9

- to be forbearing
- to be sensitive
- to associate with religious persons
- to have timely dialogue on religious issues

Verse 10

- to exercise self-restraint
- to practise holy living
- to perceive the Noble Truths
- to realize Nirvana

Verse 11

- to be unshaken by vicissitude
- to be free from sorrow
- to be cleansed from defilement
- to have a secure mind

Verse 12

- The person who has done all of the above wins success and happiness everywhere and at all times; this is the Highest Mangala.

they are systematically related to one another and offer a holistic approach to Buddhism. Beginning with the most external and physical, the sutra gradually introduces ethical principles and guidelines for living life as a good person, up to the most advanced quality of mind (one free from sorrow, defilement, and fear).

Unlike the logic of karma, which uses phenomena in the past to justify the present situation, the concept of *mangala* is directly related to prosperity and wholeness in the future. The sutra thus shows the practical relationship between one Buddhist principle and the other, conveying the entire process of spiritual development. Each *mangala*, once practised, can lead to the higher ones.

Since the Mangala Sutta links the present to the proximate future, we can see the relationship between personal and social ethics. Buddhists are to take care of parents, children, spouses, friends, and relatives. In other words, the sutra shows that individuals are not isolated but bound to one another by morality which, when practised, increases the common good of society. Hence, the connectedness of each member of the society is seen. Through the lens of the Mangala Sutta, vice in society is a *bad omen*. It will corrupt society and cause a spiral of social and spiritual decay. It is the responsibility of every member of society to take action and reverse the bad omen. This is the answer to the question about the neighbourhood brothel, mentioned earlier, that I raised to the Buddhist audience. The sutra promotes social awareness and collective responsibility to solve social problems.

This interpretation is consistent with the model of Dependent Origination, commonly accepted in the Buddhist world to explain the processes of chain-reactions that lead to the rise and fall of suffering and pain. Our lives are conditioned by others, and our success or failure is dependent on conditions associated with our moral actions. Thus, when one *mangala* is performed, it conditions another *mangala* to come into existence. And when all the *mangalas* are practised, happiness and success in life are assured. Therefore, the aphorism is a systematic teaching of social ethics in Buddhism, and provides a social dimension in which both personal happiness and success in life, and the collective good of society, depend upon an individual's morality.

The Buddha as an Agent for World Transformation

Through the lens of the Mangala Sutta, the Buddha can be seen as an ideal person. He lived his life according to this sutra, and practised what he preached. He perfected all the *mangalas* in his life; indeed, he is the First Good Omen of the world. In Buddhist legend, the Buddha was formerly a *bodhisattva* (someone on the way to enlightenment) who had accumulated an enormous amount of merit in his past lives, enough to enable him to win supreme enlightenment as described in the aphorism. Siddhartha Gautama was born into a royal family but chose to renounce his princely life. This moral decision is seen as a blessing that allows him to fulfill his spiritual quest.

Because Siddhartha left his wife and family to pursue enlightenment, some people may criticize him for not being a good husband or father. Yet the Buddha never completely abandoned his responsibilities; he returned to his family after he had accomplished his objective. In this sense, he fulfilled all the good omens that he taught in the aphorism and elsewhere in the Pali canon. The life story of the Buddha reveals that he practised all thirty-eight good omens on different occasions. Each moral decision that he made gave rise to other blessings. Together, the *mangalas* fostered change in society. Thus, the Buddhist community from the beginning was committed to propagating the teachings of the Buddha to encourage spiritual civilization in humankind.

The Mangala Sutta and World Politics

When people practise the Mangala Sutta, they are actively engaged in social development. The teachings of the Buddha are not to be followed merely for the sake of attaining Nirvana. The spiritual life cannot be lived all alone, but depends upon human interaction. The *mangalas* are conducive to the collective good of everyone in the world, as society improves by its members being devoted to decreasing suffering.

The Mangala Sutta sees individuals as being interconnected with one another and with the environment. According to this model, in a civil society people are respectful of law and order. They are beautiful friends to one another, actively engaged in various kinds of activities—arts and science, literature, philosophy, religion, and so forth. They are responsible for one another, the environment, and social welfare. Moreover, the *mangalas* are not gender specific or limited to a particular social status. They can be applied collectively in every part of the society. *Mangalas* for lay people are also good for the ordained; *mangalas* for men are also good for women, and vice versa.

Since *mangalas* or good omens are oriented toward the future, they entail a perception of society that is dynamic. Its progress or failure depends upon the common good of every member. In other words, society is a Commonwealth of Morality of individuals. The virtue that each person has accomplished maintains and mobilizes society in a positive direction.

The aphorism also supports interreligious dialogue, which is not seen as optional but as essential for the true practice of Buddhism; that is, by knowing other faiths, we know more of our own. According to the message of the Mangala Sutta, religious leaders working together would offer the strongest support for human dignity. Rather than arguing which religious institution is the strongest or the best, let's propose that the strongest are in the position to do the most good. Thus, each religion may play its part in working together for a peaceful world.

A LESSON FROM BUDDHISM: ENDORSE THE EMPOWERMENT OF WOMEN

One great lesson the world can learn from Buddhism concerns the unjust treatment of women, which I believe led to downfall of the religion in its mother-land, India. A scientific and analytical study of the Buddhist canon demonstrates that the message of the Buddha was supportive of gender equality, and that women were strong contributors to the spread of Buddhism.[21] This finding can support the process of women's empowerment and has the potential to radically reform gender issues in world politics.

Today, the status of women is much lower than that of men in most schools of Buddhism worldwide. Only the Buddhist monastic tradition in Taiwan, Soto Zen in Japan, and a few communities in South Korea accept women to be ordained as equals to their male counterparts. Elsewhere in the Buddhist world, women are not allowed to be ordained and do not have the same rights as men. The situation is worse in Theravada countries, where women are not allowed to be ordained or to enter sacred shrines; what's more, women are believed to have no ability to be enlightened and are thought to "jinx" the religion. The tradition holds that women have to be reborn as men in their next lives in order to have a chance at success in their meditation practices. In spite of the fact that women contribute more than ninety percent of the donations to Buddhist communities, they are not allowed to step into shrines and sacred areas, which are reserved for men.

In my academic research, I found that messages of the Buddha in the Tipitaka are supportive of gender equality. Buddhism as understood by Buddhists today is not the same as that taught by the Buddha, whose teaching is grounded in respect for human dignity and human rights.

Personally, my interest has never been in gender issues, and I accepted the traditional interpretation without questioning it. I became aware of the issue, however, through my research on the cause of the Buddha's death. Thirty years ago, as a young medical student, I was inspired to research his cause of death from information in the Tipitaka. In 2000, after my graduation from the University of Hamburg, I published my findings in the *Journal of the Pali Text Society*.[22] In the article, I argued that the Buddha died from mesenteric infarction, a disease of the vascular system of the bowel, which is common among the elderly. The diagnosis fit with the real-life situation surrounding the passing of Siddhartha Gautama. It also accounted for the timing and location of his death, and for the descriptions of the cremation of his body, factors that had not previously been considered by historians.

These findings prompted me to probe deeper into the social climate at the time of the Buddha's death, particularly as reflected in the First Council, which all schools of Buddhism agree was the origin of the canonization of the earliest Buddhist scriptures, the Tipitaka. These Pali texts are the foundation of Theravada Buddhism. My findings, however, challenged the Theravada tradition that the actual intention of the council was to canonize the words of the Buddha to preserve the religion in its true form. Rather, the intention of the council was to suppress the nun community.

A scientific and analytical approach to the Buddhist canon reveals that women were strong contributors to the spread of Buddhism. In the Book of Theragatha, we see that Buddhist nuns were more active than monks in the promotion of the *Dharma*. While monks tended to enjoy leading a solitary life, the nuns had stronger community ties and were very much engaged in teaching and learning. One passage even describes a nun who professed boldly to the public, "Come and listen to my teaching!"[23] Such evangelical expression is not ascribed to any monk in the Tipitaka. The Book of Theragatha is the first religious literature in the world known to be composed by women. It documents the earliest history of Buddhism, when women enjoyed equal rights with their male counterparts.

Many nuns were outstanding teachers and successful enough to enlighten some monks. Indeed, the women were so successful that many leading monks felt threatened. They waited until the death of the Buddha to take the administration of the community into their own hands and to gain control over the nun community. Members of the First Council, although honoured as saints, were faithful followers of Brahmanical Laws who were dissatisfied with the Buddha's teaching that women were equal to men. Thus, the real intention of the council was not to preserve and protect the Buddha's teachings as claimed by the tradition: it had a hidden agenda—to suppress the nun order.[24]

From the council emerged a set of Eight Rules of Heavy Duty (the *Garudhammas*) for nuns to follow for the rest of their lives. Referring to a number of texts in Jainism, law books in Hinduism, and several sections of the Buddhist canons, I found that these rules did not originate with the Buddha, but were interpolations added shortly after his death. These rules, which were oppressive and highly discriminatory against women, were enforced in the nun community through repetitions and affirmations every fortnight. Over time, the nun order was severely weakened.

The period of suppression, I surmise, lasted a few generations before the nun order finally disappeared from India. It was not long before Buddhism disappeared also. In fact, I believe that it was the suppression of the nun order that brought about the demise of Buddhism in India. This hypothesis is substantiated when Buddhism is compared to Jainism, the sister religion of Buddhism, founded by Mahavira, a contemporary of the Buddha. Like Buddhism, Jainism was seen as heterodox by Hindus and later by Muslims. The Buddhist community and Jain community share the same structure, being composed of monks, nuns, laymen, and laywomen; Buddhists worship statues of the Buddha, whereas Jains worship statues of Mahavira. While Buddhism disappeared from India, Jainism did not.[25]

Many historians still blame the extinction of Buddhism in its own motherland on oppression by Muslims and Hindus, but this theory cannot explain why Jainism was not also destroyed. The significant difference between Buddhism and Jainism lies in the treatment of women: nuns were not discriminated against in Jainism to the degree that they were in Buddhism. Even now, nuns in Jainism have the same liberty to teach as their male fellows. There are no such rules as the Eight Heavy Duties in the teachings of Mahavira!

A scientific and analytical approach to the Buddhist canon reveals a lost chapter in the history of the earliest Buddhist community in India. In light of this analysis, the evidence points to the fact that sexism in the Buddhist community was responsible for the extinction of the Buddhist religion in its own motherland. This destruction was the result of the karma committed by sexist monks in the generations following the passing away of the Buddha. Sexual discrimination or sexism was not at all part of the original teaching of the Buddha, who excluded no one.

Pieces of evidence scattered in the Tipitaka confirm that the original teaching of the Buddha did not favour men over women. The Tipitaka is a primary source of information about the early Buddhist monastic community in India. It offers a glimpse of dynamic changes in the belief system within the Buddhist community through a stretch of time no less than three hundred years. For example, the Buddha describes the origin of the human race, in which males and females emerged as a result of the continuous decay of the physical world; that is, gender distinctions do not belong to the true nature of who we are. Since gender is only the external appearance of our true nature, both men and women possess an equal ability to attain the highest enlightenment. Moreover, three references in the

Tipitaka mention visits of a king to see a *nun* while the Buddha was alive. In one episode, King Pasenadi of Kosala praises the teaching skills of nun Khema in front of the Buddha; he claimed that her teaching was as good as that of the Lord himself![26] The Book of Theragatha, as previously discussed, provides further evidence of the equal status of women.

Elements of sexism found their way into the Buddhist community soon after the passing away of the Buddha in order to reinforce men's superior status to women. Sadly, the karma of sexism remains strong in most Theravada Buddhist countries. Only some communities in Sri Lanka ordain women. Elsewhere in Southeast Asia, the ordination of women is illegal. The Ecclesiastical Council of Thailand, for example, announced publicly that any monk who supports the ordination of women is subject to severe punishment. In the Theravada tradition as a whole, sexism is followed faithfully as the authentic teaching of the Lord Buddha. Modern Buddhist communities worldwide follow these discriminatory practices. Thus, millions of women in Buddhism are treated as inferior and are not welcomed in Buddhist communities.

This analysis affirms the need for equal partnership between men and women as the foundation for a healthy community. It is also a testimony to the wrongdoing of members of the early Buddhist community, whose suppression of women was the true cause of the extinction of the religion in the motherland. Yet the lesson has not been learned in Theravada Buddhist countries, where Buddhist interpretation has never been in support of human rights and social justice. Until the religious education system in Buddhism and the interpretation of the Tipitaka in these countries is reformed, the religion will remain the biggest obstacle for the development of democracy and social justice.

The world community can learn a lesson from Buddhism. The teachings of the Buddha on gender equality, and the damage caused by ignoring those teachings, should prompt the inclusion of women's empowerment as public policy at all levels of government: local, national, regional, and international.

CONCLUSION

Buddhism, in general, is a peaceful religion with strong messages for social equality and compassion. Buddha rooted his teachings in the true nature and equality of each member of the human race. His teaching on the election of the first ruler of the world, Maha-Sammata or "the People's Choice," provides a strong foundation for democracy in Buddhist countries. Further, as a "Godless" religion equipped with the Buddha's radical rhetoric on liberation from attachment to any form of delusion, Buddhism could potentially dialogue with science and modern technology.

However, Buddhism consists of a number of schools of interpretation that have resulted in generalizations, poor social awareness, sexual discrimination, and tolerance of social injustice. In countries where Buddhists form the majority, religious faith has bolstered nationalism and given rise to xenophobic and discriminatory behaviours. These attitudes will continue to destabilize Southeast Asia if not managed carefully.

A reference for social development and activism is the Mangala Sutta, which reveals that an individual is not independent from society but has to grow as part of it. In the Mangala Sutta, in fact in all schools of Buddhist faith, development always starts with the consciousness of the person—the full realization that one needs to progress—and a commitment to improve through creative relationships with people and the environment. Through friendship and dialogue with family, friends, and religious people, and through education in the arts and sciences, a person can grow in understanding of the world and acquire higher wisdom, until the mind becomes calm and pure. As one follows the *mangalas*, one's life becomes an embodiment of the Good Omens or blessings, which are catalysts for self-development and social change. Progress is bilateral and holistic. Society progresses as people progress; social benefits increase as individuals grow and develop. Thus, the Good Omens work on both individual and social levels.

The Tipitaka is a window into a lost chapter of early Buddhist history and the original teachings of the Buddha, which were supportive of equality between men and women. After the passing away of the Buddha, sexual discrimination against ordained women arose as a means of maintaining male power and dominance, as the monks were threatened by the dynamic force of women in Buddhist education and community service. The suppression of Buddhist nuns lasted for several generations before Buddhism was weakened and finally disappeared from India. The same message of sexual discrimination does not exist in Jainism, a sister religion of Buddhism. The Tipitaka documents the great contribution of the nuns; the women were at the forefront in the propagation of Buddhism.

The teachings of the Buddha can and should be used to promote gender equality, the empowerment of women, democracy, social justice, and peace.

NOTES

[1] Because Theravada Buddhism is based on Pali scriptures, Pali spellings are preferred over the Sanskrit except for names and terms that have become part of the English language (e.g., the Buddha is commonly known as Siddhartha Gautama in English; but Tipitaka, the Pali spelling for the Theravada scriptures, is used instead of Tripitaka, the Sanskrit spelling).

[2] *Digha Nikaya*, Pali Text Society edition, DN III, 83-97; see also Maurice Walshe, *The Long Discourses of the Buddha: A Translation of the Digha Nikaya* (Boston: Wisdom Publications, 1995), 407-415.

[3] Department of Myanmar Language Commission, *Myanmar-English Dictionary* (Ministry of Education, Union of Myanmar, 1994), 520.

[4] Donald W. Mitchell, *Buddhism: Introducing Buddhist Experience* (Oxford: Oxford University Press, 2002), 288.

[5] Melford E. Spiro, *Buddhism and Society: A Great Tradition and Its Burmese Vicissitudes*, 2nd ed. (Berkeley: University of California Press, 1984), 31-63.

[6] Spiro, 66-128.

[7] Walshe, "Lion's Roar on the Turning of the Wheel," 395-407.

[8] Spiro, 168.

[9] Spiro, 168.

[10] The responses agree with Spiro's findings and analysis in his anthropological survey of Burma in 1961. See Spiro, 1984 (2nd ed.).

[11] Bhikkhu, "Effervescent Corruption in Karma-cola," *Bangkok Post*, May 25, 2005.

[12] Bhikkhu, "Buddhist Nationalism and Social Strife," *Bangkok Post*, April 7, 2007.

[13] Stanley J. Tambiah, *Buddhism Betrayed? Religion, Politics and Violence in Sri Lanka* (Chicago: University of Chicago Press, 1992).

[14] Bhikkhu, "Nationalists Tap a Source of Empty Pride," *Bangkok Post*, February 7, 2007.

[15] *Komchadluek* [a Thai national newspaper], April 9, 2007.

[16] "Monks Push for Buddhism to be Named Thailand's National Religion," *Gulf Times*, June 12, 2007. Accessed February 21, 2008, at http://www.gulf-times.com/site/topics/article.asp?cu_no=2&item_no=154565&version=1&template_id=45&parent_id=25

[17] "Drafters Reject Buddhism as State Religion," *The Nation*, July 1, 2007. Accessed February 21, 2008, at http://www.nationmultimedia.com/search/page.news.php?clid=5&id=30038509

[18] "Buddhist Groups, Monks Halt Campaign Against Draft Charter," *The Nation*, August 12, 2007. Accessed February 21, 2008, at http://www.nationmultimedia.com/search/page.news.php?clid=35&id=30044738

[19] Slightly adapted from *Sutta-Nipita*, trans. V. Fausboll (Oxford: Clarendon Press, 1881), pp. 43-4.

[20] I am indebted to a lecture by Dr. Charles Hallesey in a course on Theravada Buddhism at Harvard University, 1991, that inspired my interpretation of the aphorism.

[21] Bhikkhu, "Was the Lord Buddha a Sexist?" *Bangkok Post*, May 9, 2006.

[22] Bhikkhu and O. von Hinüber, "The Cause of the Buddha's Death," *Journal of the Pali Text Society* 26 (2000): 105-17.

[23] Pali Text Society, *Buddhist Pali Tipitaka* Thig: 54-6; see also Bhikkhu, *Hed Kued Por Sor Nung* [After the Buddha], 2nd ed. (Bangkok: Dokya Publishing Company, 2005), 168.

[24] Bhikkhu, *Hed Kued Por Sor Nung*, 126.

[25] Bhikkhu, *Hed Kued Por Sor Nung*, 171.

[26] Pali Text Society, *Buddhist Pali Tipitaka*, SN IV: 380; see also Bhikkhu, *Hed Kued Por Sor Nung*, 169.

SHIA ISLAM AS A FACTOR IN WORLD POLITICS

Abodolkarim Soroush

I come from Iran, the citadel of the Shia branch of Islam. I am not going to discuss the history of Shiism or Shia dogma. That's a very long story, and there are a number of books on the subject. What may be more useful to consider is the particularity of Shiism as a branch of Islam, and perhaps some of the differences in law and theology between Sunnis and Shiites. The differences are small but significant; in fact, some of these differences are crucial and have important practical implications.

RATIONALISM IN SHIA CULTURE

Let me begin with the importance of reason. Rationality is a much-loved element in Shia culture. Most Muslim philosophers have been Shiites. Avicenna was a Shiite. Mullah Sadra was a Shiite. Al-Farabi was a Shiite. I should also mention Sohrevardi. All of these individuals either hailed from Shiism or from Iran. Reason has always been an important factor in Shiism.

About a century and a half after the death of the Prophet, we in the world of Islam experienced a conflict or perhaps a divide between Asharite theologians and Mutazilite theologians. The Asharites were traditionalists who thought that believers should follow the tradition fully and virtually abandon their reason. The Mutazilites, on the other hand, were the rationalist camp. And although the

This paper was presented at the InterAction Council High-Level Expert Group Meeting on "World Religions as a Factor in World Politics," held May 7–8, 2007, in Tübingen, Germany.

Bridging the Divide: Religious Dialogue and Universal Ethics, ed. T.S. Axworthy.
Montreal and Kingston: McGill-Queen's University Press, Queen's Policy Studies Series.

Mutazilites were Sunnis, Shiites were actually closer to Mutazilism. Shiism has been sometimes considered an offshoot of Mutazilism, because of this rationality factor.

An emphasis on reason is one of the things that perhaps distinguish the two branches of Islam. Many of the compatriots of our dear friend Kamal Aboulmagd, author of the 1991 manifesto of the New Islamist school—like Hassan Hanafi, professor of philosophy in Cairo and an expert advisor to the InterAction Council—are Sunnis. They are Egyptians. They are very good Muslims. They are reformers, but I will tell you what their reform is. Their reform amounts to turning their backs on Asharism and, in a sense, moving closer to Mutazilism. In other words, reform in the Sunni world of Islam is taking the shape of turning away from traditionalism and moving closer to rationalism. This is very important.

Shiism is open to rational arguments about matters of faith, as I can tell you from my own experience. About fifteen years ago I wrote a book, which has been translated into Arabic and will hopefully be published in English, entitled *The Expansion and Contraction of Religious Knowledge*. In the book, I argue for the changeability and historicity of religious knowledge. It was a very provocative book, and it created many problems for me in Iran. It was even more provocative than Nasr Abu Zayd's *Mahfum al-Nass (The Concept of the Text)*, published in 1990. Abu Zayd, a professor at Cairo University, also argues for the historicity of the text of the Qur'an, and its changeability. We both made the same argument without knowing anything about one another at the time. We later met for the first time in Germany, and he told me his story. Abu Zayd had had a bitter experience in Egypt, where he had been accused of apostasy. He had to leave his country, and he is still in The Netherlands, where I, too, am based at the moment. So, fate has brought us both to The Netherlands. However, I was never accused of apostasy. Of course, the book created a great deal of trouble for me, but nobody—none of the grand ayatollahs, none of the minor ayatollahs—ever suggested that my ideas amounted to apostasy.

This whole experience of openness, of encounters with different ideas, has always existed in Shiism, which is fortunate. The leader of the Islamic Revolution, Ayatollah Khomeini, was himself philosopher. Of course, he was also a theologian and an Islamic jurist, as well as a mystic. This was the way in the seminaries; people used to study many subjects and practise various professions. He was the top-ranked theologian. Had it not been for his support for my ideas, I would have been killed. His daughter-in-law, a student of mine in the Philosophy Department of Tehran University, showed him some of my writings, and he said amicably, "This is okay. These ideas are not to be worried about." That saved me. Without his support, the counter-reactions would have been much harsher.

Ijtihad

Rationalism includes the concept of *ijtihad*, the formulation of reasoned opinions on matters of Islamic law. *Ijtihad* not only means adjudication; it means struggling—struggling with the law—in order to bring it into line with changing situations, changing conditions. This practice is very strong in Shiism, as you may know, and many grand ayatollahs have attempted to make big changes in the law to align it with new and changing circumstances that have occurred over the passage of time. This process has been continuous. It is important to note that there is always plurality of *ijtihad*, which keeps pluralism alive in Shiism.

Now, there are more than ten grand ayatollahs in Iraq. They each have their own school of law, with a distinct code of dress and behaviour. Each school is different, but not totally different, from the others. This plurality of *ijtihad* has always existed within Shiism, and it does not have a major counterpart in the Sunni world. In the Sunni world, supposedly, the gate of *ijtihad* is closed.

I would say that in Shiism the gate is wide open; a grand ayatollah has the power and authority to change Islamic law. Ayatollah Khomeini went further than this, to the extent that had he not been the grand ayatollah and the leader of the Revolution, he would have been accused of being a heretic. He maintained that virtually all of the power, privilege, and authority that the Prophet enjoyed, an Islamic jurist enjoys—this was his revolutionary idea. The Prophet was a legislator and, in Khomeini's view, any big jurist or grand ayatollah is a legislator, too. He argued that the jurist even has the power and authority to proclaim legislation that contradicts the explicit decrees of the Prophet or the Qur'an; if he thinks that it is good for Islamic society, he can do it. Imam Khomeini based these ideas on the Shiite principle of jurisprudence.

Of course, this policy is a double-edged sword. On the one hand, it can be very positive, but on the other hand, it can be very, very negative. A jurist has to be careful not to abuse this power. It is a great power—to give the power of Prophethood, the power of legislation, a God-like authority to somebody who is, after all, the leader of a revolution. But again, this principle illustrates the deep-rootedness of rationality within Shiism and the extent to which we can exercise our reason. I must add that there are jurists who do not see matters in this way and who disagree with Khomeini. Nevertheless, this tradition is now an important part of Shiism.

THREE RIVALS OF REASON

It is clear that rationality is highly regarded in Iran and in Shia culture. Yet Shiism also values forces that seem to run contrary to reason. Again, let me share my own experience. I have studied philosophy more than any other discipline. I trained in Britain in traditional analytical philosophy as well as in Islamic philosophy. I had been a scientist before I became a philosopher and a theologian, and so I have been involved in all of these fields. I am fond of reason, of course, as is any philosopher. But reason has had three rivals in my own life: revelation, love, and revolution.

Revelation

For theologians, revelation has always been considered a rival to reason. Many believers, too, feel that they either have to be good believers and give full authority to the Prophet, to revelation, to the Book that has been revealed to them, or they have to depend on reason and its products, such as philosophy, science, and so forth.

The conflict between science and religion in sixteenth- and seventeenth-century Europe is well known, but the world of Islam did not have such an experience. This is not something that is to our credit; science simply did not develop among us and, in view of this, there was naturally no conflict between science and religion. But, of course, we are well aware of the conflict that occurred in Europe.

In fact, I experienced this conflict firsthand as a member of the Cultural Revolution Institute. I had been appointed by Imam Khomeini after the Revolution. Reconciling science and religion or revelation was at the top of my agenda. I well remember when a reporter from Italy stationed in Iran called me and asked, "What are you going to do with the Darwinian theory of evolution?" I told her that this problem had not occurred to us. I can tell you quite frankly that it was absent from the minds of the people who had been given the task of revolutionizing culture or culturizing the revolution. It was simply not an issue for any of us.

This particular conflict between science and religion has not been a high priority for us Iranians, either before the Revolution or after it. Nonetheless, among scholars it has been always been debated, and various solutions have been suggested.

Love

The second rival of reason that I have experienced is love. In Islamic mysticism—and no doubt other mystical traditions are similar—love has always been considered a rival of reason. Lovers must somehow abandon their reason. The story of love and reason is the perennial story of mysticism. This is what Rumi wrote about: the story of Rumi's *Mathnawi* is the story of love. The year 2007 was declared by UNESCO as the International Year of Rumi, marking his 800th anniversary. I am supposed to be an expert on Rumi, and I can recite many of his verses and poems about love. I always say that if the Qur'an is the book of awe, the book of fear, Rumi's book is the book of love. It is a complement to the Qur'an, although this might strike some ears as an unacceptable thing to say. Nevertheless, I dare say that the *Mathnawi* is complementary to the mission and message of the Qur'an. The Qur'an is not a book of love; it is a book of fear. It is not a book of rights; it is a book of duties. Duty is an inflated idea in all religions, I suppose, especially in the Abrahamic religions of Islam and Judaism. We are infatuated with obligations and responsibilities and duties, but rights have been given short shrift.

Most Muslim mystics have been anti-theology. One reason for this is that mysticism is inclusive, whereas theology, by its very nature, is exclusive: I am a theologian of Islam, so I am, per force, in the right. I am here in order to prove that Islam is right, that it is the truth, and to disprove Christianity, Judaism, and other faiths. This is the mission, this is the business, this is the profession of any theologian. And this is why I see some defects in the present Pope, which I have expressed in writing. The previous Pope was a philosopher, and philosophy is inherently more pluralistic than theology. With all due respect to theologians, theology is not a good carrier of pluralism. Now, some Muslim mystics disliked theology because of their disdain for reason. They believed that theology was mutilating their religion as they saw it, that it was trying to rationalize something that could not be rationalized. In mysticism there is love, and there is pluralism.

Revolution

The third rival of reason, in my own life, has been revolution. Westerners have written about the conflict between revolution and reason. I, too, have written about it, but I have also lived it: I have seen it and touched it firsthand. Revolution is an outburst. It is an explosion of emotions, occasionally of hatred. It means combating, crushing, and destroying whatever is not revolutionary. In contrast, reason is cool and unemotional. It watches carefully, in order to analyze, to give everything its due, and so on.

The idea of revolting against the ruler is absent in Sunnism. Once somebody is a ruler, by virtue of being a ruler, he is seen as legitimate. But in Shiism, because of the martyrdom of Imam Husayn, the Prophet's grandson who led a revolt in 680 CE, no ruler becomes automatically and immediately a legitimate one. People can rise up against him. Many Sunnis have criticized Husayn's refusal to accept the regime, arguing that he did not have the right to revolt because the ruler was legitimate. This interpretation is a matter of dispute between Sunnis and Shiites.

Do we have the right to take up arms against the state? For Shiites, the answer is simple: "Yes, we do, if the ruler is illegitimate." That is what Khomeini did. But Sunnis are ambivalent. Sometimes they might say "Yes" and sometimes "No." One of the Sunni leaders expressed his lament to me over this issue at a conference in London after the Revolution. He said, "You Shiites are fortunate because you have a clear precedent and tradition that allows you to rise up against a ruler— you have Imam Husayn. But in the Sunni world, we have to make a lot of calculations and wade through a lot of legislation and litigation in order to perhaps come to an ambivalent conclusion that a revolution is valid." The validity of revolution in Shiism is a central truth, because of historical precedent.

MARTYRDOM

To give you a full picture, another aspect of Shiism is martyrdom. The martyrdom of Imam Husayn at the hands of the ruling regime was a pivotal event in the history of Islam, because it divided the Muslim community and gave rise to Shiism. For Sunnis, the story is merely a part of their history. But for Shiites, Husayn's martyrdom has become a rallying cry, inspiring them to fight against their enemies. The Revolution in Iran was fuelled by the idea of martyrdom. Were it not for the grandson of the Prophet and his martyrdom, there would not have been an Islamic Revolution. His martyrdom was invoked again and again, to the extent that everybody had to virtually recreate himself in the image of Imam Husayn. People believed that martyrdom was the greatest virtue—the most important virtue—for a Shiite, for a Muslim. That idea drove the Revolution.

Imam Khomeini was very careful in using this idea, because after the Revolution, when he reintroduced the annual commemoration of Imam Husayn's martyrdom, he emphasized that this event was not to be used for political ends. He basically said, "Okay, political demonstrations are fine and everything, but the commemoration of the third Imam, Imam Husayn, is a different thing, and so you must perform this independently. Do not mix it with political demonstrations. It has to be kept separate, and it has to be kept among the leading Shiites." Nevertheless, before the Revolution this Shiite principle of martyrdom, combined with left-wing ideas, actually produced the Revolution.

APOCALYPTIC SENSE

Shiism also has an apocalyptic aspect. According to Shiites, the Prophet was succeeded by eleven descendants who served consecutively as pontiffs and interpreters of the Qur'an. The twelfth descendant is hidden and will reappear one day together with Jesus. When he returns, he will lead the revolution, and Jesus will assist him. This messianic tradition follows in the footsteps of Christianity and Judaism. They, too, are looking for a saviour to come at the end of time, to make everyone happy and to establish justice on earth.

This apocalyptic sense has ebbed and flowed over the centuries. Sometimes the apocalyptic tide is high, very high, as it is in Iran today, and sometimes it is low. Before the Revolution apocalyptic sentiments were not that strong, but since the Revolution, and especially now under President Ahmadinejad, this issue is very real. Ahmadinejad thinks that Western civilization is doomed to failure and that its demise is imminent, perhaps only a few years away. This belief is the basis of some of his foreign and domestic policies, and he has many supporters.

So apocalyptic thinking comes from Shiism. But for some Shiites, apocalypticism means pacifism. Since somebody will come at the end of time, and will do everything for us, we just have to sit and watch. And if corruption increases in the world, so much the better according to pacifists, because then the Twelfth Imam will reappear sooner. I know this because I belonged to an association of Iranian Shiites who had precisely this idea, and that was precisely why I broke with them before the Revolution. Under the Shah and Western influence, they thought that all we have to do is sit and wait for the Twelfth Imam to return and set everything right. But now, active apocalypticism is at work in Iran under President Ahmadinejad. Khomeini was not like that; he never invoked a hidden Imam. But Ahmadinejad is very much inclined to do so.

GOLDEN RULE

Finally, I come to what Hans Küng and others have written a great deal about, the Golden Rule of all ethical systems. You find it in Confucianism. You find it in the Bible. But I would like to tell you that you do not find it in the Qur'an; you find it in the Books of Shiites: "Treat others as you would like to be treated yourself." This is the Golden Rule; this is the heart of justice. Again, you do not find this rule as such in the Qur'an. I am not suggesting that the Qur'an is against it, but it is not mentioned explicitly there. But in the sermons of the first Shiite Imam (Imam Ali), yes, there you find it. You are the scale and you are the measure, and you can say what is good and what is bad. The Golden Rule is common to all traditions, religious and non-religious, and must be taken very seriously for the sake of justice and happiness among all human beings.

I remind you that I have deliberately emphasized the particularities of Shiism. This brief discussion is not meant to contradict the fact that about ninety percent of Shiite and Sunni beliefs overlap. Historically, the main disagreement was over the Prophet's successors and who was the legitimate caliph or ruler. That is now a bygone era that no one wants to dwell on. But there are, of course, different traditions and particularities that continue today, which I have outlined. I hope that this outline will help give you a more accurate image of Shiism.

ISLAM AS A FACTOR IN GLOBAL POLITICS: SEARCHING FOR COMMON VALUES TO GUIDE A GLOBALIZING WORLD

Kamal Aboulmagd

The need to reintroduce Islam as a religion, a way of life, and a main source of legislation guiding, if not governing, the lives of more than a billion men and women in our time, is justifiable in light of two considerations:

The first consideration is that most Muslim countries are witnessing a "wave of religiosity" among their populations. More Muslims are trying their best to abide by the teachings of Islam, observing more carefully its rituals and becoming more keen to shape the totality of their daily lives according to the requirements of Islam as conceived by them and as elaborated by their religious leaders, whether these leaders are recognized scholars of the Islamic science, or self-appointed preachers who entertain a sense of mission to spread the word of God and to implement the principles of Islam. A diversity of attitudes prevails among these preachers and is reflected in the behaviour of their followers, and a similar diversity of ideas is advocated by contemporary groups of Islamists; thus a first priority is to try to better understand the reasons for such diversity and to identify who is who and who wants what in the present extremely rich but extremely confusing picture of contemporary Muslims and their understanding of Islam.

This paper was presented at the InterAction Council High-Level Expert Group Meeting on "World Religions as a Factor in World Politics," held May 7–8, 2007, in Tübingen, Germany.

Bridging the Divide: Religious Dialogue and Universal Ethics, ed. T.S. Axworthy.
Montreal and Kingston: McGill-Queen's University Press, Queen's Policy Studies Series.
© 2008 The School of Policy Studies, Queen's University at Kingston. All rights reserved.

The second consideration making the endeavour to reintroduce Islam to the world a matter of urgent necessity is the rise of mistrust, suspicion, and phobia toward Islam and its followers. The word *Islamophobia*, often used to designate this regrettable attitude, is not, in my view, accurate. It describes only the psychological and subjective elements of this negative attitude, and falls short of highlighting the resulting unfair and discriminatory treatment inflicted on millions of Muslims who happen to live in non-Muslim countries. In light of this observation, I believe the alternative expression *anti-Islamism* would be more accurate in describing this regrettable phenomenon. A combination of stereotyping and anti-Islamism nurtured, in some cases, by political motivation has created a psychological wedge between all Muslims on the one hand, and all peoples of different religions, nationalities, and political affiliations on the other. If exploited, denied, or neglected, this wall of "psychological separation" may deteriorate into a real "clash of civilizations" between large groupings who, in fact, have much in common that could lead them to join hands in a concerted effort of cooperation and mutual support in the face of very real dangers threatening their safety, security, and aspirations to live together in peace and harmony.

Unfortunately, the fact that many suspects in the tragic events of September 11 were either Muslims or Arabs gave undeserved legitimacy to the myth that there is something inherent in the religion of Islam that makes all Muslims potentially or actually violent. I find no better answer to this sweeping but baseless condemnation of Muslims and Islam than the wise words of Hans Küng in his most constructive paper on "The Three Abrahamic Religions," where he states that most Muslims reject "archaic inhumanities":

> They suffer from the fact that sweeping condemnations are made of Muslims and Islam, without differentiation. . . . Those who make Islam responsible for kidnappings, suicide attacks, car bombings, and beheadings carried out by a few blind extremists ought at the same time to condemn Christianity and Judaism for the barbarous maltreatment of prisoners, the air strikes and tank attacks carried out by the US Army, and for the terrorism of the Israeli army occupation in Palestine.

It is against this background that I wholeheartedly welcomed the opportunity to participate in this awesome gathering of distinguished experts and scholars, each of whom is well known and appreciated at home and worldwide for long-standing commitment to the spirit of reconciliation and for the recognition and acceptance of diversity as a law of God that works to enrich the march of human history through the exchange of knowledge and experience, without being in any way a threat to any particular faith, creed, or way of life.

Moving now to the substance of this paper, namely, reintroducing Islam as a factor in world politics, I find it both necessary and proper to state my position on two issues that shape the context within which these discussions take place: globalization and dialogue.

Globalization

In order to avoid straying too far from the subject at hand, it is sufficient to clarify my own perception of those elements of globalization that are relevant to our shared hopes for the consolidated positive impact that religions can have on world politics. I believe that a distinction must be made between globalization perceived as a *description* of certain revolutionary changes that have taken place during the last four decades in the fields of science and technology—particularly advances in the technology of transportation, information, and communication—and globalization as a *prescription* for enlarging the market for commodities and services, an enlargement that has benefited mainly rich countries and multinational corporations. The unprecedented technological revolution has resulted in a progressive shrinkage of the barriers of time and space that separated different nations and other human groupings for many centuries. The new developments have led to a much greater mobility of people, commodities, services and, above all, ideas and values. Even in the field of law, which is recognized as perhaps the slowest normative order to change, drastic changes have taken place.

Perhaps most relevant to our discussion is the gradual collapse of the traditional strict line of demarcation separating the national jurisdiction from the international. The concept of the inviolable sovereignty of the state within its national territory is consistently giving way to the right of the community of nations to monitor and interfere in national matters. This aspect of globalization has been utilized to create larger markets for every manufacturer and service provider. Giant multinationals and other investors are flourishing and becoming more powerful. However, the social consequences of this type of giantism remain to be more carefully studied and more critically evaluated. Power corrupts, and absolute and unfettered power is likely to corrupt absolutely. The economic implications of globalization, however, are outside the scope of this paper.

Much closer to our concern here are the cultural aspects of globalization. Changes that occur easily and rapidly in the economic and trade fields are not accepted with the same equanimity when it comes to cultures, values, traditions, and ways of thinking. Cultural changes are inherently slow, because they touch upon the identity of people both as groupings and as individuals. People are usually

very reluctant to accommodate, let alone welcome, any changes in their ways of thinking, their ways of life, and the deep-rooted values that shape their relations with
individuals in their own community and with others belonging to different cultures.

However, events in recent years have demonstrated that the time is up for cultural isolation. Ideas and values different from the ones entertained and followed
over the centuries by members of any given culture are gradually crossing territo-
rial boundaries and interacting slowly but consistently with traditional ideas and
values with little difficulty or no difficulty at all. The real problem has become
one of finding a modus operandi for this inevitable meeting of ideas and values, and to
agree both nationally and internationally on a criterion to guide the process of selec-
tion between those traditions and values representing the essential elements of a culture
or religion—elements that should never be abandoned or compromised—and those
non-essential elements that may, consequently, be abandoned and sacrificed to be replaced by more useful, more humane, or more efficient ones.

This *problematique* facing religious people lies at the heart of the present tension within and between religious communities and within each and every religious
individual. The search for an acceptable criterion to distinguish the essential, un-
changeable elements of a culture from the non-essential ones must be addressed
within each religion in order to sustain its moral legitimacy vis-à-vis all other
members of the community. The best approach to undertaking this search within
each religion, and on an interfaith and international scale, is to engage in genuine
and open bilateral and multilateral dialogue.

Dialogue

But what is dialogue, after all? In 2000 the General Assembly of the United
Nations passed a resolution declaring 2001 to be the year for dialogue among
civilizations. Hundreds of conferences, seminars, and workshops were held nationally and internationally to discuss cultural relations and to promote and
encourage better understanding of the cultures, values, and ways of life of other
people. Thousands of people travelled to far away places to discuss intercultural
and interreligious issues. But apparently what went on was not dialogue in the
real sense, but rather an engagement in two or more parallel monologues, the outcome of which was to deepen one's fixed ideas about one's own culture and religion
and to dismiss, even more vigorously than before, any claims to wisdom or validity by any other culture or religion.

An external structure for debate was set up in a rush without genuine psychological and intellectual readiness on the part of participants to acknowledge ideas

and values embraced by others; consequently, the parties engaged in a process of pseudo-dialogue that kept them far apart, and the search for common values and common ethics to guide the globalizing world was regrettably delayed. For dialogue, in the proper sense, to be resumed and to bear its contemplated and hoped-for fruits, all parties must first recognize that:

- the existence of other ideas and values are manifestations of God's will to inculcate diversity on earth and within all human communities. This law of God shall continue to be with us till the end of time;
- wisdom and righteousness are not the monopoly of any one nation or culture or community, let alone a single individual; and
- people of different cultures and religions will continue to need each other, and can learn from and complement each other.

The aim of dialogue is not to convince participants to convert to a different position but to bring all parties to a better understanding of the positions and views of others, and to benefit from that enriched understanding. Maintaining one's own identity guarantees diversity, which, in turn, is a blessing to all parties. Particularly in the case of interreligious dialogue, no parties are required or expected to give up their religious identity and affiliation, nor should dialogue cover the field of "dogma" and its theological components. This issue is addressed by a verse in the Qur'an stipulating that "you have your religion and I have mine" (Surah 109:6).

The purpose of interreligious dialogue is to discover and identify the essential elements common to all religions, and through these common elements to bring leaders and followers of all religions to join hands in a mutual effort to promote peace, reconciliation, respect, and dignity, and to protect humanity against the evils of excessive materialism, exploitation of the weak, and all kinds of unfair and discriminatory treatment.

In an attempt to end the present campaign against Muslims and Islam, the following concepts of Islam as a religion, a way of life, and a system of law need to be clearly presented to the world at large. Although these components are recognized and endorsed by mainstream Muslims, they are not adequately highlighted by the present Islamic discourse addressed to Muslims as well as to non-Muslims.

1. Islam, in a Broad Sense, Is Not a New Religion

Islam is, in essence, the religion of all the prophets preceding Muhammad (The Prophet of Islam). The Qur'an highlights this essential element of the Islamic religion in the most unequivocal terms. The particular bond making the Abrahamic religions a special category and designating the followers of Judaism, Christianity, and Islam as "People of the Book" is emphasized in many verses.

> He has established for you the religion that He had recommended to Nuh [Noah], and that we have inspired to you, and that which we had recommended to Ibrahim [Abraham], Musa [Moses] and Isa [Jesus] saying that you shall proclaim this true religion, and you shall not divide into schisms concerning it. (Surah 42:13)

> Those who believe, those who profess Judaism, the Christians and the Sabians, who believe in Allah and the last day, and who do good deeds, shall have their reward with their Lord, and they shall suffer no fear or sorrow. (Surah 2:62)

> The Apostle believes in what is sent down to him from his Lord. So do the believers: each one believes in Allah and in his Angels, Books and Apostles. They say "we make no distinction between his Apostles" and they say "we hear and obey." (Surah 2:285)

It is on the basis of this broad meaning of the true religion that the messages of Abraham and Jesus are categorized in many verses of the Qur'an as "Islam." Thus I strongly recommend introducing the new term *Judaic-Christian-Islamic heritage* in lieu of the misleading term Judaic-Christian heritage, which implies that Islam as a faith, a way of life, and a culture is alien to the common values and ethics of Judaism and Christianity. The practical and political consequences of such a correction are too obvious to need further elaboration.

2. Human Dignity Is Recognized in Islam as a Cornerstone of the Faith

According to several verses of the Qur'an, "mankind" has been chosen as the "honoured" creature, irrespective of race, religion, gender, or any other differences. The Qur'an explicitly states that the children of Adam are "honoured and preferred" by the Almighty: "We have honoured the Children of Adam and carried them on land and sea; and we have sustained them with good things, and preferred them to many of those whom we created" (Surah 17:70). Interestingly, the honour bestowed on human beings is balanced by responsibility for creation; the Qur'an holds the children of Adam responsible before God for the consequences of this trust.

> We have offered the trust to the skies, the earth and the mountains, but they refused to keep it, and they feared it. Yet man has accepted to keep it. Verily he is very unjust [to himself] and ignorant [of the graveness of what he has accepted]. (Surah 33:72)

3. Muslims Are Not a Chosen People in an "Exclusivist" Sense

Muslims are not exempted from any law of God; each person is account-able and shall be treated according to his or her actions. It is a central article of Islamic faith that reward and punishment are based exclusively on one's own be-haviour and on the quality of one's own deeds. This principle is a direct reflection of God's absolute justice, a reflection that allows no exception. The absolute equal-ity of all individuals before the law of God is declared in the most crystal clear manner.

> The matter of reward and punishment does not depend on your wishes, or on the wishes of those who were given the Book. He who does evil shall be punished therefore, and he would find no guardian or supporter to protect him from Allah. (Surah 5:123)

> He who has done a particle's weight of good shall see it. And he who has done a particle's weight of evil shall see it. (Surah 99:7–8)

It is most significant and relevant to the subject of this conference to note that this principle of attaching the reward and punishment of individuals to their actions is not considered unique to Islam. The Qur'an confirms that it was ordained by the scrolls of the prophets Moses and Abraham. All nations are equal before the law ordained by God:

> Or has he not been informed about what was written in Musa's Scrolls, and in those of Ibrahim, who had fulfilled his missions?
> That no soul shall bear the sin of another,
> and that man shall have nothing but what he had achieved. (Surah 53:37–39)

4. Islam Prescribes the Sanctity of Life, Honour, and Wealth

Contrary to what the behaviour of some extremists and zealots may mistak-enly suggest, Islam unequivocally prohibits the killing of human beings regardless of race, creed, or religion. Both the Qur'anic verses and the Sayings of the Prophet speak against killing: "Do not kill a human soul which Allah has made sacred, except for a rightful cause" (Surah 17:33).

In his famous sermon on his last pilgrimage, the Prophet confirmed the Qur'anic prohibition against killing in the most explicit language: "O, you people, your blood, your honour and wealth are hereby declared immune from aggression. They are as sacred as this sacred day, in this sacred city." It was in this spirit of peace and respect for the inalienable right to life that the Prophet of Islam and his companions had to wait for direct authorization by God to defend themselves against the aggressors: "Permission is granted to those who are unjustly assaulted to fight back, and certainly Allah is capable of supporting them. Those who were driven off their homes for no rightful cause except that they say 'our Lord is Allah'" (Surah 22:37).

This categorical prohibition against killing is a clear condemnation of the criminal behaviour of a limited number of misguided contemporary Muslims, who flagrantly misinterpret the concept of jihad. Jihad is a form of worship expressed by readiness to sacrifice one's own life for any good and noble cause under Sharia (Islamic Law). It is a sacrifice authorized or required only in certain exceptional circumstances and was never meant to be a licence to kill, motivated by an evil spirit of destruction that runs in opposition to and in violation of the most basic principles of Islam.

5. The Relationship between Muslims and Other Nations Is One of Peace and Cooperation

It takes more than a superficial reading of the Qur'an to identify and understand Islam's position on relations with other nations—a question of extreme importance to the present growing suspicion toward Muslims and their faith. The point of departure that illustrates Islam's position is how it looks at *diversity* in the world community. The Qur'an considers diversity to be a law of God and a blessing (*ayat*) that should be celebrated in order to enhance good relations and encourage competition in performing good deeds. Two clear-cut verses of the Qur'an testify to this position.

> Oh you human beings, we have created you from a male and a female, and we have made you peoples and tribes so that you may know one another. Those who are dearest to Allah among you are the most righteous. (Surah 49:13)

> To each one of you, we have set up a code [of legislation] and a way [of worship]. Had Allah willed, He would have made you one nation, but He did not, in order to test you in what He has given you. Therefore, race for the performance of righteous deeds. Your return is to Allah, who will inform you concerning your differences. (Surah 5:48)

Muslims are obliged to lean toward peace if, in a situation of clash and confrontation, the other side offers them a peaceful settlement of the dispute. Again, two verses of the Qur'an are quite clear in illustrating Islam's keenness to promote peace:

Oh you who believe, enter into peace altogether, and do not follow the footsteps of Satan. Verily he is an avowed enemy of you. (Surah 2:208)

If they incline towards peace, you shall incline to it and trust in Allah. (Surah 8:61)

The principle of diversity as a law of God, together with free will (a unique faculty of human beings), accounts for the strict prohibition against coercing any individual or group of people to embrace Islam. Muslims are forbidden from any attempt to impose uniformity of faith by force; there is no coercion in matters of faith (Surah 2:256), and God does not accept belief from an unwilling person who is forced to profess it. Pluralism of ideas is the natural and divine law in this world. Muslims have to accept this diversity and leave the judgment about who may be right or wrong to the one who knows the circumstances of every individual. Instead, people should cooperate, complement, and compete with one another locally and universally in doing good.[1]

Early Muslim scholars (*ulama*) who classified the different countries into the "Land of Islam" and the "Land of War" were mistaken or, at best, were reflecting the historical context in which people in most of the countries beyond the one Muslim State of those early days had not converted to Islam. It cannot be inferred from that short-sighted classification that war is the rule in designating the relations between Muslim states and the rest of the world. In our view, this classification is obsolete and untenable; it does not respond to developments in international relations and the changing needs of modern states.[2]

6. Islam Advocates the Establishment of Democratic States Based on Popular Participation and the Rule of Law

In order to substantiate this claim that Islam advocates a democratic form government, certain clarifications as to the nature of the Muslim state are indispensable. Neither the Qur'an nor the Sunnah (sayings and deeds of the Prophet) prescribe a precise form of government to be strictly followed by Muslims; rather, these two main sources of Islamic Law stipulate that certain political and legal principles be implemented and respected in any government established in a Muslim community. These principles are as follows:

The principle of participation in public affairs through the process of consultation or Shura. Two verses of the Qur'an require all Muslim leaders to make use of consultation in order to fulfill their duties as rulers:

Forgive them [your companions], ask Allah's pardon for them, and *consult them in the conduct of affairs.*" (italics added; Surah 3:159)

> Who respond to their Lord, and keep prayer, *whose affairs are conducted on the basis of mutual consideration*, and who spend from what we give them. (italics added; Surah 42:38)

Needless to say, participation in public affairs by members of the community at the time of the Prophet and his companions was exercised in a relatively primitive way compared to the elaborate procedures of modern states. However, contemporary political scientists and jurists have distinguished the essence or substance of a principle from the means (techniques) of its implementation and the structure that embodies it. The means of implementation are likely to develop in complexity in parallel with the advancement and development of political and social structures. But the essence or content of these principles remains basically the same. We do not subscribe to the reservations raised by some Muslim writers denying any similarity between modern democracy and the Islamic concept of consultation or *Shura*. These reservations relate to non-essential elements of democracy and reflect certain coincidental features that prevailed during some stages in the historical development of Muslim states and their governments.

The caliphate is not a particular form of government with prescribed features. Muslim governments carrying this name during the early days of Islam were simply representing the unity of all Muslims, but the specific features of such governments varied greatly from one place to the other.

The essence of the *Islamicity* of any government is to guarantee the consent of the people as the basis and criterion for the legitimacy of political power and authority. Both early and contemporary Muslim scholars and jurists are in agreement that the procedure of *bayat* used in electing the head of state represents a sort of contract between the elected head and those who gave their consent. This is the position of Sunni Islam, as distinguished from Shiite doctrines that accord a special status for scholars (*ulama*), endowing them with a right to rule Muslim communities under the doctrine of *wilayatu faquih*—the prerogative of the *ulama* to rule. Although an in-depth analysis of this and other concepts of Shiite theology and jurisprudence is better left to Shiite scholars, I would like to point out that doctrines on the role of the *ulama* in political life are witnessing interesting developments in the direction of adapting to modern changes. It was Ayatollah Khomeini who triggered this wave of innovation within modern Shiite jurisprudence. It is not unrealistic to assume that the spirit of innovation, if expanded to other doctrines and practices, will lead to greater rapprochement within Islam and between Islam and the world at large.

The principle of legality or the Rule of Law. Several Qur'anic verses confirm that the Prophet of Islam, through whom the revelation of the Qur'an took place, was himself subject to the laws revealed to him; thus the Qur'an is the first and supreme source of Islamic Law. Muhammad is reminded that the core of his mission is to communicate Allah's message to the people and, should he fail to do so, his mission will not be fulfilled: "Oh Apostle, communicate all that has been sent down to you from your Lord. If you do not, you will not have delivered his message. Allah shall protect you from people" (Surah 5:67). Indeed, the Qur'an spells out in most severe language the Prophet's accountably for the honest communication of God's message:

> Had he falsely attributed some sayings to us
> We would have taken him by the right hand
> And then we would have cut his Aorta Artery
> None of you can then protect him from us. (Surah 69:45–47)

The same principle of subjecting all individuals to the rule of law must apply, without exception, to every Muslim community. In a most illuminating *Hadith* (saying), the Prophet tells his companions, "Some of those who came before you were destroyed because of their practice to exempt the powerful and prestigious who steal from bearing the prescribed punishment, while inflicting said punishment on the weak and the poor. By God, if Fatima, the daughter of Muhammad, committed a theft, Muhammad would cut off her hand."

7. Islamic Law Is Not a Closed System Detached from the Changing Needs of Society

One psychological barrier distancing non-Muslims from Islam and its followers is the confusion regarding Sharia or Islamic Law, and the role it fulfills in Muslim communities. Sharia is often presented, sometimes even by Muslims, as a fixed and closed system of law that specifies in minute detail the answer to every possible legal problem. A legitimate question immediately arises as to the reality and seriousness of such an extravagant claim. In order to understand the real situation, and the role actually played by Islamic Law, certain basic facts have to be recognized.

First: No system of law, be it revealed by God, or made by individuals and institutions, can continue to serve the interests of any given society unless it changes from time to time in response to changes within that society. Change is a law of God, and for any legal system to survive as an effective means of serving the interests of individuals, it must adapt to changing societal needs through the use of mechanisms recognized and approved by legal scholars within the community.

Without such adaptability, any claim that a system of law has an absolute and continual ability to meet the actual needs of society would be a hollow contention.

Second: It is a recorded fact that throughout history, Islamic Law continued to serve Muslim societies as the law of the land and the main source of legislation. Until the second half of the nineteenth century, Islamic Law was the only system of law governing relations between Muslim individuals and, to a lesser extent, relations between Muslim and non-Muslim citizens of Islamic countries.

Third: The inevitable conclusion to draw from the above premises is that the two main sources of Islamic Law based on revelation—namely, the Qur'an and the Sunnah—must have been complemented by secondary sources that linked these sources of religious origin to new situations that unfolded in society.

Looking more deeply into the process of development of Islamic Law from the days of the Prophet and early Islam to the present, one discovers that since the establishment of the very first Muslim state in the city of Yathreb (Medina) in the tenth year after Hegira (the Prophet's migration to that city), the Prophet himself was cognizant of the need to complement the two main sources of law by recognizing other sources that were directly related to arising problems and needs. The aim was to serve the real interests of the community without violating the essential elements and principles of the whole body of Sharia. Thus before the Prophet sent one of his companions, Muäaz Ibn Gabal, to Yemen as a judge and representative of the government in Medina, he asked him how he would render a decision when asked to solve a dispute. Muäaz replied, "I will base my decision on the Qur'an." The Prophet then asked, "What if you do not find the answer therein?" Muäaz responded, "I will look for the answer in the Sunnah." The Prophet again asked, "What if you do not find the answer therein?" At this point Muäaz said, "I will resort to *ijtihad* (reasoning and innovation) and do my very best." Expressing his satisfaction with Muäaz's answer, the Prophet said, "Praise be to Allah who guided the messenger of God's messenger to satisfy Allah and his Apostle."

The great significance of this precedent is that it sanctions the use of complementary sources based on reason in order to find answers to new questions that reflect the continuous development of societies. The science of Islamic jurisprudence developed during the first four centuries after the death of the Prophet. New complementary sources of law were recognized, approved, and widely used by scholars of the six schools of jurisprudence: Hanafi, Maliki, Shafei, Hanbali, Zahiri, and Shia (both Jafari and Zaidi).

As these schools of jurisprudence flourished and matured, near the end of the fourth century after Hegira some Muslim scholars claimed that the door of *ijtihad* must be declared "closed." This claim, however, did not materialize, and followers of the founders of these schools continued to come up with innovative answers to new and old questions. Subsequent centuries, however, did witness a slowing down in *ijtihad*, marking the beginning of traditionalism and the mere following of old opinions within each school of Islamic jurisprudence.

Contemporary Muslim scholars are almost unanimous in advocating a revitalization of Islamic jurisprudence by exercising *ijtihad* with greater audacity, using all complementary sources of Islamic law. Without these complementary sources, the adaptation of Islamic Law to new situations and circumstances, new problems and challenges, will never be satisfactorily attained. In particular, most contemporary Muslim scholars strongly recommend the use of the following complementary sources:

(a) basic values, principles, and objectives (*Maquas'd*) behind the particular religious imperatives. There is a clear similarity between the approach of this school of Islamic Law and that of modern jurists belonging to the school of "sociological jurisprudence."

(b) custom (*urf*) and established practice. Acceptance of custom and practice as complementary sources of Islamic law reflects awareness of the great diversity of situations that Muslim scholars and judges are called upon to address.

(c) the general welfare and the interests of Muslim communities.

In my view, accepting the interests of the community as a major guideline in interpreting the sacred texts of the Qur'an and the Sunnah is one of the most effective means of adapting the whole body of Islamic Law to the needs of individuals in new and unprecedented circumstances. Such acceptance was reached early in the history of Islamic jurisprudence by scholars of the Maliki school and by certain scholars of the Hanbali school. The jurist Ibn Qauyyim al-Jawziyya (d. 1350) acknowledged in two of his works that basing Islamic legal opinion on the need to satisfy the interests of the community was one of the most ticklish questions arising under Sharia. But he insisted that scholars who refrained from utilizing this source, imagining that solutions derived from it would be repugnant to Sharia, rejected useful solutions. In fact, he continued, such solutions were not repugnant to Sharia but were at variance only with what those scholars understood to be the meaning of Sharia. According to Ibn Qayyim, this negative attitude stemmed from failure to profoundly understand the real objectives of Sharia and to grasp the real weight and impact of new factual situations.

It is obvious that this sociological approach to the role of Islamic Law in society is at variance with the formalist and textual approach that prevailed during

certain stages in the history of other legal systems, and that continues to be practised by some traditional jurists. The positivist school of jurisprudence in
Anglo-American legal history and the approach of the French school known as
L'ecole d' l'exigesse are but two examples of a more traditional approach to jurisprudence that continues to be followed, but to a lesser degree than previously.

ISLAM'S VIEW OF ART AND ARTISTS

Scholars belonging to a new school of Islamists based in Egypt are articulating a "mainstream vision"[3] that meaningfully engages Islamic faith and practice
with the modern world. Contemporary historians and analysts refer to this school
as "centrist Islamist intellectuals" or the "New Islamist Trend."[4] I am one of the
founding members of this group of diverse intellectuals, which includes a journal-
ist, a judge and historian, and several lawyers and religious scholars. We think of
ourselves as "an outgrowth of the centrist mainstream,"[5] as distinguished from
substreams of extremists, literalists, and advocates of strict and mechanical
abidance by the religious texts. We co-authored a manifesto in the early 1980s
that was eventually published in 1991 in the book *A Contemporary Islamic Vision*.
In this and other works, we seek to engage the major themes of Islamic faith,
culture, politics, economics, foreign policy, and community life.

One essential aspect of our vision is the need to embrace the arts. We have
argued that "an Islamic community without art is unimaginable," and we articulate in our writings an "aesthetic of belonging."[6] Our work is perhaps best
summarized by Raymond Baker in his book *Islam Without Fear*. Allow me to quote
my own words, as cited in Baker's book:

> Who is the artist? He is a person to whom God has granted a special gift, capabil-
> ity, and talent that allow him to receive things with an extraordinary sensitivity. He
> expresses himself with an accuracy and richness not granted to others. Whether a
> poet, writer, or painter, the artists see in the rhythm of things louder voices and
> clearer expressions that he is able to capture in a special, unique way. . . . It is
> unimaginable that Islam would be against this.[7]

Baker continues,

> Abul Magd [alternate spelling] reminds Muslims that one way to worship is to
> praise the manifold gifts of God. Who could worship better than the artist, he asks,
> "with his refined sensitivity and developed imagination that responds to the beau-
> tiful over the ugly?" Muslims, confused by the militant attacks on the arts, are

reassured that "there is no convincing evidence in Islam that would forbid art, song and music . . . and one should not feel he is doing wrong by listening to music, singing, or admiring the arts." Meeting the militants confidently on the grounds of faith, Abul Magd argues: "To pay tribute to God is the best way of worshipping in all religions. However, this can never take place without genuinely feeling the real gifts of God. How can one feel those gifts without differentiating between beauty and ugliness? . . . Those who prohibit the arts can never themselves feel the gifts of God."[8]

THE ROLE OF MUSLIMS IN THE WORLD SEARCH FOR PEACE, COOPERATION, AND BETTER HUMAN RELATIONS: CONCLUDING REMARKS

The foregoing discussion of certain elements of Islam and the culture and ways of life deriving from its overall philosophy and code of ethics is directed toward both Muslims and non-Muslims with a twofold objective. First, it is addressed to Muslims in an effort to bring them out of isolation and encourage them to be partners with the rest of the world in securing a more peaceful future and in promoting a culture of inclusion and cooperation based on a sincere and genuine belief in the blessings of diversity and the ways in which diversity enriches all aspects of human life. Second, it is meant to help put an end to the present wave of anti-Islamism by enhancing global understanding of the religion of Islam and the culture built through the ages around its basic values and ethics. Readers are reminded that Muslims should not be seen as one solid block of individuals who are likely to act and react in the same way.

Like all other religions and communities, the world of Islam is full of very different schools of thought, attitudes, and ways of abiding by the sacred injunctions prescribed in the Qur'an and the Sunnah of the Prophet. Most analysts and observers of religious and cultural change agree that the Muslim world is witnessing a resurgence of religiosity; there is a new spirit of willingness among Muslims to shape their lives according to the moral standards of behaviour prescribed by Islam.

The descriptions and interpretations of Islamic principles presented in this short paper may not be representative of the views of all contemporary Muslims. Rather, this paper represents the views of the New Islamists, whose approach, as a member of this group, I wholeheartedly support. Baker notes that our "work poses the central question . . . whether an Islamic project of the centre, speaking for an Islam without fear, can address effectively the demands of our global age."[9]

It is my contention that it is precisely the leaders of this New Islamist movement and all Muslims who share their views who are best equipped to guide the mainstream within the world of Islam in the direction of widespread dialogue, a spirit of moderation and reconciliation, and a celebration of cultural and religious diversity. This group, together with similar groups in other religions and cultures, is called upon to play a leadership and pioneering role in shifting the march of history away from a possible "clash of civilizations" to a paradigm of inclusion and cooperation. This hoped-for shift would be more easily attainable if based on an objective discovery of a list of agreed upon and cherished values and beliefs common to all cultures and followed by hundreds of millions of men and women of our generation.

As a starting point for further dialogue, I propose the following list of beliefs and values—beliefs common to the monotheistic faiths, and values shared by many people regardless of religious affiliation:

1. The belief that this world is the work of one absolute creator who is all knowing, all powerful and, above all, all merciful and compassionate. Theological differences in grasping the manifestations and attributes of the one God do not change a bit the essence of belief in God. We can all afford to live forever with theological differences without letting them impede our cooperation or our competition along the pathway of good deeds.

2. Belief in the dignity of the human individual, male or female. All human beings were created from a male and a female. They were created equal and must be treated equally by all human institutions. Each person is endowed with certain inalienable rights that must be respected and protected against all kinds of violations.

3. Belief in a day of judgment, when each individual shall receive some kind of reward or punishment commensurate with his or her deeds and achievements during the short life on earth.

4. Awareness of the drastic changes imposed on our lives as a result of accelerated advances in science and technology, and the dire need to adjust to the requirements of this new and unprecedented situation. Some aspects of the technological revolution represent a threat to peace and to the ability of individuals to relate in a loving and friendly manner to others.

5. Belief in genuine dialogue as an effective means of exchanging knowledge, wisdom, and expertise.

6. Acceptance of the fact that the growing religiosity within all groupings and nations is having such an impact on our lives not because of the conceptual

and textual components of a religion, but because it is inspired by the attitudes of individuals and groups toward their creator, toward themselves, and toward others. Intellectuals and leaders within each religion and culture are called upon to ensure that religious dialogue invites mutual recognition and respect, and celebrates diversity, peace, caring, and love.

7. Recognition that we are short of time and that it is incumbent on all of us to promote peace and cooperation. There will always be individuals and groups who are bent on violence, destruction, and the spreading of hate. But it is our responsibility to engage in a worldwide competition to guarantee that the balance will ultimately tip in favour of reconciliation and friendliness rather than clash and confrontation.

In evaluating Islam's role in contemporary world politics, one has to recognize the overall deterioration in the relations between Muslims and most non-Muslim nations. Tracing the origins and manifestations of this deterioration is beyond the scope and objective of this paper; however, it is useful to refer to three pivotal events.

The first and most deeply rooted event—and one still very much alive in the minds and hearts of Muslims and Arabs—is the creation in 1948 of the State of Israel, and the almost unconditional siding of many Western nations with the newly born state to the detriment of the interests and right to self-determination of the Palestinian people. The events that have unfolded since 1948, including the recent Israeli invasion of Lebanon and the West Bank, an invasion condoned by the Americans and by the West in general, have contributed tremendously to widening the gap between all Arabs and Muslims on the one hand and the Western world on the other.

The second development is the rise in Western countries of a wave of anti-Islamism based on the assumption—deliberately inflated by some media centres—that Islam and Muslims are to be equated with violence, fundamentalism, and terrorism.

The third and most recent manifestation of anti-Islamism is an escalation in many Western countries of speech and other forms of expression demonizing Islam and insulting Muslims and the Prophet of Islam. This unfortunate occurrence has negatively affected Muslim–Western relations and has created an atmosphere of suspicion and mistrust between the two sides.

As a Muslim participant in this international endeavour to achieve peace among religions, I was pleasantly surprised to find that the papers written by scholars and followers of other religions focus on common principles and beliefs rather than on the particularities of the different religions. The tone of each paper is one of tolerance, reconciliation, and a genuine desire to join hands with representatives of other religions to promote peace and understanding. In the case of Islam and Muslims, a preliminary step is indispensable in order to cross a psychological barrier and to restore a sense of togetherness with the followers of other faiths. After this necessary step, Muslims would willingly join the campaign for peace among religions as a prerequisite for peace among nations. The point of departure for such a campaign would be a full awareness of the common dangers facing humanity as a result of the negative effects of globalization and technological revolutions in information and communication. Excessive dependence on technology has led to a corresponding deterioration in the ability of many people to relate to others, a change conducive to selfishness, egocentricism, and increased violence and confrontation. It is in the face of such alarming dangers that believers of different faiths are called upon to revive our mutual responsibility and moral commitment. No follower of any religion may be exempted from joining this common cultural march toward a better quality of life based on peace, love, and justice for all.

NOTES

[1] Fathi Osman, *Concepts of the Qur'an* (Los Angeles: MVI Publication, 1999), 82.

[2] See Muhammad Selim al Awa, *Islamic Jurisprudence – On the Pathway of Innovation*, 3rd ed., in Arabic (2007), 300.

[3] Raymond W. Baker, *Islam Without Fear* (Cambridge, MA: Harvard University Press, 2003), 1.

[4] Baker, 1.

[5] Baker, 1.

[6] Baker, 59.

[7] Kamal Aboulmagd, *Rose al Yusuf*, September 4, 1989, as cited in Baker, 60.

[8] Kamal Aboulmagd, *Sabah al Kheir*, April 27, 1989, as cited in Baker, 60.

[9] Baker, 1.

MAHAYANA BUDDHISM AS A FACTOR IN WORLD POLITICS

Osamu Yoshida

INTRODUCTION

I feel very honoured to be invited to this conference to share in the discussion of issues critically vital for our global life system with distinguished participants dedicated to a global ethic. I sincerely hope that together we can take cooperative and concrete steps toward solving the global problematique endangering the future of all life systems. The global problematique is the intertwined problems of ecological deterioration, resource depletion, species extinction, wars, poverty, terrorism, and so forth. The sixth mass extinction of global life forms has been set in motion by the human race, a single species out of thirty million. Human beings, self-proclaimed the best of creatures, are annihilating the only known life sphere of the universe in an atomic, biological, and chemical holocaust. A famous biologist recently predicted that if steps are not taken to reverse this calamity, the human race will be decimated to one percent of the present population.

Given this dire prospect, I feel obliged to contribute to the solution from the Mahayana Buddhist perspective and practice. I would like to share an approach toward politics and other problems from both a Buddhist and a general religious perspective.

This paper was presented at the InterAction Council High-Level Expert Group Meeting on "World Religions as a Factor in World Politics," held May 7–8, 2007, in Tübingen, Germany.

WHAT IS BUDDHISM?

In the following metaphor, Buddha Gautama illustrates the human situation. The story is particularly relevant to our own time as diverse traditions and trends mix in the globalization process, with religions often functioning as fanatical and ferocious factors in world politics.

> King Ādassa summoned blind men to feel an animal and to tell what they found. One blind man said it was like "a snake," another "a hose," another "a pillar," another "a winnow," another "a wall," and so forth. They insisted they were right and then started to fight for their own truths.

The Buddha said that the "absolute truths" people claim only demonstrate that those truths are not absolute. Then, fights over the "truth" worsen the human situation. The solution is first to stop fighting, then to start frank, fair, and free dialogue—talk and walk together in peace. As other participants have said, we must stop misinterpretation, monologue, and superstition. It is crucially important to transcend old selfish ways and advance into new holistic ones. We need a decisive paradigm shift from ego to eco, from separation to synthesis.

Buddhism means to become awakened from the blindness of such delusion and devastation. Essentially all errors and ensuing sufferings come from mistaking a part for the whole, the relative for the absolute. *Buddha* means an awakened one. Buddha Gautama was awakened to the *Dharma* of Dependent Origination, to the realization that all phenomena are interdependent—the origination of everything is dependent upon causes and conditions. His awakening led to an understanding of the limitless causal relationships and relativities among phenomena. *Dharma* means norm (*Dharma*) and form (*dharma*). The Law of Dependent Origination is the "norm of all forms" (phenomena). It applies not only to the natural world but to the human world as well—to feelings, mental states, ethics, and spirituality. Thus the "self" is part and parcel of the world of phenomena, the dynamic function of the total system in time and space. In Buddhism, the idea of an independent and eternal self is a fiction, and attachment to it is the source of *samsara* (the total flow of change, birth-death), strife, and suffering (cf. original sin).

The principle of Twelve-Limbed Dependent Origination illustrates how we are involved in this process of identifying our body-mind as "self," which is the cause of suffering.

The circular structure of the diagram illustrates our conventional life obsessed by delusional attachment and appropriation of "the self," and the resulting suffering (*dukkha* or wrong-going) in impermanence. However, this formula, which was compiled for learning and teaching, has been misinterpreted for millennia in many countries as "reincarnation and transmigration of the soul" because of a dominant Hindu idea of *samsara*. Karma, shown as "formation" here, has been misinterpreted as fate, not only in the Theravada tradition but also in the Mahayana tradition; however, karma can be the key to change.

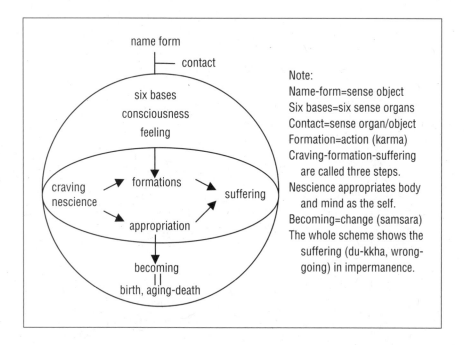

The Buddha's teaching is not the only religious wisdom that has been misunderstood. In all religions of the world, misinterpretations of the founders' teachings have caused enormous problems—dogmatism, sectarianism, fundamentalism, and nationalism. Fighting about these mistaken ideas is like fighting over a finger pointing to the moon (mental fabrication) rather than the moon itself (truth). In times of war, nationalistic and fundamentalist movements degenerate and defame religions. These movements must be rationally dissuaded and peacefully mediated by politicians and religious practitioners; leaders must not use these movements for their own selfish purposes.

Once awakened, the Buddha appreciated and acted according to the truth, beauty, and goodness of limitless life, light, liberation, and love. This way of life was the solution to the delusion of self and other, life and death, peace and war. His life example was echoed by his followers, including political figures such as King

Asoka (268–232 BCE) and Prince Regent Shotoku (574–622 CE). King Asoka of India, a cruel and ruthless ruler, converted to Buddhism after the calamitous Kalinga war and established a reign of *Dharma* (Truth). He erected stone pillars inscribed with the edicts of *Dharma* all over India and sent *Dharma* envoys to countries near and far (Sri Lanka, Syria, Macedonia, Egypt, and so forth). In Japan, Prince Shotoku embraced Buddhism and unified the country, putting an end to tribal feuds between powerful clans and establishing the world's first constitution whose first article is "Harmony is honoured." Both King Asoka and Prince Shotoku went beyond politics, establishing the future course of their countries upon a foundation of harmony.

The Buddha's renunciation of his political status and ordinary life symbolized a return to total truth. He was awakened to the fact that total truth and perfect practice can end selfishness and suffering. His life and teachings tell us that neither prognosis (knowledge) nor practice accrue from partiality and partisanship. He defined religion as "cultivation" from self to system, from sin (which means separation) to reunion with the holy (the wholesome whole). He was one of the greatest initiators of religions.

The Buddha was the forerunner of the Axial Age; he inaugurated a revolution from civilization to culture. Civilization is urbanization (from the Latin *civitas*, Greek *polis*, Sanskrit *pura*, German *burg*, French *bourg*, and so forth), from which come politics and policies. Civilization saw the rise of city-states and pyramidal systems that promoted separation with walls, wars, classes, gender, slavery, and many more divisions. Civilization promotes competition for limited "matter and power" and is entangled in the five calamities of delusion, bondage, discrimination, exploitation, and extermination. Culture is the cultivation of limitless "mind and life" endowed with the five blisses of awakening, freedom, equality, love, and peace along with truth, beauty, goodness, and holiness.

Solutions for social and global problems will never come from fallacies and fighting, selfishness and suffering. Solutions will come only from a paradigm shift from selfishness to holiness in genuine religions. By genuine religions, I mean universal ones beyond all delusion, dogmatism, selfishness, and sectarianism. Religious fundamentalism and sectarianism are nothing but parts separated from the whole, like bubbles from the sea.

The well-known Mahayana Buddhist Dogen (1200–1253 CE), who recommended *zazen* (sitting and thus stopping all karmas), admitted only one Awakened Way without subsects or schools. He summarized actualization of the Awakened Way as follows:

> To learn the Awakened Way is to learn the self. To learn the self is to forget the self. To forget the self is to be verified by all *dharmas*. To be verified by all *dharmas*

is to drop off the body and mind of the self and others. The trace of awakening is ceased. Traceless awakening is furthered on and on.

He said, "If it is not with all from the very beginning, it is not the Mahayana," and recommended that people cultivate "the mountain, river, great earth mind." He clearly indicated that it was laughable to discriminate against women in sacred places, saying that even a girl of seven years can lead the world, if awakened. He expressed his worldview in a poem, one of his many poems on the Way:

> Mountain colours and valley sounds altogether are
> The figures and voices of the Shakyamuni Buddha.

But Dogen was puzzled by a paradoxical question: If we are all provided with a Buddha-nature (as claimed by Mahayana), why do we have to cultivate our bodies and minds? He left Japan in search of an answer and returned empty-handed, simply witnessing to the truth of eyes horizontal and nose vertical. For Dogen, the practice of sitting was itself a moment-by-moment attainment of awakening—the journey and the goal were one and the same. It is the karma we accumulate in this world and in society that separates us from the inseparable holy life—from our true Buddha-nature—and makes us selfish and sanguine. He found the "come and see" way to be awakened to karma and unconditioned by it, through simple sitting and stopping all karma in truth and peace. No possession is non-possessedness, limitlessness (cf. the way of poverty, in poverty blessed).

Maha-yana means Great Vehicle or Great Way. It is a way that includes all beings in one harmonious, unified community (*sangha*) like water and milk, allowing everything and everyone to become buddhas who attain unsurpassed awakening (*anuttara-samyak-sambodhi*) and unconditioned peace (*nirvana*, calmed wind). As a Mahayana practitioner, I consider that our genuine life is like the ocean—not bubbles on the surface—with water, wind, light, language, gravity, genes, and so on and so on, limitless in time and space. We share and sustain the truth, beauty, goodness, and holiness of our limitless life.

Buddhism acknowledges two truths of human life: conventional and ultimate. Conventional "truth" embraces the fictitious idea of an independent and eternal "self," resulting in the problems of civilization (e.g., conflicts between sovereign states). Ultimate reality is the selfless, holy system of nature, like trees living thousands of years benefiting all and benefited by all. These two levels show that we can solve our problems by returning to the ultimate realm of truth from the conventional realm of fiction. We are, however, feeling creatures, blocked by walls. We are like winnowed chaff trapped in the treadmills of karmas, concepts, and cravings, thus not fulfilling the *dharma* (truth) world. So, we must read the heavenly law, rather than millions of books.

WHAT IS RELIGION?

Religion has been defined in different ways—as dogma, faith, ritual, and morality. Karl Marx called it the opium of the people. Otto Schrader defined it as the Holy. Etymologically, religion means re-union from the Latin word *re-ligare*. From an historical perspective, there has been development from tribal to ethnic to world religions, a movement from coarse to subtle, from particular to universal in space and time, form and content. We can see a shift in the practice of religion from a "way *of* life" to a "way *to* life," from an unconscious, collective way of limited life in a certain time and place to a conscious way to limitless life. Thus, we can define religion as the process of reunion with the holy. Religion is to return to the origin, to the holy harmony of body-mind, self-other, life-death, time-space—to wholeness and wholesomeness.

From the development of religions in the Indo-Iranian tradition in particular (which preserves proto-Indo-Aryan literatures from the Veda-Avesta to the Veda-Anta, the end of Veda), and from the development of world religions in general, we can observe the trend from local gods to universal ones, from limited members (e.g., age, race, gender) to unlimited ones, and from polytheism, henotheism, kathenotheism, and monotheism to monism (cf. prana, pneuma, ether, life in *Brahma-atma-aikyam*, unity of Brahman and self).

Monotheism, in contrast to monism, has an anthropomorphic God. Monotheism is good for human intimacy with God, but it is not good for human interpretations of God. Praying to God can change to playing God. God-imposters have been waging wars and promoting superstitions. Interpretations and interpolations can create self-centred beliefs in a chosen people, and in God-given power and practice. Homocentric ideas of God need to be reconsidered in order to solve the emerging ecological problems. An absolutist belief in *my* God and in scripture as the literal words of God blocks true understanding and interferes with action for dynamic development. Violence in monotheistic religions seems to accrue from power struggles over partial truths.

Monotheistic religions tend to fortify selfhood, but monistic religions are inclined to selflessness. Monotheistic religions teach respect for life but often stop short of extending this respect to other people, let alone to other species, generations, and the total life system. Universal religions must transcend self-centredness and self-righteousness to become holy and wholesome.

Universal religions tell us to return to the holy (wholesome whole) from sin (separated self) in prognosis (knowledge/science) and practice (action/ethic), so that we can realize peace, compassion, happiness, and blessing. They teach One World (i.e., Truth, Tao, Dharma, Dyau, Deus, Jovis, Jhvh, Allah, El) with aspiring and aspired "friends" (Mitra, Metteyya, Miroku, Messiah, Mazda) for all. Actually all living beings, animals, and plants are relatives with shared genomic patterns that have been living for four billion years, neither as aliens nor foes. No one has the right to harm this limitless life, as prescribed in the Five Buddhist Precepts:

- do not kill
- do not steal
- do not indulge in sexual misconduct
- do not make false speech
- do not take intoxicants.

These precepts have been incorporated into the global ethic developed by the InterAction Council and Parliament of the World's Religions.

If we could only transcend our selfishness and discrimination, we would find our life limitless in true conviviality, intimacy, beauty, and holiness. This holy perspective and holistic practice is seen in the abundance of flowers in the valleys and birds in the skies, in mountain colours and valley sounds, and in the lives of selfless saints and people free from possessing and being possessed.

WHAT IS POLITICS?

To understand economics, politics, religion, and ecology, we need to widen our perspective of historical processes. Over the course of human history we have experienced three major revolutions—economic (matter), sociopolitical (power), and spiritual (mind-life)—that make humanity unique and extraordinary:

Revolution:	Economic	Sociopolitical	Spiritual
1st stage: years ago:	Farming (10,000)	Urban (5,000)	Religion (2,500)
2nd stage: years ago:	Industrial (250)	National (200)	Ecological (25)

These revolutions were caused successively by environmental, social, and human conditions. Each revolution occurred in two stages. The first stage of the sociopolitical revolution saw the rise of city-states and the beginning of pyramidal society or civilization (*civitas, polis*), characterized by the five calamities of delusion, bondage, discrimination, exploitation, and extermination. *Politics* refers to the power struggle over policies to control the *polis* that are self-serving and often other-sacrificing.

To correct these calamities, spiritual revolutions were initiated by religious practitioners to restore the five blisses of the holy natural system: awakening, freedom, equality, love, and peace. German philosopher Karl Jaspers called this period of revolutionary thinking in world outlook and life values the Axial Age. Unfortunately, masses of people preferred matter and power to mind and life, despite the examples and teachings of the awakened ones (cf. the temptation legends, Sermon on the Mount). This failure to embrace the spiritual revolution has caused ongoing corruption and catastrophe. Therefore, we now need a fourth revolution—we might call it a Life Revolution—to summon our attention to the critical situation we now face and to change our attitude toward the universally linked life of all.

In order to solve the global problematique, we must awaken to the holy truth and act quickly and decisively to put an end to errors in perspective and priority. Religion is not a simple factor in politics, but it is the essential factor for it. For religions and politics to function fully in an inseparable system, religious and political leaders must reflect seriously upon their duties and return to the original wholesome whole, reforming the present systems and functions. Separation and selfishness are against the wholesome system and the symbiosis of satisfaction and sanctity. Politics must broaden its focus from small *polis* and nations to the globe, making peace the great policy of the whole global life community. As done before by King Asoka and Prince Shotoku, policy-makers must awaken to the global problematique and act for the global ethic.

WHAT WE SHOULD DO?

The Declaration Toward a Global Ethic (1993) and the Universal Declaration of Human Responsibilities (1997) developed by the Parliament of the World's Religions and the InterAction Council respectively are great achievements in the advancement of our ethical history. We are thankful for the efforts of Dr. Küng and other dedicated members of the Global Ethic Foundation and the InterAction Council. We are especially grateful to the InterAction Council for listening to the voices of scholars and practitioners from all of the major world religions at this critical juncture. We must implement the former declaration and urge the United Nations to adopt the latter one. If it is enacted by the United Nations, the Declaration of Human Responsibilities will reinforce the practice of the universal ethical principles expressed in the Universal Declaration of Human Rights.

We are confident that so many influential people working together through the InterAction Council and Parliament of the World's Religions will be able to change the course of global history and ethics. We must summon the necessary resources and dedicate our utmost effort to this work on behalf of our shared life. I propose the following global life principles for consideration:

- five *S*s of the global system: Systemic, Sustainable, Saving, Safe, Simple
- five *L*s of the global ethic: Law, Life, Love, Liberation, Lie-lessness
- five *R*s of material flow: Reduce, Reuse, Recycle, Rearrange, Restore
- five *A*s of information flow: Access, Assess, Agree, Act, Advise

We must practise these principles of truth and ethic in relation to all life forms and systems, seeing beyond the separation of religions, nations, politics, and economics. Acting on these principles throughout the world is essential at this time of global crisis. It is high time for us all to return to the holy life and to realize a policy for universal wholeness—a global policy and ethic for the holy world.

CONCLUSION

We must wake up and work together to stop the imminent global catastrophe. For this purpose, Mahayana Buddhism reveals the essential oneness of everything, already or originally awakened in Dependent Origination. So we can return to the original holy state, if we wish, and let our actions flow out of it. Buddhism ensures unsurpassed awakening and unconditioned peace through the law of Dependent Origination. Buddhist system theory and its selfless truth and ethic are great contributions to the needed paradigm shift, with concrete practices to attain this holy state. Religions aspire to friendship, love, and compassion, and to one world under one law (truth and wisdom, as expressed for example by Dao, Dharma, Jhvh). Religion offers politics a paradigm shift from selfishness (sinfulness) to selflessness (holiness), from the five calamities to the five blisses. This shift entails a return to the *natural, cyclical system* from an *artificial, pyramidal one*. We know that money, power, and possessions cannot buy mind, life, and nature. Only limitless life and light render limitless harmony and happiness. We need a second Axial Age for a total paradigm shift, a spiritual mass movement. We need planetary prognosis (knowledge) and practice, policy-makers and religious practitioners. Everyone must participate; a paradigm shift depends on each person's practice. Without it, we are doomed.

May all live in harmony and happiness, attaining limitless life, light, liberation and love, awakened to the unsurpassed truth and attaining the unconditioned peace!

Part Two

RELIGIOUS INFLUENCE: TOWARD A UNIVERSAL ETHIC OR GLOBAL DIVISION?

As His Eminence Archbishop Damianos reminds us, Mount Sinai, "austere and precipitous, is forever revered as the place where the great, sacred events and theophanies of the Hebrew Bible took place." Here is the site of the burning bush, the place where God granted to Moses and the people of Israel his divine law. *Jebel Musa*, or "Mount Moses," the Jebeliyah Bedouin call it. In the Qu'ran, the Prophet Muhammad, in the fifty-second and ninety-fifth *suras*, swears by Mount Sinai. Revered by Jews, Christians, and Muslims, the holy mountain of Sinai is a symbol of unity.

Helmut Schmidt reveals that he first began to understand the unity of religions because of the inspiration of Anwar Al Sadat, and one of Sadat's favourite metaphors for this unity was Mount Sinai. Indeed, the Prophet Muhammad granted a Letter of Protection to the monks of Sinai, a remarkable document establishing that Christians and Muslims should live in peace.

The unity of Sinai is a fitting testament to the universality of ethics, since it was here that the Decalogue of moral imperatives first became known to humankind. All religions have a common core of ethical norms. There is harmony without uniformity. The ancient foundations of human dignity, human rights, and human responsibilities present to the world a shared ethic of universal validity.

As the authors in Part Two argue, these ancient norms are as relevant today as they were at the time of Confucius, the Buddha, Christ, or Muhammad. In our global age, we need to be responsible global citizens. Thus, as TU Weiming states, religious leaders must master two languages: "the language of their respective faith communities . . . and the language of global citizenship." This imperative is evident in modern problems such as preservation of the environment. The human species is just one of thirty million species—we are part of one global family. That is the message of Sinai. We must be stewards of the earth rather than its exploiters.

CHRISTIANITY AS A FACTOR IN GLOBAL POLITICS

Hans Küng

There is more than one Christianity, just as there is more than one Judaism and more than one Islam. Different "Christianities" have emerged from different historical constellations that have very different forms and also very different political effects: Roman Catholic, Orthodox, and Reformation Christianity, to mention only the main forms. But Christianity in particular must also be seen in the context of other religions, since there are some principles that apply to them all.

PRELIMINARY REMARKS ON THE RELIGIONS AS A FACTOR IN GLOBAL POLITICS

1. *A distinction must be made between religion and superstition*: The Marxist critique of religion identified religion with superstition. However, religion does not recognize as an absolute authority anything relative, conditional, or human but only the Absolute itself, which in our tradition since time immemorial we have called God. By God I mean that hidden Reality, first of all and last of all, that is worshipped not only by Jews and Christians but also by Muslims, and that Hindus seek in Brahman, Buddhists in the Absolute and, of course, traditional Chinese in Heaven or in Dao. Indeed, the adherents of all religions express it, each with their own concepts and ideas.

This paper was presented at the InterAction Council High-Level Expert Group Meeting on "World Religions as a Factor in World Politics," held May 7–8, 2007, in Tübingen, Germany.

By contrast, superstition recognizes as the ultimate authority something that is relative and not absolute (and that requires blind obedience). Superstition divinizes material realities (money, power, sex), human beings (Stalin, Hitler, Mao, the Supreme Head of State, the Pope), and organizations (Party, Church). In this respect, any cult of persons also shows itself to be a kind of superstition! Clearly, not all superstition is religion; there are irreligious, and also very modern, forms of superstition. Conversely, not all religion is superstition; there is true religion. But any religion can become superstition wherever it makes a non-essential essential, turns a relative into an absolute.

2. *Freedom of religion holds for both believers and non-believers*: No one can be physically or morally compelled to accept a particular religion or ideology. People must be allowed to leave the community or change their religious beliefs. Article 18 of the Universal Declaration of Human Rights has stated this in a binding way. There was not always freedom for atheists; but atheists must be given freedom of thought, speech, and propaganda even in countries where the constitution has a religious orientation. Nor was there always freedom for religious people; but believers of all religions must be given freedom of thought, speech, and propaganda in all countries, whether these countries are secular, socialist, Islamic, or any other orientation.

3. *Any religion can be exploited and misused politically*: In our day religion is again appearing as an agent in global politics. It is true that religions have far too often shown their destructive side in the course of history; they have stimulated and legitimated hatred, enmity, violence, indeed wars. But in many cases the religions have stimulated and legitimated understanding, reconciliation, collaboration, and peace. In his big book on the potential of the religions for peace, Dr Markus Weingardt of the Global Ethic Foundation investigates six central case studies and more than thirty examples of mediations in conflicts with a religious basis. And in a book published in the 1990s, Dr. Günther Gebhardt emphasizes the potential for education toward peace in religious peace movements. In recent decades, all over the world heightened initiatives of interreligious dialogue and collaboration have developed. In this dialogue the religions of the world have discovered that their own basic ethical statements support and deepen those secular ethical values contained in the Universal Declaration of Human Rights. At the 1993 Parliament of the World's Religions in Chicago, more than two hundred representatives from all the world religions declared their consensus for the first time in history on some shared ethical values, standards, and attitudes as the basis for a global ethic.

4. *The three monotheistic religions are particularly exposed to the temptation of engaging in violence*: All three prophetic religions—Judaism, Christianity, and Islam—find themselves confronted today with the accusation that as monotheistic religions they are more tempted to engage in violence than polytheistic and non-theistic (Buddhism) religions. Could it be that while every religion as such contains aspects of violence, because of their tie to a single God monotheistic religions are especially intolerant and ready for violence?

It is sobering to note that ever since there have been human beings there has been religion, and ever since there have been human beings there has also been violence. A non-violent, paradisal society has never existed in this human world, which grew by evolution out of the animal world. Down the generations human beings had to try out and test elementary ethical norms, including having reverence for the life of others and not killing people with base intent—in other words, *not murdering*.

However, time and again religions have legitimized and waged wars, indeed, even declared "holy wars." By holy wars I mean offensives waged with a missionary claim on behalf of a deity. Whether this offensive is in the name of one God or several gods is of secondary importance. Of course, it would be wrong to say that all the wars waged by "Christians" in recent centuries have had religious motivations. When white colonialists in South and North America and in Australia killed countless Indians and Aborigines, when German colonial masters in Namibia killed tens of thousands of Hereros, when British soldiers shot Indian protesters in large numbers, when the Israeli army in Lebanon or Palestine killed hundreds of civilians, or when Turkish soldiers killed hundreds of thousands of Armenians—these atrocities, not to mention the two World Wars, truly should not be foisted on belief in one God.

5. *Every religion must reflect critically on its own religious tradition*: In a time when, unlike in antiquity and the Middle Ages, humanity can destroy itself by novel technological means, all religions, and in particular the three prophetic religions that often are so aggressive, must be concerned to avoid wars and promote peace. A differentiated *rereading of one's own religious tradition* is unavoidable here. Two pointers stand out: First, the warlike words and events in one's own tradition should be interpreted historically, on the basis of the situation at the time, but without excusing them. That applies to all three religions.

- The cruel "wars of Yahweh" and the inexorable psalms of vengeance in the Hebrew Bible can be understood from the situation of the settlement and from later situations of defence against far superior enemies.

- The Christian missionary wars and the "crusades" are grounded in the situation of the church ideology of the Early and High Middle Ages.
- The calls for war in the Qur'an reflect the concrete situation of the Prophet Muhammad in the Medinan period and the special character of the *surahs* (chapters) revealed in Medina. The calls to fight against the polytheistic Meccans cannot be transferred to the present time to justify in principle the use of violence.

Secondly, the words and actions that make peace in each tradition should be taken seriously as impulses for the present. The following ethical principles on the question of war and peace should be noted with respect to a better world order:

- In the twenty-first century, as in the past, wars are neither holy nor just nor clean. Given the immense sacrifice of human lives, the immense destruction of infrastructures and cultural treasures, and the ecological damage, modern "wars of Yahweh" (Sharon), "crusades" (Bush), and jihad (al-Qaida) are irresponsible.
- Wars are not a priori unavoidable: better coordinated diplomacy supported by efficient arms control could have prevented the wars in Yugoslavia and the two Gulf wars.
- An unethical policy of national interests—say over the oil reserves or for hegemony in the Middle East—amounts to complicity in war.
- Absolute pacifism, in which peace is the highest good to which everything must be sacrificed, cannot be realized politically and can even be irresponsible as a political principle. The right to self-defence is explicitly affirmed in Article 51 of the UN Charter. Peace at any price, if say a new Holocaust or genocide threatens, is therefore irresponsible. Megalomaniac dictators and mass murderers (Stalin, Hitler) must be resisted.
- Crimes against humanity must be brought before the International Court of Justice, which hopefully the American administration following that of George W. Bush will finally support in the best American tradition.

I now want to look more specifically at the roles of the Roman Catholic Church, then of the Eastern Orthodox Church, and finally of the Protestant churches in politics. In what follows, I will be referring to the macroparadigms in the history of the Christian faith that I introduce in my chapter on "The Three Abrahamic Religions." An historical analysis of these paradigms—the entire constellation of beliefs, morals, rites, and so on shared by the community—gives us insight into a past that persists into the present:

    I: the Jewish apocalyptic paradigm of earliest Christianity;
   II: the ecumenical Hellenistic paradigm of Christian antiquity;
 III: the medieval Roman Catholic paradigm;
 IV: the Protestant paradigm of the Reformation;
  V: the paradigm of modernity oriented on reason and progress; and
 VI: the ecumenical paradigm of postmodernity.

THE ROMAN CATHOLIC CHURCH AS A POLITICAL FACTOR

The Roman view of Christianity (Paradigm III, which is fond of claiming to be *the* Catholic view) was planted in the fourth and fifth centuries, theologically by Augustine and politically by the Roman Popes, after the imperial residence was transferred to Constantinople. It was implemented in the eleventh century by the Popes of the Gregorian Reform with the help of the Pseudo-Isidoran forgeries. At the centre of the Roman vision stands the Bishop of Rome, the Pope, who with an appeal to God and Jesus Christ claims absolute universal rule over the church (and for a time claimed rule over society as a whole): both a normative competence in interpreting doctrine and a legislative, executive, and judicial authority in the life of the church.

As early as the eleventh century this absolutist claim to power (of course together with other factors) led to conflict with the German emperors (the Investiture Controversy) and a split between a Latin church in the West and a Byzantine-Orthodox church in the East; then in the sixteenth century to the splitting of the church in the West into the churches of the Reformation and the Counter-Reformation Roman Church; and finally, in the nineteenth and twentieth centuries, to the polarization, to the alienation, indeed to the conflicts between the Roman hierarchy and the Catholic people and clergy, all of which is also reflected in theology.

In the second half of the twentieth century the Second Vatican Council adopted many of the central concerns both of the Reformation (Paradigm IV) and of modernity (Paradigm V), but as a result of the compromises and half-measures extorted by the Roman Curia, the Council in many respects failed to realize a consistent Catholic vision of the church for the twentieth century. The collegiality of the Pope with the bishops that had been resolved upon in 1965 as a counterbalance to the definition of primacy by the First Vatican Council (1870) was ignored by the Roman Curia after the Second Vatican Council, and papal absolutism was restored and staged in grand style with the help of the mass media.

Almost all over the world the Catholic Church has remained a spiritual power, indeed, a great power, which neither Nazism nor Stalinism nor Maoism could annihilate. Quite apart from its grand organization, on all fronts it is unique in its breadth of communities, hospitals, schools, and social institutions, in which an infinite amount of good is done despite all the difficulties, in which many pastors wear themselves out serving their fellow men and women, in which countless women and men devote themselves to young and old, the poor, the sick, and the disadvantaged. This is a worldwide community of believers and committed people. Such commitment is time and again effective politically; in many situations of oppression and injustice it is the commitment of Christians grounded in faith—sometimes even at the cost of their lives—that brings about change. For example, Catholic groups and individuals played an important role in overthrowing dictatorships in South America and in the Philippines.

However, the history of the Catholic Church, like that of other institutions, is also ambivalent. We all know that behind the efficient organization is an apparatus of power and finance that often operates with extremely worldly means. Behind imposing statistics, great occasions, and liturgies involving vast crowds of Catholics, there is all too often a superficial traditional Christianity that is poor in substance. A set of clerical functionaries who always have an eye on Rome, who are servile to those "above" and high-handed to those "below," manifests itself in the disciplined hierarchy. A long-outdated, authoritarian, unbiblical scholastic theology is evident in the closed, dogmatic doctrinal system. And the highly praised Western cultural achievement is accompanied by far too much secularization and deviation from the real spiritual tasks.

A pastoral ministry of the Bishop of Rome to the whole church, following the example of the apostle Peter, can be meaningful if it is exercised selflessly in the spirit of the gospel. Indisputably, the Papacy has done great service in maintaining the cohesion, unity, and freedom of at least the Western churches. And the Roman system has often proved itself to be more efficient than the somewhat loose alliance of the Eastern churches. To the present day, wherever the Pope has credibility, he can address the conscience of the whole world as a moral authority. But the dual spiritual-political role of the Vatican as church government and sovereign state is highly ambivalent. A baneful mixture of the two surfaces when the Vatican attempts to impose its moral ideas as policy in dealing with such problems as AIDS or birth control. The 1994 World Population Conference in Cairo is one example of this.

So the weaknesses and defects of the Roman system are apparent, and considerably limit the influence of the Pope, even in his own "sphere of rule." Many Catholics, too, criticize the Roman claim to power, pointing out that the Roman system has time and again strayed from the original Christian message and church order. Since the High Middle Ages, the negative aspects have been evident. Since then, there have been complaints about the authoritarian-infallible behaviour of the Papacy in dogma and morality; impositions on laity, clergy, and local churches, down to the smallest detail; and the whole fossilized absolutist system of power, which more closely resembles the Roman emperors than Peter, the modest fisherman from Galilee.

Opportunities for the Catholic Church

From the *Roman perspective* it is not denied that often a crumbling church is hidden behind the brilliant Catholic façade. The tremendous crowds that gather on church occasions give the impression, which can easily be deceptive, of an inner power of faith that holds together the Catholic Church as the most significant religious multinational in the world. In Rome it is thought that the reforms called for by many would not advance the Catholic Church any further than the Protestant churches, which have met these demands for reform and are no better off as a result. Rather, the church grows where it draws on its own positive sources of life, where its great impulses are experienced as a present power derived from looking toward God and encountering Jesus Christ.

From an *ecumenical perspective* it is a matter of course to affirm the need to concentrate on the essentials of Christianity—God and Jesus Christ. But because the evangelization campaign initiated decades ago by John Paul II was bound up with long-outdated dogmatic positions and moral demands and was in practice a campaign of re-Catholicization, it has failed. Despite an immense number of documents, speeches, and trips and a vast amount of media propaganda, the Pope did not succeed in convincing a majority of Catholics of the Roman position on any of the disputed questions, especially those of sexual morality (contraception, sexual intercourse before marriage, and abortion).

So there should also be a warning against *false hopes*: The crowds present at great church events should not disguise the fact many who come are not only curious or looking for meaning, but above all are from traditional folk Catholicism. The young people come from those conservative *movimenti* native to Spain, Italy, and Poland, which stand out for their veneration of the Pope, not for following his moral commandments or for their greater commitment to Christian service in their home communities. Despite decades of indoctrination, only a small minority even of these young people observe the prohibition against pills and condoms. The abortion figures are alarming, particularly in countries where the church has banned the pill.

The traditional Greek-Hellenistic dogmas of the fourth and fifth centuries, like those of the Counter-Reformation dogmatics of the sixteenth century, are virtually unknown to the average Catholic. Moreover, the four relatively new Vatican dogmas—the Immaculate Conception (1854) and Assumption (1870) of Mary, and the primacy of papal jurisdiction and infallibility (1870)—are largely ignored, if not called into question, in the Catholic Church. Thus a great emigration from the Catholic Church has taken place, particularly in traditionally Catholic countries. Because of the rejection of marriage for priests and ordination for women, and the authoritarian Roman system, soon half of all parishes worldwide will be without a pastor, and the pastoral care built up over centuries will collapse. In Latin America, countless millions of Catholics have transferred to Pentecostal churches (which cannot be dismissed as "sects") because there they found inspiring preachers and living communities ready to help.

The fundamental deficiencies in the Roman system, which is to be distinguished from the Catholic Church as such, make reconciliation with the Orthodox churches of the East and the Protestant churches of the Reformation seem difficult.

THE ORTHODOX CHURCH OF THE EAST AS A POLITICAL FACTOR

The Orthodox Church of the East is beyond doubt closer to earliest Christianity in many respects. The foundations of the Greek-Hellenistic paradigm of the old Roman imperial church (Paradigm II) were laid by the apostle Paul, and gradually replaced the Jewish apocalyptic paradigm of earliest Christianity (Paradigm I). This early church still had no centralist government like that of the later Roman Catholic Church of the West (Paradigm III). It allows at least priests to marry, though not bishops, and so the latter are mostly taken from monastic orders. In the Orthodox Church the faithful receive the eucharist in two forms, bread and wine. And the Orthodox Church has held out under all political systems, in Russia even surviving seventy years of persecution under the Communist regime, with thousands of martyrs. The Orthodox Church has lasted above all because of its splendid liturgy and hymns. All this strikes even someone from the West.

However, we cannot overlook the fact that on the other hand the distance from earliest Christianity is enormous. The average believer has difficulty recognizing Jesus' last supper in the Byzantine and Russian court liturgy. One particular danger of the Orthodox Church, though, lies in the fact that it is a *state church*, in which under emperors, tsars, and general secretaries the church could become a pliant instrument of the state or the party. The symphony model of state and church that came into being in Byzantium shows clearly that the dependence of the Russian Orthodox Church on the political regime of the time, a dependence that still exists today, has a particularly long and hallowed tradition. It is not only in line with the Muscovite state church that formed in the fifteenth and sixteenth centuries but also has deep roots in the Byzantine tradition, indeed, dating back to Emperor Constantine's conversion to Christianity in the fourth century. The Byzantine-Slavonic state-church tradition also explains why most Orthodox churches proved mistrustful of the ideas of 1789—the ideas of democracy, the separation of church and state, freedom of conscience and religion, and so on.

This danger is accentuated in modern *nationalism*. Granted, for the people under Ottoman rule, the church for centuries formed the last stronghold for the memory of their own identity and independence, and so the church had the function of constituting and legitimizing the nation. But in the more recent history of Orthodoxy, the nationalistic ideology which emerged from that period has served often enough to inflame ethnic rivalries rather than to dampen them down and keep them under control. Developments in former Yugoslavia assumed such fanatical dimensions not least because for centuries the churches had encouraged nationalism instead of taming it: the Catholic Church encouraged the nationalism of the Croats, the Orthodox Church that of the Serbs. Certainly there is also nationalism in Poland, Ireland, and certain Protestant countries. But if there is a special temptation and danger in the Orthodox world of the East, it is less authoritarianism (Roman Catholic) or subjectivism (modern Protestant) as in the West, than nationalism!

Opportunities for the Eastern Orthodox Church

From a *Roman perspective*, the Eastern churches stand relatively close to the Roman Catholic Church. Because of their common past in the first millennium, both have a common structure: episcopal churches that are founded on the apostolic succession, an uninterrupted chain of laying on of hands in the ordination of bishops and priests. Because of its strong dogmatic and liturgical identity, Orthodoxy is relatively peaceful, though it too is affected by the pressure of secularization; for example, the former Soviet empire alienated more and more people from it. On top of this there is the classic problem of all autocephalous churches (churches with their own supreme head): they are always in danger of political dependence and identification with the nation, whether the Greek, Russian, Serbian, or any other nation. Precisely for that reason a reunion with the

great Catholic Church—of course under Roman supremacy—would be very useful for the Orthodox churches and is a goal to be striven for by churches on both
sides. That is how people think in Rome.

From an *ecumenical perspective*, an abolition of the mutual excommunication
and a restoration of communion in the eucharist—expressed in theory after Vatican II but not realized in practice—would be a task of the first order. Given the
necessary respect for frontiers and the Orthodox self-awareness, a course shared
with the Catholic Church would avoid the dangers of a national or an ethnic religion. Moreover, the anthropological foundations of human dignity, human rights,
and human responsibilities would be more recognizable from a shared Christian
faith and would thus present to the world a shared ethic with universal validity.

Here, too, it is necessary to warn against *false hopes*: All the features of dogma,
liturgy, and church law that the Roman Catholic Church and the Orthodox Church
have in common cannot disguise the fact that Rome's claim to primacy over the
East, which has been made since the eleventh century, is the central insuperable
obstacle to a reunion, supported by an infallibility in doctrine defined in the nineteenth century. Broad areas of Orthodoxy see these new dogmas as the real heresy
of the Roman Church, in conflict with the New Testament and the joint Christian
tradition of the first millennium. And the arbitrary appointment of Roman Catholic bishops on Russian territory after the political change, in Siberia and even in
Moscow, and thus the establishment of a Roman hierarchy in parallel to the Orthodox hierarchy, has confirmed all the East's fears of Roman imperialism.

So a papal visit to Moscow has so far not been wanted (there has been no invitation from Putin). And Benedict XVI's visit to the Patriarch of Constantinople
did not bring any real progress apart from fine ecumenical speeches and gestures.
For this Pope, too, did not give any indication that one could replace the medieval
primacy of jurisdiction—which exists in any case only in Roman theory—with an
unpretentious, practical pastoral primacy.

Of course, all this does not exclude the possibility that for opportunistic reasons there could be a political alliance between the first Rome and the second
(Constantinople) and, above all, with the third (Moscow). But such an alliance
would not represent real ecumenical unity, which would presuppose the reciprocal recognition of ministries and eucharistic fellowship. It would even be "unholy"
if it were directed against democracy, freedom of religion and conscience, the
dignity of women (the rejection of the ordination of women), Protestantism, or the
World Council of Churches. Such a political alliance would further reinforce the
impression that the Orthodox Church primarily represents a hierarchy that appears

through its liturgy, in which in practice the proclamation of the gospel is neglected, as is pastoral work in the community and critique of society.

THE CHURCHES OF THE REFORMATION AS A POLITICAL FACTOR

The great strength of Protestantism lies in its constantly renewed confrontation with the gospel, with the original Christian message. Concentration on the gospel is the true core of "Protestantism," and this is quite indispensable for Christianity.

In the twentieth century, people have had the surprising experience that with the Second Vatican Council the Catholic Church, which had appeared to be completely fossilized in the Counter-Reformation and antimodernism, has made a move toward the other Christian churches: it has finally undergone the paradigm change of Protestant Christianity from the Middle Ages to the Reformation in fundamental dimensions. Without giving up catholicity, the Catholic Church has begun to concentrate on the gospel and thus integrate the Protestant paradigm of the Reformation (Paradigm IV). A whole series of central Protestant concerns have been taken up by the Catholic Church, in principle and often in practice: a new regard for the Bible, genuine popular worship in the vernacular, the revaluation of the laity, the assimilation of the church to different cultures, and a reform of popular piety. Finally, Martin Luther's central concern, the justification of sinful men and women on the basis of faith alone, is today as much affirmed by Catholic theologians as is the need for works or acts of love by Protestant theology.

Opportunities for the Church of the Reformation

From a *Roman perspective*, world Protestantism is engaged in a process of rapid change that to many people seems a disturbing process of decay. The classic confessional churches are rapidly shrinking. They have somehow been able to preserve their significance as vehicles of culture, but they are losing their importance as religious homes. Frequent attempts are made to lead the churches out of this crisis with modern management and marketing methods. But the real forces by which the churches live and on which their being or non-being depend are barely visible. And the more Protestant churches continue as mere factors in culture and society, the more they submit themselves to a radicalized enlightenment, the more they dissolve. That is how people think in Rome.

From an *ecumenical perspective* it would be welcome if the Protestant churches were to sharpen their profile and present their substance more clearly. Every church should preserve its identity and remain a religious home. It should not subject itself to the dictates of a radicalized enlightenment and, even worse, adapt itself or fit in with modern society. The great mistake is not that Protestantism has carried through urgent reforms (the marriage of priests, a more understanding sexual morality, more democratic structures), but that at the same time it has not tackled its poverty of substance and lack of profile decisively enough.

Here, too, Rome has *false hopes*: A church should not chain itself to its own tradition—it should put neither medieval nor Reformation theology and church law above the confession of Jesus Christ and the discipleship of Christ. For centuries, having witnessed the constant splitting up of Protestantism, Rome has anticipated the spiritual emptying and dissolution of Protestantism—in vain. A comparison of Catholic and Protestant theology alone shows how often Catholic theology and the Catholic Church have lagged behind; all the decisive advances in exegesis were first made in Protestant theology. Protestantism is by no means dead; there are living communities in Europe and North America, and in other parts of the world.

THE THREAT FROM MODERNITY AND FUNDAMENTALISM

Within the framework of the Protestant paradigm of the Reformation, the fundamentalist movement formed in the nineteenth and twentieth centuries in reaction to modernity (Paradigm V). A fundamentalist is someone who in today's world confesses the verbal inspiration and therefore the unconditional inerrancy of the Bible; someone who in precritical times understood the Bible in an uncritical, naïve, and literal way is not a fundamentalist.

Fundamentalism took shape in the face of a twofold threat to the traditional understanding of faith. On the one hand, modern science and philosophy (especially Darwin's theory of evolution) opposed the picture of the world presented in the Bible. On the other hand, scholars of modern biblical criticism, working since the Enlightenment with historical-critical methods, have investigated the origin of the books of Genesis and the five books of Moses, and also the complex history of the origin of the three synoptic Gospels and the Gospel of John, which is very different from Matthew, Mark, and Luke. So fundamentalism in the authentic sense is a product of both a defensive and an offensive stance against modern science, philosophy, and exegesis, aimed at rescuing the verbal inspiration and inerrancy of the Bible from the threat posed by modernity.

In the nineteenth century, Roman theology, too, with the usual time lag, largely appropriated the doctrine of the verbal inspiration and inerrancy of scripture (which had already been systematized by Protestant orthodoxy). But just as the Roman

Inquisition discredited itself with processes against Galileo and others, so too American fundamentalism failed when it attempted to prescribe its theory of creationism (the creation of human beings directly by God) in state schools.

Most recently, the term *fundamentalism* has also been extended to other religions, above all Islam and Judaism. Muslims themselves call exclusivist, literalistic Islam *Islamism*, and Jews call exclusivist, literalistic Judaism *Ultra-Orthodoxy*. But if one wants to characterize negatively a rigid literalistic faith and a legalistic observance of the law, which are often combined with political aggressiveness, then one speaks of Muslim and Jewish fundamentalism as one speaks of Christian fundamentalism. Of course, geopolitical strategies are developed only by Christianity ("Crusade for Christ," "Re-Evangelizing Europe") and Islam ("Re-Islamizing the Arab world"). Here the thought patterns of American evangelical hardliners and Islamic radicals are similar: the political opponent is *the* embodiment of evil. And the battle of good against evil legitimizes even military attacks and invasions. Nor should one forget the fundamentalist streams within the religions of Indian and Chinese origin. Hinduism (against Muslims, Christians, or Sikhs) and Confucianism (against non-Han Chinese) can also behave in an exclusivist, authoritarian, repressive, fundamentalist way. In other words, fundamentalism is a universal problem, a global problem.

Opportunities for Fundamentalism

What is the source of the enormous effectiveness and thrust of the different forms of fundamentalism? Three factors are heightened and work together:

- *Consistency* – a basic religious value or a basic idea is constructed consistently and protected zealously in fear of a debilitating compromise.
- *Simplicity* – ways of thinking, attitudes, and systems are simple and transparent; more sophisticated perspectives are largely excluded.
- *Clarity* – the interpretation and doctrinal structure are unambiguously set out; any subtle interpretation is rejected as a deviation from pure doctrine, indeed, as heresy.

But here, too, we should have no illusions: Is there any future in putting forward the doctrine of the verbal inerrancy or infallibility of holy scripture, whether of the Hebrew Bible (Halacha), the Qur'an, or the New Testament (or under certain conditions even the infallibility of the Pope and reformers of the Vatican Council) as the dogma of dogmas, the formal central dogma on which all other truths of faith depend? Like Judaism and Islam, Christianity seeks to communicate a basic orientation for human life in an age that is poor in orientation. But how can a fundamentalist Christianity offer in the long term an interpretation of existence and the world—an interpretation that embraces all aspects of living in a time stamped through and through by modern science, technology, and culture—if it is tied to a literal understanding of the account of creation and last judgment, fall and redemption?

This reactionary religious view of the world has proved particularly baneful where it has been combined with a *reactionary foreign policy*. Anyone who admires the America of Lincoln, Kennedy, and Martin Luther King; the America of the New Deal, the Marshall Plan, the Peace Corps, and the Peace and Civil Rights Movements; and the America of the Nobel Peace Prize–winner Jimmy Carter—all representatives of the democratic and humanitarian America that has lasted for centuries—was and is dismayed at the reactionary reorientation of American foreign policy, the work of a neoconservative clique of journalists and power politicians (orchestrated by the power of the media). They allied themselves not only with the powerful Israel lobby (AIPAC), but increasingly with the Protestant fundamentalists of the southern states, who under the leadership of neoconservative intellectuals became George W. Bush's important power base, with masses of foot soldiers. However, since the last congressional elections and in view of the hopeless Iraq war, with its victims in the thousands and debts in the billions, the day has again begun to dawn in the United States.

Hidden religious structures have provided the points of reference in these remarkable new alliances. Secularist Jewish neoconservatives ("neocons") could thus ally themselves with fundamentalist Protestants ("theocons") who, for their part, like George W. Bush, regard the war against terrorism as an apocalyptic fight against "evil" generally and, on the basis of a literalistic understanding of the Bible, see the whole of Palestine as the "holy land" given by God to the Jews; for fundamentalist Protestants, however, the state of Israel is merely the presupposition for the return of Christ announced by the New Testament, with the subsequent total conversion of all Jews! The Jewish side often tacitly accepts this anti-Jewish ideology as long as it is of political benefit to the State of Israel and its policy.

But this fundamentalist world view has also combined with certain positions of American domestic policy: against abortion, stem cell research, and same-sex marriage. Since the election of President Reagan, the religious right—those politically active evangelical Christians—has played a major role in the Republican Party and helped Bush Junior to be elected twice. But recently a backlash can also be noted in domestic politics. Individual leaders of the religious right are showing more understanding of the problems of AIDS, euthanasia (the Terri Schiavo case), and the threat to the environment from climate change.

THIRTEEN STEPS FOR PEACE: ON REREADING A JEWISH PRAYER

Rabbi Jonathan Magonet

It is very difficult to speak of peace in such troubled times in the Middle East. Indeed, the word *peace* itself has become a kind of slogan or even a weapon in the propaganda that accompanies conflict. Each side is able to use it to justify their own position and at the same time dismiss the wishes of those on the other side. The psalmist's words, "I am for peace, but whenever I speak it they are for war" (Psalm 120:7), take on a hollow ring. Today they sound too one-sided, too self-seeking. And yet so many individuals and groups are working for peace, cross-ing boundaries, taking risks, entering into dialogue with those perceived to be the enemy. Everything must be done to support such efforts.

There are also deep questions to be addressed to the three Abrahamic religious traditions. There is a kind of pious defensiveness that suggests that our own reli-gion is pure, innocent, and peace-loving. If there have been aberrations, then they do not belong to the "authentic" tradition but to human failures or abuses of the faith. Perhaps it is necessary to retain the belief that the tradition is ultimately able to deliver its promises of peace, but this belief should not exclude a self-critical approach to past and, indeed, present failures to live up to such values. The word of God may be divine, but the interpreters of the word are human, all too human, and bound by time and circumstances.

This paper was presented at the InterAction Council High-Level Expert Group Meeting on "World Religions as a Factor in World Politics," held May 7–8, 2007, in Tübingen, Germany.

Bridging the Divide: Religious Dialogue and Universal Ethics, ed. T.S. Axworthy.
Montreal and Kingston: McGill-Queen's University Press, Queen's Policy Studies Series.

I would like to look at an aspect of the Jewish tradition that may help us in our quest for peace. It belongs to the daily prayers of the Jewish people. This prayer is such a basic part of our worship that we may no longer be listening closely to what it says. Yet with a particular emphasis and interpretation, it may speak afresh to the conflict that divides the descendants of Abraham from one another and destroys human lives and hopes.

The prayer is known as the Amidah or "standing prayer," and at its heart are thirteen blessings, effectively petitions to God. The origins of these petitions go back almost two thousand years. They express what was most desired by the Jewish people following the destruction of Jerusalem and the Temple, our national and spiritual centres. Throughout the centuries of exile, the words of this prayer have sustained us and encouraged us to retain our dignity and hope. Today I want to reread them as helpful stages toward another kind of hoped-for future, one of reconciliation and peace between Israelis and Palestinians, and harmony among Jews, Christians, and Muslims in a restored Jerusalem.

The first blessing affirms that through God's grace all human beings have access to *de' ah binah v' haskel,* "knowledge, discernment, and wisdom." Each of the terms has a particular resonance: *de' ah* suggests emotional knowledge and understanding. We have insight into the emotions that stir and move us, and so we do not need to be their slave, but rather their guide. *Binah* means the ability to analyze, to discern, to distinguish, to discriminate, to differentiate between good and bad, wisdom and folly, friend and foe. *Haskel* suggests all the intellectual and practical knowledge needed to conduct a war or to work for peace. God has given to human beings all the necessary tools, and so there are no excuses. The first step is to accept our responsibility for the ways in which we create and destroy, and to bring every aspect of understanding to bear on the goal of reconciliation.

What do we learn with this knowledge? The second blessing suggests that we discover our human weaknesses and failures, and our distance from God. We may define this perception in theological terms, or simply recognize the distance we have strayed from our goal or ideal, or even from some basic recognition of our shared humanity with those we define as the other. The key term of this blessing, *teshuvah,* is often translated "repentance," but the Hebrew word speaks more directly of "turning"—turning around, turning back, turning away from what is false. Just as we are asked to acknowledge the mistakes that have led us away from God as an essential step in returning to God, we must also acknowledge past failures, mistakes, and deliberate abuses in our relationship with the other as the first step in any attempt at reconciliation. This is the price demanded by the knowledge we have been granted. Moreover, Jewish tradition insists that *teshuvah,* that "change," is always possible whatever the circumstances, no matter what past wrongs seem to stand in the way. Another direction can always be chosen. Without *teshuvah*, little of long-term value can be gained.

The third blessing follows logically: the request for forgiveness from God. Jewish tradition assumes that ultimately only God can forgive. The dead cannot forgive the wrongs done to them, nor can anyone else do so on their behalf. What is possible is to accept the *teshuvah* of the other as a genuine sign of change, and expect the same in return. If someone has made the effort to apologize and seek forgiveness, that in itself is a painful undertaking that must be taken at its face value and welcomed. Although such acceptance may seem naïve, it is nevertheless the requirement of Jewish teaching during the great penitential season of the New Year, and the lesson is universal.

These three opening blessings establish the inner commitment and understanding required for everything that follows. Reconciliation begins with an inner revolution that makes something possible, though never certain.

The fourth blessing asks God to look upon our suffering, to take up our cause and bring redemption. Yet surely the God who knows everything knows of our suffering! Again this blessing points to our human failure. For in a conflict, both sides employ a system of denial: our own suffering is sacred and unique, but that of the other cannot be acknowledged, because then the "other" would become "persons" like us and we would become truly complicit in causing their pain. Nevertheless, this recognition of the suffering inflicted by our actions is required as one of the earliest stages in our own redemption.

When the damage we have caused is acknowledged, then we can ask God for our own healing, the fifth blessing in the sequence. In any conflict the wounds, both physical and emotional, are deep and easily reopened. But that does not preclude the conscious effort to do what can be done to repair the damage, to replace what cannot be repaired, to compensate for what cannot be recovered, and simply to be there in support of those who cannot in some ultimate sense find healing. Paradoxically, our suffering in the "disease" of conflict is what unites us across the boundaries. Many individuals, even in the present conflict between Israel and Palestine, have shown that the suffering shared by victims on both sides can be transformed into an active quest for peace.

The sixth blessing asks for a good harvest and restoration of the land. In its original context, it seems to have been a necessary prerequisite for the return of the Jewish exiles and the renewal of a viable economy and ecology. In a part of the world totally dependent upon the rains for survival and sustenance, the hand of God was seen in the presence or absence of rain. In our context, the restoration of the land implies healing on a broader scale. Houses have been demolished, social infrastructures destroyed, communities disrupted, trees uprooted, and land laid waste. This blessing calls for the necessary reparation that will help rebuild community and society. Restoring the human society will restore the land that sustains it. Both must go hand in hand.

The seventh blessing goes to the heart of Jewish hopes during the almost two millennia of exile from the land of Israel: the hope that those scattered throughout the world would be able to return. The blessing begins with a call to blow the *shofar*, the ram's horn, to proclaim our liberty. Here is an echo of the Biblical Jubilee where every fifty years all slaves were to be set free, and people could return to the land that had been part of their tribal allocation since earliest times. The combination of freedom and return to the land points to the value system that is to operate in this newly restored nation: a free, independent people sustained by the produce of the land. It also reflects directly on the question of how to acknowledge and address the particular needs of the displaced and refugees. Where restoration is not possible, then adequate and appropriate compensation is required. Freedom begins with certain basics—food, clothing, and shelter—but goes beyond these physical necessities to a reinstatement of human dignity and responsibility. The extent to which freedom is accorded to others is a measure of the civilization of any society. The Biblical record is clear on this to the point of bluntness: "The land shall not be sold in perpetuity [says God], for the land belongs to Me, for you are merely guests and tenants with Me" (Lev 25:23).

The eighth blessing calls for the restoration of judges. Originally, it must have meant an end to foreign, namely Roman, rule and the return of political autonomy. But at a deeper level, it is a call for the rule of law, for justice to be the basis on which the many consequences of conflict—misdeeds and follies, atrocities and counterattacks—can be adjudicated, responsibility determined, and restoration undertaken. The Hebrew term *mishpat* implies more than just determining who is right and who is wrong; it includes an attempt to restore wholeness and harmony between the disputing parties. After judgment comes healing, but the latter cannot be reached without the former.

The ninth and tenth blessings are extensions or consequences of the restoration of law. Those whose actions set them outside what is acceptable, even in war, whose deeds destroy the human dignity of victim and perpetrator alike, must be found, exposed, and punished. Conversely, the heroism and humanity of those who resisted the temptation of barbarism, or who sought ways of meeting the other when such a road was not popular or desired, need to be acknowledged for their human decency and courage. They are the models we need if we are ever to step outside the endlessly repeated abuse of our humanity.

Only then, after the human dimensions have been addressed, do we turn in our sequence of blessings to the issue of religious sanctuaries—the holy sites, the holy places, the holy cities that have proven to be so troublesome. This issue comes late in the sequence because the term *holy*, as commonly understood, enforces a kind of absoluteness on all that we seek to do. If God stands behind the sanctity of a place, where is there room for negotiation or compromise, for cautious sharing and wholehearted respect? There is a narrow divide between piety and idolatry, one that becomes even narrower when holy places are involved. For they represent a great temptation and a great trap. Thus the eleventh blessing focuses on Jerusalem, but only after much human understanding and reconciliation has been achieved.

The twelfth blessing, which speaks of the coming of a future king, a descendant of the Biblical King David, takes this lesson further. People can so easily become intoxicated by charismatic leaders who promise that through them, and them alone, will all problems be solved, all answers found—if only they had the power at their command. Yet the sequence of blessings suggests that this figure will appear only when everything else has been achieved. The longed-for messianic king has had dramatic appeal in Jewish experience over the centuries. Yet every pretender to the title has, in the short or long term, proven to be a disaster, either as a direct result of his actions or because of the disruption and inevitable disappointment that his failure brings. For this reason it is a wise tradition that locates the arrival of this leader at the end of the process, not at the beginning. When together we have established a world based on justice and mutual respect, then we can expect and welcome the right kind of symbolic leadership, so that just and fair rule is bequeathed to subsequent generations.

The thirteenth blessing is one of thanksgiving to God, in anticipation that all of the above will come to pass. It is a thanksgiving and, at the same time, a plea for God's compassion. May God listen to our prayers. But these prayers are not offered in a vacuum. The Hebrew word, *tefillah*, carries a sting in its tail, for the basic sense of the word is self-judgment. Our prayer will be acceptable to God only if we have done the necessary work on ourselves.

It is difficult to sustain a religious position of any integrity in the face of the conflict we seek to address. All too often the effect of a religious word is to harden attitudes, encourage fanaticism, and diminish responsibility for our actions. Or we may feel only the impotence of prayers, talks, sermons, conferences, and general good intentions in the face of hard and bitter political realities, of facts on the ground and blood in the streets. If our respective traditions are to be of help, we must challenge the problems they bring to the table and explore the resources they can offer for mutual understanding and respect across the boundaries of conflict. Instead of fear of the other, we need to discover in a new way the awe and fear of God. Alongside the love we feel for our own, we need to remember the love of God, the love that extends to each and every human being, who is created, exactly like ourselves, in the image of God.

BEYOND THE ENLIGHTENMENT MENTALITY: AN ANTHROPOCOSMIC PERSPECTIVE

TU Weiming

The Enlightenment can be perceived as a cultural movement, as an ideal for the human community yet to be fully realized, or as a mentality characteristic of the modernistic modus operandi throughout the world. The focus of this chapter is the Enlightenment mentality, arguably the most powerful ideology in world history. Both socialism and capitalism grew out of the Enlightenment; so did market economy, democratic polity, and civil society. As advanced economies are knowledge-based, the dominance of science and communication technologies has become more pronounced. Max Weber's prophetic view that modern society will be controlled by experts and managers seems self-evident, and the rise of technocracy in the military, government, multinational corporations, social institutions, and even in non-governmental organizations seems inevitable. Furthermore, the values underlying the Enlightenment—such as liberty, rationality, human rights, and due process of law; and the dignity, independence, and autonomy of the individual—are widely recognized as universal values. The rhetoric of the Enlightenment mentality, suggesting that there is only one option for the future of the human community, seems persuasive.

This paper was presented at the InterAction Council High-Level Expert Group Meeting on "World Religions as a Factor in World Politics," held May 7–8, 2007, in Tübingen, Germany.

Bridging the Divide: Religious Dialogue and Universal Ethics, ed. T.S. Axworthy. Montreal and Kingston: McGill-Queen's University Press, Queen's Policy Studies Series.

However, the Enlightenment mentality is also seriously flawed. Confined in anthropocentrism, dictated by instrumental rationality, and driven by aggressive individualism, it is a form of secularism that suffers from inattention to religion and destructiveness of nature. Without a fundamental restructuring of its worldview, the Enlightenment can hardly provide guidance for human survival, let alone for human flourishing. A comprehensive reflection on and critique of the Enlightenment, especially the pervasive mentality it has engendered throughout the world, is in order. Building upon the insights already accumulated by feminists, environmentalists, postmodernists, communitarianists, and religionists, I intend to offer a humanistic vision, both as a sympathetic understanding of the contemporary significance of "the age of reason" and as a judicious assessment of the blind spots of this de-natured and de-spirited mentality. The purpose is to explore the authentic possibility of a new world order based on a continuous and sustained dialogue among civilizations.

It is vitally important to note that in the *cultural tradition* of the modern intellectual, the Enlightenment mentality is so ingrained in the life of the mind that *traditional culture* has been relegated to the background, a distant echo in the habits of the heart. The political and cultural elite is particularly committed to the Enlightenment project in developing countries such as China, where the struggle to develop a full-fledged market economy, a publicly accountable democratic polity, and a vibrant civil society is far from complete. China is not yet ready to go beyond the Enlightenment mentality; indeed, in its developmental strategy, it takes the traditional Western model as the point of departure. As the pervasive rhetoric goes, for a developing society it is too much of a luxury to hark back to the cultural legacy for inspiration. Yet, ironically, for the survival and flourishing of the human community, it is imperative for intellectuals, including Chinese intellectuals, to go beyond the Enlightenment mentality. From an historical and comparative civilizational perspective, the surest and soundest way to accomplish this challenging enterprise is to tap all the spiritual resources available to the human community in order to formulate a humanistic vision that can transcend anthropocentrism, instrumental rationality, and aggressive individualism without losing sight of the liberating ideas and practices of the Enlightenment as a movement, an ideal, and a mentality.

The upsurge of interest in the Axial Age civilizations symbolizes a "spiritual" turn in philosophy. The "epistemological" and "linguistic" turns have been successful in making the academic study of philosophy in the English-speaking world a truly respectable professional discipline. However, by consigning aesthetics, ethics, and the philosophy of religion to a marginal position of analytical concern, academic philosophers comfortably and snobbishly confined themselves for decades to cocoons of technical competence. Not surprisingly, their style of philosophizing has not had much relevance to issues defining the human condition. As a result, very few philosophers became public intellectuals, and the voices of those who did aspire to public service were often overwhelmed by theologians, cultural commentators, social critics, and political economists. The time is ripe for a fundamental philosophical reorientation. Asian and comparative philosophy can play a significant role in this critical moment.

Historically, none of the major Axial Age civilizations in Asia—Hinduism, Buddhism, Confucianism, and Daoism—made a clear distinction between philosophy and religion. Virtually all philosophical contemplation was embedded in religious insight and cultivation. Indeed, without spiritual disciplines, sophisticated intellectual reflection is impossible. The interplay between philosophy and religion, or more precisely the confluence of disinterested analysis and experiential understanding, is a defining characteristic of Asian modes of thinking. As philosophically seasoned historians such as the French academician Pierre Hadot have convincingly demonstrated, to the Greeks philosophy was a way of life exemplified by spiritual exercises. Harvard professor Hilary Putnam approaches the study of Maimonides, Rosenweig, Buber, and Levinas from a philosophical and religious perspective in his lecture course on the "Four Jewish Thinkers," an approach that is equally relevant to major Islamic thinkers since Avicenna and al-Ghazali. It seems obvious that the revival and flourishing of philosophy as a subject in liberal arts education is in part predicated on its renewed attention to spiritual traditions. Through close collaboration or friendly competition with colleagues in religion, philosophers can recover a highly productive way of philosophizing in the twenty-first century. Needless to say, this undertaking is also a wholesome return to the core and source of the philosophical enterprise: self-knowledge.

The New Humanism rooted in self-knowledge, beyond the secular humanism of the Enlightenment mentality, is historically significant as the spirit of our time. It addresses the ideal of a universal ethic in the reality of cultural diversity. At least eight general principles are involved:

1. As a comprehensive and integrated anthropocosmic vision, it encompasses nature and religion in its humanistic concerns.
2. It assumes that a concrete, living person is at the centre of relationships. Individual dignity, independence, and autonomy are essential features of the person as the *centre* of relationships; sociality is indispensable for personal identity *in relationships*.

3. The concrete, living person is rooted in body, home, community, world, and cosmos and yet seeks to transcend egoism, nepotism, parochialism, racism, and anthropocentrism to reach the highest level of self-awareness. This interplay between rootednes and public-spiritedness characterizes the richness and complexity of the human condition.

4. Nature is, in Thomas Berry's felicitous phrase, "not a collection of objects" but a "communion of subjects." We cultivate a sense of reverence for all beings without imposing the exclusive dichotomies of body/mind and spirit/matter on our life-world. New humanism envisions continuity and consanguinity among all people and all things.

5. Our life in its lived concreteness embodies self, community, nature, and Heaven in an ethic of care and responsibility.

6. Humanity as the core value embodies "Heaven, Earth, and the myriad things" in its sensitivity and consciousness.

7. Although cultural diversity is taken for granted, our quest for "harmony without uniformity" enables us to be an integral part of the "great unity" (the human community) in which all people are recognized as global citizens.

8. Global citizenship signifies primarily a political idea but is suffused with spiritual values and grounded in nature. The humanism that sustains the world order is informed by spiritual and naturalistic concerns.

Global citizenship, predicated on the anthropocosmic vision, is neither a utopian ideal nor wishful thinking but a common aspiration, indeed, a practicable idea with profound ecological, ethical, and religious implications. In this vision, all four dimensions of the human experience—self, community, nature, and Heaven—are incorporated in a holistic approach to the life-world. Integration of the body, heart, mind, soul, and spirit of the person, fruitful interaction between self and community, a sustainable and harmonious relationship between the human species and nature, and mutuality and mutual responsiveness between the human heart and mind and the Way of Heaven are standards for the human community as a whole. They are not abstract ideas but defining characteristics of the necessary path for human survival and human flourishing. This path is diametrically opposed to closed particularism. It also rejects abstract universalism.

The belief that there is a single way to establish a world order is impractical and dangerous; it is likely to generate tension and conflict. Unilateralism is flawed in both theory and practice. It fails to understand that economic globalization enhances as well as homogenizes cultural diversity. The imposition of secular humanistic ideas on the rest of the world, without understanding and appreciation of other core values that are equally desirable and necessary for cultivating global citizenship, is short-sighted and misinformed. Liberty without justice, rationality without sympathy, legality without civility, rights without responsibilities, and individual dignity without social solidarity cannot bring about an enduring world order nurtured by a richly textured culture of peace. All five core values in the Confucian tradition—humanity, righteousness, propriety, wisdom, and trust—are relevant as a reference for universal ethics. Islam, Buddhism, Christianity, Judaism, Hinduism, and other spiritual traditions also offer rich resources for global citizenship. Only through "dialogue among civilizations" can a thick description of universal ethics emerge. Dialogue as mutual learning is the best practice.

Ordinary human experience tells us that genuine dialogue is an art that requires careful nurturing. Unless we are well-prepared intellectually, psychologically, and spiritually, we are not in a position to engage fully in a dialogue. Typically, we relish the joy of real communication only with true friends and like-minded souls. Is it possible for strangers to leap across the civilizational divide to take part in genuine dialogue if the "partner" is perceived as the radical other, the adversary, the enemy? It seems simple-minded to believe that civilizational dialogue is not only possible but also practicable. Surely, it may take years or generations to fully realize the fruits of dialogue. Yet, the benefits of dialogical relationships at personal, local, national, and intercivilizational levels are readily available in our ordinary, daily existence.

If these common experiences are conscientiously cultivated and universally shared, we can learn to transform a common sense of the benefits of dialogue into a good sense of guardianship of global public goods. Ecological consciousness is an obvious example. Our sense of urgency about the sustainability of the environment and the life prospects of future generations enables us to take not only an anthropological but also a cosmological attitude toward all our resources—mineral, soil, water, and air. Through education, this ecological sensitivity can encourage us (perhaps in the beginning we will be only a tiny minority) to mobilize the positive forces of globalization to enhance the material, moral, aesthetic, and spiritual well-being of those underprivileged, disadvantaged, marginalized, and silenced by current trends in economic development. Dialogue among civilizations also encourages wholesome quests for personal knowledge, self-understanding, individual identity, group solidarity, and communal trust.

We have learned from a variety of interreligious dialogues that tolerance of difference is a prerequisite for any fruitful communication. Yet, mere tolerance is too passive; it does not enable us to leap beyond the "frog in the well" mentality. We need to be acutely aware of the presence of the other before we can actually begin communicating. Awareness of the presence of the other as a potential conversation partner compels us to accept our coexistence as an undeniable fact. This awareness leads to the recognition that the other's role (belief, attitude, and behaviour) is relevant and significant to us. In other words, there is an intersection where the two of us are likely to meet to resolve divisive tension or to explore a joint venture. Only when the two sides have built enough trust to meet face-to-face with reciprocal respect can productive dialogue begin. Through dialogue, we can appreciate the value of learning from the other in the spirit of mutual deference. We may even celebrate the difference between us as the reason for expanding both of our horizons.

Dialogue, so conceived, is neither a tactic of persuasion nor a strategy of conversion, but a way of generating mutual understanding through discovering common values and creating a new concept of the meaning of life together. As we approach civilizational dialogues, we need to suspend our desires to sell our ideas, to persuade others to accept our beliefs, to seek approval of our opinions, to gain agreement on our course of action, or to justify our deeply held convictions. Rather, the purpose is to learn what we do not know, to listen to different voices, to open ourselves to multiple perspectives, to reflect on our own assumptions, to share insights, to discover tacit agreements, and to explore best practices for human flourishing. A salient feature of civilizational dialogue is interreligious communication.

The advent of modernity fundamentally transformed all religions. Max Weber defines modernization as rationalization. A distinctive marker of rationalization is secularization. Unlike premodern communities, the overwhelming majority of contemporary societies are managed by secular governments. The United States, perhaps the most religious country in the West, maintains the separation of church and state. In the political process, religion is perceived as a matter of the heart and therefore as a private affair inappropriate for public debate. Educational institutions are wary of religious advocacy and jealously protect their neutrality in religious disputes. But this situation is undergoing a fundamental transformation with substantial consequences for politics and civil society at large.

The need for religious leaders to become bilingual is obvious. They are naturally proficient in the language of their respective faith communities, but they must also learn to be proficient in the language of global citizenship. In other words, they cannot abandon their responsibility to assume the role of public intellectuals. Ideally, bilingualism enables them to bring their own spiritual resources to bear on the vital issues of the global village: protecting the environment, alleviating poverty, eliminating gender inequalities, and abolishing child labour, just to mention a few. In this information age, even if religious leaders choose to concentrate on the spiritual well-being of their faith communities, they cannot be immune to the major events confronting the world.

Experts and professionals in other fields should also feel obligated to become proficient in two languages: the language specific to their profession, and the language of the public intellectual. They must be able to address themselves to two overlapping communities. Unless they are capable of rising beyond their own interest groups as global citizens, they cannot properly situate their expertise in a knowledge-based economy and society. Indeed, religious leaders as well as other experts are confronted with a major challenge. Yet, religious leaders have a comparative advantage. Once they become seasoned in the language of global citizenship, they can bring the ecumenical language of the heart to public discourses. In so doing, they can help to create a new ethos of communication, networking, and negotiation, with profound significance for the market economy, democratic polity, and civil society.

One of the necessary conditions for shaping a world order through dialogue among civilizations is the demand that religious leaders assume their responsibility as public intellectuals. However, the idea of the public intellectual, which recently has attracted a great deal of attention, historically has been relegated to the background. The term *intellectual* first appeared in nineteenth-century Russia. It does not seem to have any antecedent in the Hindu, Buddhist, Judaic, Greek, Christian, or Islamic traditions. The Hindu quest for union of the real self with the cosmic reality, the Buddhist salvation as delivery from worldly attachments, the Jewish covenant with God as the source of all values, the Greek search for truth through the contemplative life of the mind, the Islamic devotion to Allah, and the Christian faith in the Lord in Heaven presuppose the existence of a spiritual sanctuary essentially different from, if not diametrically opposed to, the world here and now. The engagement in and management of worldly affairs is either by choice or default overlooked.

Not surprisingly, the role of the intellectual, as we understand it today, is not the functional equivalent of the guru, monk, rabbi, philosopher, priest, or mullah. The minimum requirement for an intellectual—politically concerned, socially engaged, and culturally sensitive—is fundamentally at odds with a person passionately devoted to the service of a higher reality beyond the mundane concerns of the secular world. Although all spiritual traditions are inevitably intertwined with the ordinary lives of their devotees, the rupture of the chain of being by privileging the "Pure Land" or the "Kingdom of God" outside of the daily routine of human existence is undeniable.

The study of religion has significantly enriched liberal arts education in modern universities; however, the time is ripe for religious leaders and scholars to become engaged in a joint venture to bring the spiritual dimension to economic, political, and social discourses. Religious leaders must be able to address the global community as concerned global citizens. The United Nations Millennium Conference of religious leaders in 2000 was a disappointment because the overwhelming majority of participants used the forum to preach the superiority of their distinctive approaches to life and salvation rather than to articulate a shared vision of spirituality indispensable for human flourishing. Religious leaders are in a position to sensitize other public intellectuals to become religiously musical in their consideration of critical global issues. Indeed, major international organizations are becoming more sensitive to religious matters. For example, religion featured prominently in recent annual meetings of the World Economic Forum at Davos. Even the World Bank is not immune to religious input in its regular programs. The preparatory work of the United Nations Secretariat for the 1995 Social Summit initiated a process whereby ethical and religious dimensions are integrated into discussions of development. This good practice features prominently in the final report of the Copenhagen Seminars devoted to a multidisciplinary inquiry on social progress. Obviously, by becoming public intellectuals, religious leaders can help bring religious concerns to bear on policy discussions of economic, political, and social issues. Furthermore, they can sensitize other public intellectuals to become musical to religious voices.

Decades before the rhetoric of the coming "clash of civilizations" became prevalent in international politics, religious scholars and leaders had been involved in interreligious dialogues. Those seasoned in religious discourse are acutely aware of the great potential for peace or violence in virtually all religious traditions. As the foci of powerful forces, religions are never neutral. They are confluences of dynamic processes of human self-realization and concentrations of creative energies for human self-transcendence, but they are also instruments of mass destruction and vehicles of persistent violence. Without harmony among religions, the chances for a culture of peace are slim. Our quest for a universal ethic, a common ground for peaceful existence among divergent cultures, must take interreligious dialogue as a point of departure.

Recreating a world order through dialogue among civilizations is time-consuming and painfully difficult. Yet, as the politics of domination is replaced by the diplomacy of conversation, a dialogical civilization based on mutual tolerance, recognition, respect, deference, and learning is emerging. The anthropocosmic vision underlying this new humanism, in the words of a great Confucian thinker, enjoins us to "form one body with Heaven, Earth, and the myriad things."

HINDUISM AND POLITICS: THE ROLE OF RELIGIOUS ANTAGONISMS IN INDIAN HISTORY AND POLITICS

Stephan Schlensog

In the first part of this chapter, I propose to give an overview of the interaction between religion and politics and to describe the ambivalent role played by religion on the Indian subcontinent in the course of India's long history. I shall then concentrate on the rise of nationalistic, right-wing Hindu movements since the beginning of the twentieth century and describe their ambivalent role in Indian politics through to the present day.

India's economic and political significance is a subject of much controversy these days. Many political observers believe that, in the coming decades, world politics will be dominated above all by Asian powers: alongside China, by India in particular. As Harald Müller, director of the Peace Research Institute Frankfurt, observes,

> India is the largest democracy in the world; its stability has been proven in almost sixty years of its existence. It has survived numerous shifts of power and even a dangerous, though brief period of emergency rule in the mid-Seventies. It has gone through several wars and suffered prolonged internal violence—terrorism included—in a society which is socially, ethnically and religiously extremely heterogeneous, and yet it has remained a democracy nevertheless.[1]

This paper was presented at the InterAction Council High-Level Expert Group Meeting on "World Religions as a Factor in World Politics," held May 7–8, 2007, in Tübingen, Germany.

In addition, analysts prognosticate for India in the next ten to fifteen years the highest rate of economic growth worldwide, more even than Malaysia and China. They reckon six percent per year. India's economy, no longer dominated by the old noble dynasties, is producing a steady stream of new millionaires and multi-millionaires, who are often called the "new maharajas." According to current estimates, the Indian subcontinent could become the *third largest national economy in the world* after the United States and China—despite the fact that today almost seventy percent of Indians still live below the poverty line, eking out a living by subsistence farming, handicraft and small trade, in large part without access to education, and tied down in archaic cultural and religious bondage.

To understand India, one must above all understand Hinduism and its role in the political and social development not only of India but also of neighbouring countries.[2] Today, eighty-two percent of Indians are Hindus. Approximately twelve percent are Muslims, while Christians and Sikhs each account for two percent, and Buddhists and Jains each comprise less than one percent of the population. Hinduism is the *dominant culture* in India; scarcely any other country in the world—particularly those of corresponding political and economic importance—is so thoroughly imprinted and influenced by its predominant religious culture. For this reason, we must begin with the question: What is Hinduism?

WHAT IS HINDUISM?

For non-Hindus, India and Hinduism are often difficult to comprehend: innumerable gods, thousands of castes, hundreds of languages and dialects, and the thicket of life views, religious ideas, philosophical concepts, ethical norms, and social conventions are unfathomable to most outside observers. Hinduism has no founder to whom it traces its institution as a religion and as a culture with a religious message; it knows no binding dogmas and recognizes no binding teaching office. Beyond a core of common beliefs, there is bewildering diversity. There are innumerable regional variations, as each cultural-linguistic area has its own tradition and local gods and goddesses, all of whom are but limited portrayals of the unlimited, ultimate reality (*brahman*) that is formless, nameless, and without personality.

As you may well know, underlying this diversity is a core of common beliefs among Hindus based on ancient scriptures and sacred writings such as the four Vedas, the Upanishads, the two great epics Ramayana and Mahabharata, and the Sutras, Puranas, and other texts. Hindus believe in the doctrine of birth, rebirth, and reincarnation or transmigration of the soul (*atman*); they believe in the law of *karma* (action), the moral law of causation, which determines the sequence of rebirth. Hindus follow the provisions of a rule called *dharma* (duty or conduct), which is related to caste (a social grouping determined by birth). For Hindus, the final goal of human existence is liberation from rebirth, which means escaping from the bondage of individual existence and becoming one with the ultimate reality, *brahman*.

Like every other religion, Hinduism has undergone epochal transformations in the course of its several thousand-year-old history. Such paradigm shifts have modified existing philosophical and religious ideas—notions of humanity, conceptions of the world, images of the divine, concepts of salvation—and given rise to new ideas. For this reason, it is just as impossible to speak of Hinduism *as such*, as it is to speak of Christianity or Islam as such.

Hinduism is primarily concerned with the salvation of the individual, and less with the shaping of society and politics; nevertheless, the Hindu ethic—like the ethics of all other religions—is clearly focused on how human beings get on together. The central idea of Hindu ethical thinking is the notion of *dharma*, from which was derived, particularly in the medieval *Dharmashastras,* specific rules and duties applying to human beings in all classes and walks of life.

Naturally, in the course of Indian history, various attempts have been made to develop models of government according to traditional notions. Notorious is the *Arthashastra*, a manual of statecraft presumably written by a certain Kautilya, a high official of the Maurya King Candragupta (320 BCE). This work proclaims an unscrupulous doctrine (*shastra*) about what is useful (*artha*) for kings and for the state: Success in foreign politics is achieved by corrupting the enemy through espionage and bribery, and success in domestic politics is achieved through a centralistic organization and merciless suppression of all opposition. Granted that the *Arthashastra* inspired the fantasies of many rulers down through the Middle Ages, it is not representative of India. Being more Machiavellian than Hindu, it is of little use for our present considerations.

India is today and always has been a multiethnic state. Be they Greeks, Persians, Turks, Mongolians, Afghans, Muslims, or Christians, in all epochs of its history India and Hinduism have been confronted with foreign peoples and cultures. Religiously and politically, India and Hinduism have reacted to these influences, with ramifications often extending well beyond the Indian subcontinent.

In the political sphere, interactions with Islam and Sikhism both past and present have had important political consequences. Equally important is the rise of "political Hinduism" or "Neo-Hinduism," which emerged at the beginning of the nineteenth century in response to the confrontation with British colonialism. In this tradition stand those religious and nationalistic forces that in recent decades have shaped India's politics and its relationships with its neighbours and the rest of the world. It is to these forces, their mutual dependence and their political consequences, that I will devote the rest of this chapter.

HINDUISM AND ISLAM

Islam has been present politically on the Indian subcontinent since the eighth century. It soon developed into a cultural and political force in the northwest. In 1192, Afghans of Turkish extraction defeated a Hindu confederation and, in 1206, erected the Sultanate of Delhi. This was the first independent Muslim empire, extending over the whole northern region of the subcontinent; its life, however, was of short duration. Thus it was the Moguls, a dynasty of Turkish rulers, who established the first enduring Muslim empire, ruling over most of India from 1526 to 1707. Alongside the founder of this dynasty, Babur, his grandson Akbar, called "the Great," rose to fame not least because of his religious policy aimed at conciliation and rapprochement.

As the Muslim rulers succeeded each other, their policy toward their Hindu subjects and those of other religions varied: some rulers were rigorous, forcing Hindus to convert and plundering or destroying their temples; others were tolerant, granting religious freedom, albeit at the price of protection money. In the early years of Muslim rule an intensive interchange took place in science, art, and literature; the rules of Akbar the Great and his two successors, in particular, were marked by a blossoming of Hindu-Muslim culture in religion, art, architecture, literature, and lifestyle.

This empire formally ended in the mid-nineteenth century with the onset of British rule in India. To stabilize their control, the British colonial rulers practised a policy of "divide and conquer," especially by introducing a system of "communal" and "special" representation and separate electorates, which increased religious hostility and undermined the National Congress's effort to speak for both Hindus and Muslims. Political radicalization increased on both sides, and tensions between Hindus and Muslims intensified in the years preceding independence. Nevertheless, religious differences did not per se cause violence, confrontation, and enmity between the two communities. Rather, the Muslim league used religious differences to mobilize popular support for the creation of an independent Islamic state, and the Congress leaders contributed to the process by their unwillingness to accommodate Muslim demands.

Just before independence and the partition of India, violence escalated between Muslims and Hindus. The often arbitrary demarcation lines between India and

Pakistan drawn up by the British sharpened the situation and led to the ongoing conflict in Kashmir, which is claimed by Pakistan although the Hindu majority desires incorporation into India. Despite several wars and ensuing peace efforts, a stable political solution to this conflict has yet to be found.

Until the late 1960s, Muslims and Hindus lived peaceably with each other in India. India's secular constitution aimed at neutrality in religious questions and the secular Congress party strove for equal treatment of the religious and ethnically mixed population. However, with the rise of religious and nationalistic Hindu organizations and parties, tension between Hindus and Muslims has grown. Tragic highpoints of this tension are the destruction of the Babri Mosque in Ayodhya in December 1992 and the pogrom in Gujarat in the spring of 2002. I will return to these events later.

CONFLICT OVER THE SIKH STATE

Like the Hindu-Muslim question, the controversy over the Sikh region is a conflict with political and religious roots that has shaped Indian politics for decades.

Founded by Guru Nanak, a Hindu, at the beginning of the sixteenth century, Sikhism is, to put it rather simply, a blend of Hindu devotionalism and Muslim piety. It emphasizes the unity of God, forbids the worship of idols, and opposes the Hindu caste system. Persecuted by the Muslims, the Sikh community developed in the seventeenth and eighteenth centuries from a pacifist to a militant minority that established its own kingdom in the Punjab in the nineteenth century. This soon led to conflict, at first with the British, then with the government of independent India.

The British conquered the Sikh region in 1849. Eight years later, they needed the support of the Sikhs to put down the countrywide "Great Mutiny" of Muslim and Hindu troops in the colonial army that almost cost them their rule. What triggered this rebellion was a religious question, namely, the rumour that the British were issuing cartridges waterproofed with lard or tallow, substances that Muslims and Hindus were forbidden to touch. The Sikhs helped the British to put down the mutiny and the British rewarded them by carrying out a series of development projects in the Sikh region. But in the long run only the middle and upper classes benefited from these projects, which led to social problems and political opposition to the British. The massacre of Amritsar in 1919 effectively ended the cooperation between the Sikhs and the British; six years later the first bloody conflict broke out in connection with the administration of a Sikh temple.

At the partition of India in 1947, the boundary between Pakistan and India was drawn through the middle of the Sikh region. The result was open conflict. Muslims,

Hindus, and Sikhs were forced to leave their homes in a mass exodus of over twelve million people accompanied by horrible massacres where the streams of refugees crossed each others' paths. For decades, the situation of the Sikhs in independent India remained tense. The political demand for the creation of a Sikh province grew louder and was ultimately fulfilled with the creation of the Federal State of the Punjab after the India-Pakistan War of 1966.

Growing economic problems and emerging religious demands—the call for recognizing Amritsar as a holy city, the call for a Sikh state with its own religious orientation—led in the 1980s to a violent confrontation between the Sikh organization Akali Dal and the central government under Indira Gandhi. Terror escalated on both sides. In June 1984, the attempt to storm the Golden Temple in Amritsar ("Operation Blue Star") proved a disaster for Indira Gandhi. In October she was shot by two of her Sikh bodyguards. There followed open violence between Hindus and Sikhs throughout the country and even beyond India. In 1985, Rajiv Gandhi reached an accord with moderate Sikh leaders, and in 1989 the Indian government gained a major victory over Sikh terrorism with its "Operation Black Thunder." In the wake of the difficult election in 1992, the Sikh question is far from being resolved politically, but by and large the tension between Hindus and Sikhs has quieted down considerably.

POLITICAL HINDUISM: FORERUNNER OF INDIAN INDEPENDENCE

In the nineteenth century a movement formed among India's leading social forces—politicians, intellectuals, social activists, religious leaders, and charismatic figures—calling for political and cultural self-reflection, national autonomy, and religious renewal in opposition to British colonialism. This movement, which took the name Political Hinduism or Neo-Hinduism, has had several prominent representatives.

- *Orthodox Hindu Bengali Ram Mohan Roy (1772–1833)*: Influenced by Christianity, he strove for a critical, purified Reform-Hinduism and founded the Brahma Samaj. Under his successors Debendranath Tagore (the father of the famous poet Rabindranatah Tagore) and Keshab Chandra Sen, this organization eventually split when Sen called for a radical criticism of Hinduism and sought to form an ethical universal religion.
- *Gujarati Mulshankar, also known as Dayananda Sarasvati (1824–1883)*: With his "true Hinduism," the founder of the Arya Samaj sought to restore Hindu self-esteem, which had been weakened under the supremacy of

imported British and Western culture. He sought to renew Hinduism radically from its roots. This movement later split into a more traditionalistic and a more reform-oriented organization.

- *Bengali mystic Ramakrishna (1836–1886)*: On the basis of Vishnuite Bhakti and Vedanta philosophy, he developed a vision of a philosophy and spirituality encompassing and transcending all religions. His favourite disciple, Narendra Nath Datta (1863–1902), otherwise known as Swami Vivekananda, took part in the first "Parliament of World Religions" in Chicago in 1893 as an imposing representative of a pluriform, tolerant, and cosmopolitan Hinduism.
- *Bengali writer Bankim Chandra Chatterjee (1838–1894)*: He, too, strove for purification, demythologizing, and reform of traditional Hinduism. However, he linked his religious criticism with a mystical-religious Bengali nationalism and thus ranks as one of the forerunners of the Indian independence movement. Bankim venerated Bengal as a protective mother-goddess, and his hymn *Bande Mataram* (Hail to the Mother) became a war-cry against the British and in effect the Bengali national anthem.
- *Mohandas Karamchand Gandhi (1869–1948)*: Known as the "Mahatma" (great soul), he more than any other knew how to link ethical and religious convictions with political prudence and pragmatism. He was the leading figure in India on the way to political independence. The methods of civil disobedience and non-violent resistance, which he developed, have become models for millions of people around the world.
- *Bengali author Aurobindo Ghose, also known as Sri Aurobindo (1872–1950)*: He linked revolutionary agitation, including armed resistance, with a nationalistic interpretation of India's religious heritage, which he eventually developed into a worldwide cosmic spirituality.

In contrast to the Neo-Hindu thinkers and activists, many nationalistic Hindu activists went underground and founded radical groups. From these groups emerged the religious-nationalistic parties that were to become a potent political force in post-independence India.

THE RISE OF RELIGIOUS HINDU NATIONALISM IN POST-INDEPENDENCE INDIA

On August 15, 1947, India became independent, but it was divided into two separate nations. Pakistan, itself divided into a western and an eastern territory, had a predominantly Muslim population. The Indian Federation had a predominantly Hindu population, but included substantial numbers of Muslims, Sikhs, and other religionists. The failure of the moderate politics of Gandhi and Nehru to avert the partition of India played into the hands of those religious nationalists who continued to dream the unfulfilled dream of an undivided India under Hindu rule. For these groups, there were two enemies to overcome:

- Islam and the Muslims, whom they viewed as a threat to the Hindu nation and to *Hindutva* (Hinduness, the culture formed by Hinduism); and
- The notion of a secular Indian state, which the fathers of Indian independence, Nehru in particular, had pursued on the basis of past experience and which eventually came to prevail—the separation of religion and state, the neutrality of the state in religious matters, equal rights for all religious communities, and prohibition of discrimination on the basis of religious affinity as well as on the basis of race, caste, sex, and place of birth.

For the Hindu nationalists, what was at stake was the self-assertion of *Hindutva* over against everything that was not Hindu, thus above all against Islam, which since the Mogul period had been perceived as a threat to Hindu culture. For this reason, they likewise opposed secular values like religious freedom, although they claimed, on their part, to represent "the true secularism."[3]

The core of the religious nationalist movement is the Rashtriya Svayamsevak Sangh (RSS; National Corps of Volunteers).[4] Founded in 1925 by Keshav Baliram Hedgewar (1889–1940), the goal of the RSS is "to unify India under the saffron flag, a symbol of Hindu power deriving from the reign of Shivaji, an eighteenth-century Hindu prince who conducted a brief rebellion against the Muslim empire—to declare India a nation unified by a single culture and a holy land that is the same time the motherland."[5] The RSS substituted the saffron flag for the national tricolour—the so-called saffron revolution. However, the RSS understood itself initially as more a social than a political movement with the goal of uniting India under a Hindu identity. The key to its success consisted of local groups (*shaka*), networked and organized nationwide, in which young Indians could learn social solidarity, discipline, and Hindu consciousness.

After Hedgewar's death in 1940, M. S. Golwalkar (1906–1973), a disciple of Svami Vivekananda, took over the leadership of the RSS. In contrast to the founder of the movement, Golwalkar had written a number of influential, programmatic publications, so that in the literature he is often called the spiritual father of the movement. For him, geography, race, religion, culture, and language are "the five hallmarks of a national identity and unity." Thus, following Golwalkar's line, today's right-wing Hindus are above all concerned with "loyality to the land with its Hindu traditions, and to their own religion with its culture and its own sources of ethical and spiritual authority."[6] Likewise of great importance for the development of the RSS are the writings of V. D. Savarkar (1883–1966), who was actively involved in the Indian independence movement, though not a member of the RSS. Inspired by European nationalism, both Golwalkar and Savarkar believed that the decisive weakness of India lay in the absence of national and cultural identity.

The relationship of the Hindu nationalists to political Neo-Hinduism and to the Indian independence movement is ambivalent. As with many Neo-Hindus, the RSS was concerned with creating a cultural, religious and, ultimately, a national Hindu identity. Their chief adversary, however, was not the British, but rather the Muslims and Islam. It is not by chance that the RSS leader Golwalkar felt bound to the spiritual heritage of the Bengali nationalist Bankim Chandra Chatterjee, and to this day, many RSS followers chant daily Chatterjee's hymn *Bande Mataram*.

Like many Neo-Hindus, the Hindu nationalists hark back programmatically to the religious Hindu tradition, but they interpret it in a very selective and one-sided manner. Thus, for instance, appealing to the Mahabharata (Great Epic of India), they emphasize the combative tradition of Hinduism and regard Rama, the hero of the Ramayana, as the central divinity of the Hindu pantheon, reinterpreting him in terms of their own political program. Whereas Rama's enemy was originally the King of the Demons, Ravana, his enemy now becomes the Muslims, especially the Moguls, whose ruler, Babur, had in 1528 built a mosque, the Babri Masjid, over Rama's alleged place of birth in Ayodhya. An initial conflict there in 1850 was quickly put down by the British, but since 1949 Ayodhya has become the centre of increasingly violent strife. In contrast to most Neo-Hindus, Gandhi in particular, RSS activists like Golwalkar and N. V. Godse, Gandhi's murderer, reject nonviolence as being utopian, unmanly, and an expression of weakness.

After Gandhi's assassination in 1948, the RSS was forbidden and thousands of its adherents were imprisoned. A year later, however, the organization was legitimized. In the 1960s, the Hindu nationalists got a boost from India's wars with China (1962) and Pakistan (1965). In this period arose the RSS-associated movements of the Janata Sangh (People's Family) in 1960, and the Vishva Hindu Parishad (VHP; All-Hindu Council) in 1964, plus the militant youth organization Barjang Dal. In 1980 the Bharatiya Janata Party (BJP; National People's Party), the long-time political affiliate of the RSS and VHP, was founded as a successor to the Janata Party, which had absorbed the Janata Sangh; its first leader was the RSS member Atal Bihari Vajpayee, who served as the Prime Minister of India briefly in 1996 and from 1998 to 2004.

More than any other Hindu nationalist force, the Bharatiya Janata Party has influenced India's politics in recent decades. Its development reveals the potential but also the limits of Hindu nationalistic politics. Seven periods can be distinguished:[7]

1. *The moderate BJP (1980–1986)*: The BJP distanced itself from the radical RSS. But the electoral success of Rajiv Gandhi in 1984, by appealing to anti-Sikh sentiments after the assassination of his mother, showed the BJP leaders that a Hindu voting block could indeed be formed.

2. *The two-track strategy (1986–1989)*: On the one hand, the BJP opposed the Congress party and the corruption in the Gandhi government; on the other, it drew closer to the radical RSS and VHP. The divorce case of a Muslim woman brought increased political support for the party. The woman had successfully sued in the courts against Islamic law for a monthly alimony from her divorced husband. When this decision was overturned by the Gandhi government through a law passed in deference to Muslim voters, a nationwide wave of protest played into the hands of the Hindu nationalists.

3. *The militant BJP (1990–1992)*: Crucial to this period was the massive nationwide Hindu agitation against the Babri Mosque in Ayodhya, which was built by the Mogul Emperor Babur on the alleged birthplace of the god Rama.

4. *The "responsible" national party in search of power (1992–1998)*: After the destruction of the Babri Mosque in 1992, the protest of radical Hindus threatened to get out of control. The BJP then concentrated on new political themes (anticorruption, good government) and focused its campaign on the non-ideological slogan, "a vote for change."

5. *BJP in power (1998-1999)*: After two decades of struggle over India's atomic policy, ending in disappointment over the role of the nuclear powers and the nuclear armament of Pakistan with Chinese help, the BJP government in May 1998 tested five nuclear weapons, provoking the Pakistani government likewise to test nuclear devices. These tests were accepted in India across ideological and political lines, and Prime Minister Vajpayee became one of the most popular non-Congress leaders of independent India. In dealing with religious matters, the BJP government showed increasing pragmatism.

6. *The BJP caretaker government and the 1999 electoral victory*: Forging a National Democratic Alliance with twenty-three parties, the BJP expanded its basis of power across caste divisions, winning support in middle- and upper-caste groups whose interests were no longer represented by the Congress party.

7. *Return to fundamentalism and the electoral defeat in 2004*: In Gujarat in
   2002, pogroms broke out between Hindus and Muslims. At first, the BJP
   profited from this unrest, but in 2004 it lost the elections because its religious nationalist demands and its slogan "India shining" failed to convince
   many of the poor electorate. Sonja Gandhi won the election, but, as a born
   Catholic, she refrained from taking over the government herself and thus
   made the Sikh Manmoham Singh the prime minister.

The development of the BJP, like that of the RSS, shows that these groups have
only been able to play the Hindu-nationalist card successfully as long as dissatis-
faction with the secular Congress Party government prevailed—under Indira Gandhi
and Rajiv Gandhi it had become too preoccupied with maintaining its own power—
and as long as the BJP voters continued to profit politically and economically
from their allegiance. For instance, when conflict over the Ayodhya Mosque flared
up in 1990 and thousands were killed in the riots, and when a year later RSS
activists destroyed the dome of the mosque, the BJP was hard put to prove that it
was in control of the situation. "Focusing not only on ethnic-religious issues but
also on a range of economic and efficiency issues," it won the elections that same
year but was increasingly forced to play "a double rhetorical game: speaking mod-
erately to appeal to the centre and win votes, but sending a message of intense
ideological commitment to its base."[8]

Nevertheless, the *Hindutva* ideology continued to gain support, benefiting in
2002 from the pogroms in Gujarat, Gandhi's home state, which early on had been
targeted by the nationalists. Following a quarrel between Hindus and Muslims
that to this day has not been satisfactorily cleared up, a train in Godhra was set on
fire, and fifty-seven Hindu pilgrims lost their lives in the conflagration. In retali-
ation, pogroms broke out in Gujarat and neighbouring parts of Maharastra, in which
between one and two thousand Muslim men, women, and children were slaugh-
tered. The massacres were evidently organized with the help of the state
government, and the police did little or nothing to stop them. In the subsequent
elections in December 2002, the Gujarati BJP won by a landslide vote of some
seventy percent.

This success, however, was short-lived. Although the BJP in Gujarat was able
to mobilize voters from all social classes with its nationalistic ideology, "the
example of Gujarat," as Harald Müller showed, "failed to become a model for all
India, as the radical Hindutva propagandists had hoped."[9] Although the *Hindutva*
ideology has spread to the upper classes of Indian society, "the hostility of the
Hindus against the Muslims," despite the sharpness and uncompromising character

of local conflicts here and there,[10] "has not become an all-encompassing characteristic of Indian culture."[11] In the first place, such violence is concentrated in the larger cities and is not a universal phenomenon. In the second place, there are many cities in which peaceful relations between Hindus and Muslims are the rule, either because the social and sometimes religious differences are greater within the groups than between the groups or because in India there exists "a transcultural network of associations (trade unions, businessmen's associations, athletic clubs, reading circles, etc.)," which constitute "a hard to overcome barrier to mobilization of communal violence."[12] In the administration, the executive, and the economy—particularly among those elements of the population oriented to prosperity and social advancement—there are simply too many people who are against the escalation of violence, which would only enhance problems and retard development. For this reason, it is not surprising that the BJP suffered an unprecedented defeat in the 2004 elections.

OUTLOOK

These examples from Indian history not only show how Hinduism and politics have interacted in the national history of India, but also what worldwide effects these interactions have had in the past and continue to have in the present. The history of the Hindu nationalist Bharatiya Janata Party reveals the dangers and the limits of religious nationalist fundamentalism. The fact that the electoral defeat of the BJP in 2004 was hailed by many as a triumph for multicultural, multilingual, multicaste, and multireligious politics gives grounds for hope.

Whether the fundamentalists will regain the upper hand in India or whether in the long run political reason and rejection of violence will come to prevail even among the religious zealots, only the future can tell. The decisive question is whether the breeding grounds for nationalism and fundamentalism can be dried up. This means making accessible income and education to that lower third of the Indian population who, despite growing economic prosperity in the country, still live below the poverty mark. The social marginalization and discrimination of certain castes and social groups and, above all, of women in India is also a religious problem, in which Hinduism is an important political factor.

What role India and Hinduism will play in global politics and in the global economy is at the moment difficult to assess. That Samuel Huntington, despite occasional references to India and Hinduism in his much discussed "Clash of Civilizations," assigns no special role to them says more about the author than about the significance of the land and its culture. Despite the many problems, the example of India shows how a society can be rooted in its own culture and still open itself to the manifold challenges of a modern, multicultural, globalized world. In many respects, India finds itself in a dramatic process of transformation, and Hinduism appears in many respects, both internal and external, to be an important political factor. For this reason, we should come to see this huge country with its admirable culture as "a democratic partner, whose major political role in the world can help make democracy more attractive and can give to the developing countries that long needed, important voice at the table of the mighty. In the best case, the participation of India can help to dampen the notorious arrogance of the West and to make the world more peaceful."[13]

NOTES

[1] Harald Müller, *Weltmacht Indien. Wie uns der rasante Aufstieg herausfordert* (Frankfurt am Main: Fischer Taschenbuch Verlag, 2006), 8.

[2] On Hinduism and Indian history, see Stephan Schlensog, *Der Hinduismus. Glaube – Geschichte – Ethos* (München: Piper Verlag, 2006); Harald Müller, *Weltmacht Indien*; and S. Kakar and K. Kakar, *Die Inder. Porträt einer Gesellschaft* (München: Verlag C.H. Beck, 2006). For the history of India since independence, see Ramachandra Guha, *India After Gandhi: The History of the World's Largest Democracy* (New York: HarperCollins, 2007). On the relationship between Hinduism and politics generally, see E. O. Hanson, *Religion and Politics in the International System Today* (Cambridge: Cambridge University Press, 2006).

[3] As Julia Eckert argues, "Based upon the notion that Hinduism is not a religion but rather a way of life which can integrate people of different faiths without missionizing them, tolerance toward what is 'other' is seen as a fundamental principle of Hinduism." See Eckert, "Die Verstetigung des Konflikts: zur Rolle von Religion im Hindu-Nationalismus," in *Politik und Religion, Politische Vierteljahresschrift*, eds. M. Minkenberg and U. Willems, 351 (Wiesbaden: Sonderheft, 2003). The notion that Hinduism is not a religion but rather "the way of life of all Indians" has been confirmed, with fateful consequences, by a 1995 decision of the Indian Supreme Court. That pretence of an all-encompassing Hindu tolerance was but a theoretical construct has been shown by the quite intolerant history of recent Hindu nationalist politics.

[4] For the history and political activity of the RSS, see especially the recently published work of Martha C. Nussbaum, *The Clash Within: Democracy, Religious Violence, and India's Future* (Cambridge: Cambridge University Press, 2007). See also Ainslie T. Embree, "The Function of the Rashtriya Swayamsevak Sangh: To Define the Hindu Nation," in *Accounting for Fundamentalisms: The Dynamic Character of Movements*, eds. Martin E. Marty and R. Scott Appleby, 617-52 (Chicago/London: Chicago University Press, 1994).

[5] Nussbaum, 154-55.

[6] Nussbaum, 163.

[7] On this point, see the telling observations of S. K. Sahu, "Religion and Politics in India: The Emergence of Hindu Nationalism and the Bharatiya Janata Party (BJP)," in *Religion and Politics in Comparative Perspective: The One, the Few, and the Many*, eds. Ted G. Jelen and Clyde Wilcox, 243-65 (Cambridge/New York: Cambridge University Press, 2002); and S. Corbridge, "The Militarization of All Hindudom? The Bharatiya Janata Party, the Bomb, and the Political Spaces of Hindu Nationalism," *Economy and Society* 28, no. 2 (1999): 222-55.

[8] Nussbaum, 178, 183.

[9] Müller, 121.

[10] On the reasons for the increasing hardening of these conflicts, see the two informative articles (in part identical) by Julia Eckert: "Die Verstetigung des Konflikts," and "Der Hindu-Nationalismus und die Politik der Unverhandelbarkeit. Vom politischen Nutzen eines (vermeintlichen) Religionskonflikts," *Aus Politik und Zeitgeschichte* B43-43 (2002): 23-30.

[11] Müller, 121.

[12] Müller, 123.

[13] Müller, 326-27.

SINAI AS AN EMBLEM OF PEACE IN THE WORLD TODAY

Archbishop Damianos Hegumen

Mount Sinai, austere and precipitous, is forever revered as the place where the great sacred events and theophanies of the Hebrew Bible took place. Here is the site of the burning bush where God instructed his servant Moses and, when God had revealed himself ("I am that I am"), sent him to Pharaoh to deliver the children of Israel from slavery in Egypt and take them through the wilderness of Sinai to the promised land. Here is Mount Horeb, another name for Sinai, the mountain of God, the peak of the Decalogue, the place where, in the midst of divine darkness and fire, God revealed to the great God-seer Moses the mystery of the creation and divine law.

This law was established more clearly thirteen centuries later by the incarnate Son and Word of God. The summation of God's law, which is set forth in the Gospel according to Matthew (22:27–40), speaks to the heart of the three mono-theistic religions of Sinai: "Thou shalt love the Lord thy God with all thy heart, and with all thy soul, and with all thy mind. This is the first and great command-ment. And the second is like unto it, Thou shalt love thy neighbour as thyself. On these two commandments hang all the law and the prophets."[1]

This God-trodden mountain, which again received the grace of God "as a gen-tle breeze" with the coming of the Prophet Elias, is one of the few places in the

This paper was presented at the 25th Annual Plenary Session of the InterAction Council, held May 21–23, 2007, in Vienna, Austria.

Bridging the Divide: Religious Dialogue and Universal Ethics, ed. T.S. Axworthy.
Montreal and Kingston: McGill-Queen's University Press, Queen's Policy Studies Series.

world that is revered by Jews, Christians, and Muslims. It is a place settled by holy men and women who, longing for communion with God in silence and prayer, have "abandoned the city and made a city of the wilderness." The harmony among the faiths of Sinai is an emblem of unity, a testament to peace that is much needed in the world today.

The settlement of Christian hermits commenced in the late third and early fourth centuries at the place of the burning bush, beneath the Mount of the Decalogue, and spread into all the mountainous wilderness to the south of Sinai. With the construction of the monastery fortress by Justinian at the place of the bush in the sixth century, the anchoretic life received the distinctive mark of a coenobium. In this manner, the pious emperor of New Rome gathered the monastic life of Sinai into a more organized entity. It is a life that, according to our sixth-century predecessor Saint John Climacus, entails "a constant constraint of nature and an unceasing watch over the senses." According to Procopius the historian, it is "an unceasing contemplation of death."

Compunctionate prayer, tears of repentance, purification of the heart from the several passions of covetousness, vainglory, and sensuality, and the martyric blood of the righteous monks of Sinai (of whom one hundred and eighty are formally honoured by the Orthodox Church as saints), have preserved and augmented divine grace at this place. But the healing ascetical life and unceasing prayer do not bring salvation only to the ascetics themselves. This sacred place has contributed and is contributing in perpetuity to the salvation of the world through unceasing prayer and the creation of incomparable spiritual works—icons, manuscripts, and other sacred works of art that are treasured at Sinai. And this grace has sanctified those pilgrims who have come here out of piety through the centuries. Since the Middle Ages the monastery has maintained friendly relations with a multitude of pilgrims who come from the West; here, the longing of pilgrimage has outflanked even the schism!

The history of Sinai is thus forever sacred to Jews and Christians. But Sinai is forever sacred to Muslims as well. The call of Moses at the burning bush is described in the Qu'ran, as is the splitting asunder of Sinai at the revelation of God. In the fifty-second and ninety-fifth *suras* (chapters), the Prophet Muhammad swears by Mount Sinai. The Muslim faith came to Sinai in the seventh century, with the conversion of the Jebeliyah bedouin who trace their descent to the two hundred soldiers sent to Sinai by Emperor Justinian. The bedouin dwell in the vicinity of the monastery and take their name from *Jebel Musa,* "Mount Moses." Over the span of fourteen centuries, the monastery's relations with the Muslim rulers and local bedouin have been characterized by peace and mutual respect. How have the monks and bedouin of Sinai been able to achieve this lasting collaboration?

The first foundation must be the shared reverence for Mount Sinai and the revelations of God that took place at this holy site.

Another important reason is the Letter of Protection granted by the Prophet Muhammad to the monks of Sinai and Christians in the area. It is a remarkable document, establishing conditions to ensure that Christians and Muslims live in concord.[2] This letter of protection is one of many granted by the Prophet Muhammad. It is comparable to the one given to the Christians of Najran (today north Yemen), which was at that time the largest centre of Christians in Arabia.[3] The original Letter of Protection granted to Sinai was taken to the Topkapi Palace in 1517 by Selim I, the first Ottoman sultan to rule Egypt. Sultan Selim had copies made so that each of the monastery's churches could have one, and several of these letters are on display at Saint Catherine's Monastery. In addition, it became traditional for successive rulers to confirm their protection of the monastery by a *firman* (decree). The monastery possesses an important archive of these *firmans*.

Another distinctive sign of Christian and Muslim collaboration in the Sinai must be the existence of a mosque within the confines of the monastery. In 1012 a building thought originally to have been a refectory, and which dates to the seventh century, was converted into a mosque. At the same time, the campanile was converted into a minaret. From that time, mosque and church have stood side by side, symbols of peaceful coexistence. The *minbar* (pulpit) was donated by Abu 'l Kasim Shahan Shah, the powerful chancellor of the Fatimid empire. The date on the dedicatory inscription corresponds to November 1106 CE. This *minbar* is one of only three to survive in Egypt from the Fatimid era. The *kursi* (stand for reading the Qu'ran) also survives, a rarity, donated by Abu Mansur Anushtekin, a distinguished emir of the Fatimid empire.[4]

From ancient times, the monastery has given bread to the bedouin. In times past, the bedouin would gather firewood and brush for baking bread, which was drawn up into the monastery with a windlass. The loaves of bread were then let down in the same manner and distributed to the bedouin. The baking and distribution of bread is a tradition that continues to this day, in the midst of changed circumstances. About once a week, dough is prepared, and when it has risen, bedouin workers and monks gather in the bakery, and together they knead the bread and roll out the loaves. When the dough has risen sufficiently the second time, the loaves are baked, and this is also a joint effort between monks and bedouin. The resulting loaves are divided, the greater part of them being distributed among the bedouin.

The baking and sharing of bread is but one of many examples in which the ancient traditions of collaboration between monks and bedouin continue to this day. Many bedouin are employed by the monastery—in the kitchen, in the maintenance of the monastery, in the bookstores, and in many positions of assistance to pilgrims and visitors. It is worth noting that Saint Catherine's Monastery is the only Christian monastery in Egypt to have Muslims in its employment.

From the beginning the monastery has had a hospital where care was given to the sick. In the sixth century, Gregory the Great, Pope of Rome, sent an offering of blankets to the monastery hospital. Medical care has extended to the bedouin as well, and in the last few years the monastery has built a clinic just outside the walls for the benefit of the bedouin, offering first aid, diagnostics, and dental care.

The poor among the bedouin receive distributions of clothing and food from the monastery. This charity is limited only by the limited resources of the monastery, which allocates approximately one-fourth of its resources for the benefit of the bedouin. The monastery also fully supports recent efforts to encourage traditional crafts among the bedouin, and to find markets for these crafts among the many visitors to the area.

The bedouin and Muslim officials participate in special feasts at the monastery. On the feast of Saint Catherine, the bedouin sheikhs attend the beginning of the service, standing next to the Archbishop's throne in the church. On the feast of Pascha, the bedouin sheikhs and local Egyptian officials visit the monastery and are received by the Archbishop, who offers them Paschal eggs and sweetbreads. On the feast of Saint Basil, two *vasilopita* are baked. One is blessed and distributed to each of the monks and novices by name. The second is also blessed and distributed to each of the monastery workers by name.

There are occasions when the Archbishop or one of the monks is invited to attend a bedouin wedding. When a child is born, the father will ask the monastery for a set of white clothes to give to the child as a blessing. When the bedouin are ill and turn to the monastery for help, the medications they receive are also esteemed as a blessing. If the bedouin have a dispute they cannot resolve with their own elected sheikhs, they appeal to the Archbishop for a ruling, who is thus like a grandfather to the bedouin. And when a bedouin dies, his or her relatives ask for a white garment for burial and invite the Archbishop or one of the monks to attend the funeral. All of these are extraordinary examples of mutual respect and lives shared in common by the Christian monks and Muslim bedouin of the Sinai.

The monks of Sinai are Greek-speaking Christians and celibate. The bedouin of Sinai are Arabic-speaking Muslims with families. They are thus divided by language, religion, and culture, by so many differences, all of them fundamental differences, which easily make for misunderstandings and conflict and strife. And the Christians are fervent and dedicated Christians, while the Muslims are fervent and dedicated Muslims. But at Sinai there has been peace. This is due to the shared reverence for the Holy Mount and the revelations of God that took place at this holy site, and to the shared respect that the Christians and Muslims of the Sinai feel toward each other.

Some Christians reproach the monks of Sinai for not having converted the bedouin to Christianity after all these years. Others feel that it is a scandal that the Muslim bedouin can be seen saying their prayers within the monastery. And the bedouin themselves are reproached by some Muslims for their tolerant attitude toward the Christians in their midst. But the mutual respect that has been achieved at Sinai since the seventh century stands as an example for all, especially today, when the concord that exists there is so much needed in the world.

The monks of Sinai seek enlightenment from God through prayer, so that their very lives may be given over to benevolence, charity, and acts of compassion. They ask continually that God will bestow his peace upon the whole world. They strive to bear always in mind the admonitions given by the Holy Apostle Paul to the Romans,

> Let love be without dissimulation. Abhor that which is evil; cleave to that which is good. Be kindly affectioned one to another with brotherly love; in honour preferring one another; not slothful in business; fervent in spirit; serving the Lord; rejoicing in hope; patient in tribulation; continuing instant in prayer; distributing to the necessity of saints; given to hospitality. Bless them which persecute you: bless, and curse not. Rejoice with them that do rejoice, and weep with them that weep. Be of the same mind one toward another. Mind not high things, but condescend to men of low estate. Be not wise in your own conceits. Recompense to no man evil for evil. Provide things honest in the sight of all men. If it be possible, as much as lieth in you, live peaceably with all men. (Romans 12:9–18)

NOTES

[1] Bible quotations are from the King James Version.

[2] Richard Pococke, *A Description of the East and Some other Countries* (London: W. Bowyer, 1743), 268-70.

[3] Sultan Ahmed Qureshi, *Letters of the Holy Prophet* (Delhi: Noor Publishing House, 1994), 41-3.

[4] Heinz Skrobucha, *Sinai*, trans. Geoffrey Hunt (London: Oxford University Press, 1966), 61-2.

Doing Evil To Do Good: Is There An Alternative Approach to Military Intervention in the Clash of Civilizations?

Thomas S. Axworthy

Introduction

Agonizing over the dropping of atomic bombs on Hiroshima and Nagasaki, theologian Reinhold Niebuhr wrote in 1946, "How much evil must we do in order to do good?"[1] Like St. Augustine who contributed to the Just War debate by declaring, "love may require force to protect the innocent,"[2] Niebuhr defended Truman's decision as the only way to avoid potential American casualties, but he was plainly troubled by the age-old question of whether the end justified this particularly horrific means: How much evil for how much good?

Niebuhr's dilemma is at the core of today's debate over military intervention in humanitarian crises. The twentieth century has been a century of megadeath—over 160 million human beings killed in violent conflict—and one that perfected the crime of genocide. The century began with Turkey's Armenian genocide, and it ended with the Rwandan Hutu militia's slaughter of 800,000 Tutsi, and ethnic cleansing in the Balkans. In between, Hitler, Stalin, Mao, and Pol Pot had their turns dancing with the devil. The paradox of the twentieth century, write Robert S. McNamara and James G. Blight, is that we have been enormously successful in saving, lengthening, and enriching lives (average life expectancy, even in the Third

This paper was presented at a conference of the InterAction Council on International Humanitarian Law, held April 22–23, 2002, at the John F. Kennedy School of Government.

World, rose from forty to sixty-five years), while we have been incapable of preventing human slaughter. "Why," they ask, "has the killing of human beings by other human beings been immune from the overall trend toward achieving larger, more fulfilling lives that characterized so much of the twentieth century?"[3]

THE INTERVENTION DEBATE

Humankind's response to a previous century of megadeath—the seventeenth—was the development of the concept of state sovereignty and the principle of non-interference. Today, critics of sovereignty blame the concept for allowing leaders to be unjust to their own peoples and unaccountable to the international system. But the 1648 Treaty of Westphalia was a breakthrough, not only in ending the Thirty Year War, but for constructing an international system with some semblance of order. The Protestant Reformation had split the universal Catholic Church, and in that age of religious zealots, war was conducted in the name of religion. Entire populations were obliged to change their faiths on the basis of whatever army triumphed on the battlefield. Savonarola versus Calvin, Torquemada versus Knox—the seventeenth century had Osama Bin Ladens in every camp. Westphalia was to stop this merging of faith and power. All signatories confirmed the facts on the ground; that is, whoever rules determines the religion of his subjects. It was the partition principle. But Westphalia also declared that no country had a right to intervene in the process. Rulers of one faith were to refrain from inciting uprisings of their co-religionists. With religion removed as an excuse for war, non-interference became one of the critical elements regulating the conduct of states. Non-interference, the *bête noir* of human rights activists of today, was the human rights solution to the seventeenth-century religious wars that had reduced the population of central Europe by a third—more than the Black Death. By putting a lid on religious extremists, Westphalia allowed time for the virtue of pluralism to grow. In 1667, John Locke published his *Essay on Toleration*, and by the eighteenth century, the Age of Enlightenment made the earlier religious frenzy look like an aberration. The non-interference principle had worked.

For that reason, statesmen as wise as Dean Acheson believed non-interference in domestic matters "to be the primary rule of international relations."[4] Acheson wrote,

> By painful experience over the centuries there has come an understanding that each state should respect the autonomy, with respect to internal affairs, of every other state existing in the vast realm external to its own boundaries. That precept is basic to whatever hope there is for peace and order in the world. That it is occasionally violated is no reproach to its validity.[4]

Yet, basic as the principle of non-interference has been to the operation of the international system since 1648, and despite its support today by developing states still smarting from colonialism, it has allowed the most appalling abuses to occur. In Rwanda in 1994, for example, despite a plea from the UN commander Romeo Dallaire for more troops, the Security Council refused to respond positively. Invoking the principle of non-intervention in the Rwandan civil war, the great powers refused to intervene, and in three months, 800,000 human beings died, most by knives or machetes. For all those involved in this non-decision, Rwanda is, in the words of Stephen Lewis, former Canadian ambassador to the United Nations, "an almost incomprehensible scar of shame."[5]

Reflecting an emerging new consensus among human rights activists and public opinion generally, Pope John Paul declared, "The principles of sovereignty of states and not-interference in their international affairs . . . cannot constitute a screen behind which torture and murder may be carried out."[6] Many of the participants in the Rwanda tragedy, such as President Clinton and Madeleine Albright, took the Pope's lesson to heart and applied a different set of principles to the crisis in Kosovo. There NATO intervened even without the approval of the Security Council. But the result has been, according to analyst Michael Mandelbaum, "a Perfect Failure."[7] Blaming Serbia for the conflict when Serbia's army fought Kosovar Albanians intent on independence, NATO flew 34,000 sorties in seventy-eight days. Before the air war, 2,500 had died in the civil war and 230,000 Kosovar Albanians had been displaced; by the end of the war, 10,000 people had died and 1.4 million people had been forced to move from their homes. Every war has unanticipated consequences, writes Mandelbaum, "but in this case virtually all of the major political effects were unplanned, unanticipated, and unwelcome."[8] NATO waged war not for its interests but for its values, and so committed was the Alliance to this humanitarian agenda that it even decided on its own, without Security Council approval, to undertake the mission, destroying in the process the hitherto sacrosanct principle that in order to be legitimate, humanitarian missions should have the international sanction of the Charter. As Henry Kissinger concludes about the Kosovo debacle, "whatever one's view of the obsolescence of the doctrine of national sovereignty, the combination of flagrant disregard of it by an Alliance of democracies and its truculent diplomacy amounted to a departure from the many international norms on which those democracies had insisted throughout the Cold War."[9]

"Life is unfair," said John F. Kennedy, and never more so for the political and military leaders of today on whose shoulders falls the responsibility for deciding whether to intervene or not in crises like Rwanda or Kosovo.

There are no easy answers: military intervention may make the matter worse, as is the case in Kosovo, but inaction or non-interference may lead to genocide, as in Rwanda. To assist leaders in facing the moral dilemmas of humanitarian intervention, an International Commission on Intervention and State Sovereignty co-chaired by Gareth Evans and Mohamed Sahnoun was created in September 2000 by the General Assembly. Its report, *The Responsibility to Protect*, released in December 2001, states several principles to help answer the questions posed by Secretary-General Kofi Annan: "If humanitarian intervention is, indeed, an unacceptable assault on sovereignty, how should we respond to Rwanda, to a Srebrenica—to gross and systematic violations of human rights that affect every precept of our common humanity?"[10]

Proportionality of the military force employed, the necessity for legitimacy through authorization by the Security Council, and the responsibility to rebuild after the action is completed are some of the guidelines recommended by the report. But among the suggestions two common-sense ideas stand out: prevention—the responsibility to address root causes and direct causes of internal conflict, and military intervention as a last resort. To state the obvious, if the international system was better at prevention, then world leaders would be spared the impossible dilemmas that faced them in Rwanda and Kosovo. Easy to say, hard to do. But the United Nations has also endorsed the concept of human security as a principle to guide preventative diplomacy. Does human security give us a way out of the moral blind alley of humanitarian military intervention?

HUMAN SECURITY

Human security is not a new concept. It was first used by the United Nations in the early 1990s. It has been defined by a former foreign minister of Canada as "the premise that security goals should be primarily formulated and achieved in terms of human, rather than state, needs."[11] The core propositions of the human security approach can be summarized as follows:

- Security goals should be focused around human security and not state security;
- Human security entails taking preventative measures to reduce vulnerability and minimize risk, and taking remedial action when prevention fails;
- Human security must go beyond humanitarian action by addressing the sources of people's insecurity. It requires short-term humanitarian action and longer term strategies for building peace;
- Soft power, a term coined by Dean Joe Nye of the Kennedy School, is the new currency of international politics. Skills in communicating, negotiating,

mobilizing opinion, and working with multilateral bodies can be as effective as the "hard" power of the military.

The human security approach therefore focuses on human needs, not on the primacy of sovereignty. It emphasizes prevention: as Secretary-General Boutros Boutros-Ghali wrote, "In matters of peace and security, as in medicine, prevention is self-evidently better than cure. It saves lives and money and it forestalls suffering."[12] This approach seeks to address the sources of insecurity—poverty, environmental degradation, lack of status or power—and it is enthusiastic about new tools of communication to build trust and achieve consensus. The human security agenda of the United Nations is a modern version of the liberal internationalist traditions of Kant, Cobden, Gladstone, and Wilson, rather than the *realpolitik* tradition of Richelieu, Metternick, Bismarck, and Kissinger. In assessing the utility of this new formulation of liberal internationalism, how would a human security framework address one of the great conflicts of our time, the war on terror and the clash with Islam?

CLASHING CIVILIZATIONS

Tony Blair and George Bush have been careful to say that the war against terror is not a war against Islam. Osama Bin Laden disagrees: in an October 7, 2001, videotape following the start of the Afghanistan campaign, for example, he declared that the United States and the United Kingdom "have divided the entire world into two regions—one of faith, where there is no hypocrisy, and another of infidelity, from which we hope God will protect us."[13] In a tape broadcast on April 16, 2002, Ayman Zawahri, a senior official in al-Qaida, with Bin Laden beside him, states: "Those nineteen brothers who went out and sacrificed their lives for God were rewarded with this victory."[14] For good measure the pan-Arab daily *al-Hayat* revealed on the same day a statement from ousted Taliban leader Mullah Mohammed Omar that "the war against Islam and the Muslims is a flagrant crusader war."[15] We are desperately close, if we are not there already, to turning Samuel Huntington's warning about a clash of civilizations into a reality: the engagement of the Taliban in Afghanistan, the carnage in Israel and Palestine, and the war in Iraq cannot help but enrage Islamic fundamentalists. Similarly, al-Qaida's attack on the United States on September 11, the discovery of Islamic terrorist cells in Montreal, Hamburg, London, Brussels, Paris, and Madrid, and the obvious delight of many Arab commentators, and Arab public opinion generally, about the destruction of the World Trade Towers have convinced many in the West of the implacable hostility of Islam toward our secular, democratic values. With Islam and the West, as Samuel Huntington has observed, "each has been the other's Other."[16]

In one way the terrorist attacks of September 11 have little connection with the theme of humanitarian intervention. Providing guidance for heads of state faced with human protection dilemmas in other states is quite different from responding to attacks on one's own nationals. The United Nations Charter provides explicit authority for a military response in self-defence. In the aftermath of the September attacks, NATO invoked Article 5 that an attack on one state was an attack on all, and the Security Council unanimously passed resolutions 1368 and 1373 authorizing the antiterrorist campaign. But in another way the subject matter is very similar because humanitarian intervention takes place in internal disputes, usually civil wars, and a critical component of today's crisis is that the West has become part of Islam's modern civil war. As someone scribbled on a wall in Washington a few days after the September 11 attack, "Dear God, save us from the people who believe in you."

In her book *The Battle for God*, Karen Armstrong has shown that religion is anything but a spent force. With religious attendance declining for a generation in much of the West (but not in the United States), few political analysts took religion seriously, but in recent years, writes Armstrong, "the fundamentalists ha[ve] brought faith out of the shadows and demonstrated that it could appeal to a huge constituency in modern society."[17] Fundamentalists of all religions attacked secularism and liberalism on the basis of what Jean Paul Sartre acknowledged as the God-shaped hole in modern consciousness.[18] In America, fundamentalist Christians have become a political force, especially in the Republican Party; in Israel, Jews are divided not only by the Arab-Israeli conflict but also between the secular and the orthodox. Prime Minister Rabin's assassin, Yigar Amir, has been called "the only happy man in Israel"[19] because God had persuaded him that Rabin was an enemy of the Jewish people, and now the Middle East is bearing the brunt of his perverted act. But the most violent battle between fundamentalists and moderates has been in Islam.

Ibn Kaldun, the great fourteenth-century Arab historian, wrote that a recurring theme in Muslim history was the periodic assault on urban civilization by primitive and puritanical nomads of the desert. Osama Bin Laden is part of this tradition. His beliefs, drawn from Wahhabism, a puritanical version of Islam that emerged from Arabia in the eighteenth century, reflect the most narrow, extreme deviation from the broad tent that is Sunni Islam. The real targets for Islam extremists are existing governments of Muslim lands that have deviated from the path of absolute truth. The spiritual guide of the Islamic Jihad organization that murdered Anwar

Sadat in 1981, Abd al-Salam Faraj, published "The Neglected Duty" a few months after the assassination. Sadat was characterized as a "Tartar," aligned with the Mongol rulers of the thirteenth century who had supposedly converted to Islam, but who were deemed Muslim in name only. Rulers like Sadat "are in apostasy from Islam. They were raised at the tables of imperialism, be it Crusaderism or Communism or Zionism. They carry nothing from Islam but their names, even though they pray and fast and claim to be Muslims."[20] Responding to this extremist thrust, different governments have tried different strategies ranging from arresting fundamentalist leaders, to out-Islaming the Islamists as in Egypt where the prestigious university of al-Azbar issues its own brand of intolerance, to the Saudi regime which has bankrolled the extreme Wahhabi version of Islam the world over.[21] On the whole, what the existing Arab regimes have not tried is democracy and equitable government.

PREVENTION

Could the application of the human security approach have any bearing on the eventual outcome of this Islamic civil war? The first principle is prevention, and on this front there is much to be done. While the world's attention has been focused on the war in Afghanistan and Iraq, what is needed in a serious campaign against terrorists is police work, not bombing. Terrorists must be traced by patient and long-term operations of police and intelligence forces. The world knew of the threat of Osama Bin Laden long before September 11. Indeed, he announced his purposes publicly, much like Hitler in *Mein Kampf*, but no one paid attention. In Canada, for example, where a member of a Montreal terrorist cell attempted to bomb the Los Angeles airport in 2000 (he was stopped at the border), the budget of the Canadian Security Intelligence Service was cut by a third in the 1990s, and the CIA and other intelligence agencies suffered the same fate. Even with improved resources, Richard Betts reminds us that no intelligence service can succeed one hundred percent of the time. There will be another failure like September 11. Therefore, as part of a prevention strategy there must also be an equal emphasis on civil defence, medical readiness, and emergency measures: "Efforts at prevention and preparation for their failure must go hand in hand."[22]

BRIDGE-BUILDING

Facing up to the real sources of conflict is the second essential element of a human security approach. Military operations can fix a short-term problem (Serbian abuses in Kosovo), but if hatred continues unabated, what will happen when the soldiers go home? Bernard Lewis has captured the essential issue in the Islamic civil war: the critical question for Islam, Lewis writes, is what went wrong? Islam, one of the world's great civilizations for a millennium, has fallen on hard times in the twentieth and twenty-first centuries. Whatever measure one applies—economic growth, literacy, scientific invention, artistic creativity or military power—Muslim lands in general and Arab lands in particular are suffering in comparison with the West and East Asia. Different answers to the question "What went wrong?" are at the heart of the Islamic civil war:

> For those nowadays known as Islamists or fundamentalists, the failings and short-comings of the modern Islamic lands afflicted them because they adopted alien nations and practices. They fell away from authentic Islam, and thus lost their former greatness. Those known as modernists or reformers take the opposite view and see the cause of this loss not in the abandonment but in the retention of old ways, and especially in the inflexibility and ubiquity of the Islamic clergy.[23]

This is a question that only the peoples of the Muslim world can answer. But what, if anything, can outsiders do to tip the decision? Human security based on the classic liberal approach would recommend an attempt to build bridges and increase understanding between Islam and the West. A key reference point for the fundamentalists is that Western civilization is alien and pagan. Finding points of convergence between each tradition is a start toward mutual learning. Here, the InterAction Council has played a potentially useful role but with little support from human rights advocates or the United Nations' system as a whole.

In 1987, when Bin Laden was in Afghanistan fighting the Soviets, Takeo Fukuda, the founder of the InterAction Council, had the insight to convene the leaders of five major religions in Rome to see if "an understanding could be obtained from religious groups and a certain common denominator might be found."[24] Helmut Schmidt further promoted this initiative by chairing a group that produced a Universal Declaration of Human Responsibilities in 1997. The core of the Schmidt approach, guided by advisors like Hans Küng, is that the world's religions have different interpretations of the divine, and many faiths reject the separation of church and state that is the norm in the West. But the moral codes of the world's faiths are remarkably similar: every great religious tradition, for example, has the Golden Rule "do unto others as you would have others do unto you." By focusing on responsibilities, part of the Christian ethic but long neglected, the InterAction Council hoped to find common ground both with Islam and the Confucian tradition, which both place a greater emphasis on obligations instead of rights. If Fukuda's goal of gathering political and religious leaders together to discuss problems and misconceptions could become a central priority of the United Nations' system—a worldwide summit or Parliament of Religions—then slowly, ever so slowly, the caricature of other faiths promoted by extremists of all camps might dissolve. What cannot be ignored, however, is the centrality of religion in today's affairs.

If building bridges between faiths is one prong of a human security strategy, then assisting reformers to address the human needs of their co-religionists is another. Islamic extremism has a chance to thrive because the objective condition of so many Muslims is so awful. Many Muslims may reject the extreme interpretations of Islam by Wahhabism, but they rejoice in the schools, hospitals, and social security networks that the fundamentalists provide. In the debate between fundamentalists and reformers (so evident in Iran, for example) do we not have a vital stake in whether moderates succeed? If progressive, moderate, democratic-leaning Muslim regimes succeed in providing a better quality of life for their citizens, will this not contrast with the record of the Taliban in Afghanistan and thus shift the debate? Jordan, a moderate country caught in a vice between Iraq and Israel, is one candidate for maximum assistance; Indonesia, the world's most populous Muslim state (and with a gentle version of Islam) is another. Turkey, especially, is a critical case. Turkey is Muslim in religion but secular in policy. It is one of the most important states in the world because it is the hinge on which the world may avert a war between civilizations. Turkey has applied to enter the European Union. Many Europeans feel that Turkey is not part of Europe. But if the European Union can bring large advances to the economic prospect of Turks and if Europe can encourage Turkey to move along a democratic path, then admitting Turkey to the Concert of Europe might be one of the most important contributions Europe can make to the world. A prosperous, secular, democratic, Muslim Turkey allied with the West not only in NATO but also in the European Union would be a standing rebuke and an alternative path to the future Islam advocated by al-Qaida.

COMMUNICATIONS

"How can a man in a cave out-communicate the world's leading communications security?" asked Richard Holbrooke, former US ambassador to the United Nations.[25] Islamic fundamentalism may look back to the seventh century for its inspiration, but it is as thorough and up-to-date as they come in the use of communications technology. Through the use of videotape and propaganda broadcasts on the Arab-language satellite station Al Jazeera, Bin Laden's diatribes went directly to 34 million potential viewers across the Middle East and North Africa. Bin Laden is following in the footsteps of the Ayatollah Khomeini, who used sophisticated communications while in exile in France to weaken the regime of the Shah. Human security expounds the use of "soft power" of which communication is a central component. In this regard, Bin Laden, alas, has shown himself to be a master of propaganda in producing violent acts of theatre.

In the civil war within Islam, the communications challenge is simply enormous. Independent stations like Al Jazeera compete with officially sanctioned media to see who can most faithfully demonize the West and promote anti-Semitism. Day in and day out the media in the Middle East stoke the fires of Muslim outrage. A Gallup poll taken in nine Muslim countries, released in February 2002, shows the results: despite the widespread publicity on Bin Laden and his henchmen taking credit for September 11, sixty-one percent of the respondents did not believe Arab groups were behind the attacks, and a further sixty-seven percent thought the US campaign in Afghanistan was unjustified.[26] A popular canard, repeated ad nauseam throughout the Middle East, is that four thousand Jews did not turn up for work on September 11, "proof" that Mossad was behind the attacks. Not just the view on "the street," this conspiracy theory was also voiced publicly by the Syrian Defence Minister Mustafa Tlass. A poll taken today, after Israel's incursion into the West Bank, would almost certainly show an even more extreme Muslim view.

Liberal internationalists would argue that public diplomacy, especially in a new information age, is as important a tool as military power. As long as hate is broadcast daily in the Arab media, there will be little chance of moderates winning the Islamic civil war. Arab governments that control their media should be held to account when the propaganda gets too extreme. For too long there has been a quiet bargain—you supply us with oil, and we will let you play the extremist card with the masses to show your Islamist credentials. That policy contributed to the atmosphere that made September 11 inevitable. Arab-speaking Western diplomats and experts must be present to debate issues and provide another point of view. The BBC and Voice of America must be more active in Muslim lands. And, above all, it would be in the interest of everyone if there were more independent media outlets in the Muslim world. Independence does not necessarily imply balance—Al Jazeera is independent of state control. But diversity of outlets would at least increase the possibility that a diversity of views could be heard. Non-American contributors such as UNESCO or the United Nations proper should fund a program to assist the establishment of alternative media outlets in Islamic countries. The Soros Foundation introduced such a program in Central and Eastern Europe after the fall of Communism, and this model should be available throughout the Islamic world. Fighting against a Communist insurgence in Malaysia two generations ago, the British coined the phrase "battle for hearts and minds." At present, the West is not even contending for the hearts and minds of Muslims.

In the seventeenth century, Westphalia created an international system that checked the fires of religious extremism and gave tolerance a chance to grow. Today the United States is waging a military campaign against terrorism that has resulted in one war in Afghanistan and another in Iraq. Terrorism has to be confronted: with weapons of mass destruction available, there is no greater threat in the world. But along with the use of force, there should be a complementary track that focuses on prevention, building bridges, and explicitly communicating that this is not a war against Islam; it is a fight against those who would distort Islam. To defeat this enemy, terrorist infrastructures must be destroyed, but extremist ideas must equally be confronted. The compassion of the Prophet must win out over the hard men who twist his message. Demonizing Islamic fundamentalists will certainly do us no good: we must understand their fears and rage if we are to assist Muslim moderates to better convince their co-religionists. Reinhold Niebuhr, whose agonies about the bomb introduced this essay, also had some advice about how to respond to ideological threats from the Other, in his day Soviet communism. In the midst of the terrible McCarthy witch hunts, Niebuhr preached understanding and a sense of proportion that we need as much today as his countrymen did in 1952:

> For if we should perish, the ruthlessness of the foe would be only the secondary cause of the disaster. The primary cause would be that the strength of a great nation was decided by eyes too blind to see all the hazards of the struggle, and the blindness would be induced not by some accident of nature or history but by hatred and vain glory.[27]

NOTES

[1] Quoted in Richard Fox, *Reinhold Niebuhr* (New York: Pantheon, 1985), 225. Niebuhr was debating with James B. Conant, a defence policy-maker, who questioned Niebuhr's participation in a group of religious leaders who criticized the morality of Truman's decision.

[2] St. Augustine is quoted in the report of the United States Conference of Catholic Bishops, *The Harvest of Justice Is Sown in Peace* (Washington: US Catholic Conference, 1993). I am indebted to Robert S. McNamara and James C. Blight in *Wilson's Ghost* (New York: Perseus Books Group, 2001) for their excellent chapter on "Reducing Communal Killing," 113-68, which contains the Niebuhr and St. Augustine quotes.

[3] McNamara and Blight, *Wilson's Ghost*, xv.

[4] Dean Acheson, *Grapes from Thorns* (New York: W.W. Norton and Co., 1972), 172.

[5] Stephen Lewis, "After Rwanda, the World Doesn't Look the Same," *International Herald Tribune*, July 10, 2000.

[6] Quoted in the United States Conference of Catholic Bishops' report, *Harvest of Justice*.

[7] Michael Mandelbaum, "A Perfect Failure," *Foreign Affairs* (September/October 1999): 2-8.

[8] Mandelbaum, 2.

[9] Henry Kissinger, *Does America Need a Foreign Policy?* (New York: Simon & Schuster, 2001), 263.

[10] Quoted in the Report of the International Commission on Intervention and State Sovereignty, *The Responsibility to Protect* (Ottawa: International Development Research Centre, 2001), vii.

[11] Lloyd Axworthy and Sarah Taylor, "A Ban for All Seasons," *International Journal* (Spring 1998): 191.

[12] Boutros Boutros-Ghali, "Challenges of Preventative Diplomacy," in *Preventative Diplomacy*, ed. Kevin M. Cahill (New York: Basic Books, 1996), 16.

[13] Quoted in Michael Scott Duran, "Somebody Else's Civil War," *Foreign Affairs* (January/February 2002): 23.

[14] *Globe & Mail*, April 16, 2002.

[15] *Globe & Mail*, April 16, 2002.

[16] Samuel Huntington, *The Clash of Civilizations* (New York: Simon & Schuster, 1996), 208.

[17] Karen Armstrong, *The Battle for God* (New York: Ballantine Books, 2000), 317.

[18] Armstrong, 365.

[19] Helen Schary Motro, "The Only Happy Man in Israel," *Toronto Star*, April 16, 2002.

[20] Quoted in Armstrong, *The Battle for God*, 336.

[21] See Graham B. Fuller, "The Future of Political Islam,"*Foreign Affairs* (March/April 2002): 48-60.

[22] Richard Betts, "Fixing Interference," *Foreign Affairs* (January/February 2002): 59.

[23] Bernard Lewis, *What Went Wrong?* (Oxford: Oxford University Press, 2002), 156-7.

[24] Takeo Fukuda, "Preface to the Rome Statement," InterAction Council, 1987.

[25] Quoted in David Hoffman, "Beyond Public Diplomacy," *Foreign Affairs* (March/April 2002): 83.

[26] BBC News, February 27, 2002.

[27] Reinhold Niebuhr, *The Irony of American History* (New York: Charles Scribner's Sons, 1952), 174.

Part Three

POLITICS AND RELIGION: SPEAKING TRUTH TO POWER OR POWER TO TRUTH?

While the essays in Part Two demonstrate that religious movements can wield great positive influence, in Part Three the leaders of the InterAction Council caution that too often religion is exploited and abused by political leaders who take advantage of insecurity and ignorance to maintain power. The three essays in this section call for a higher ethical standard. Oscar Arias wrote, in 1997, that "it is time to talk about human obligations." Freedom and responsibility, he maintains, are interdependent. "Responsibility, as a moral quality, serves as a natural voluntary check for freedom."

In his essay "Human Rights and Human Responsibilities in the Age of Terrorism," Malcolm Fraser, writing after the climactic event of 9-11, worries that our devotion to the longstanding norms of international law has been superseded by fears about terror. This has led to the doctrine of national security pre-emption championed by the Bush administration. But how, Fraser asks, can pre-emption be reconciled with the United Nations Charter?

Helmut Schmidt, writing in 2007, observes that "the maxim of peace is an essential element of the ethics or morals that must be required of a politician." It does not serve the aims of peace, he believes, if "a religion's believers and priests try to convert the believers of another religion and to proselytize to them." He reflects, too, on the need for compromise: all democratic politicians know they must compromise. Without the principle of compromise, there can be no principle of democracy. Politicians, he concludes, have all-too-human weaknesses. When their internal restraints or consciences fail, as they inevitably will, there must be a system of accountability, of checks and balances, to prevent abuse. "We must never forget," he writes in an insight that applies to all, "that one's own reasoning can fail, and so can one's own conscience."

SOME CONTRIBUTIONS TO A UNIVERSAL DECLARATION OF HUMAN OBLIGATIONS

Oscar Arias Sanchez

IT IS TIME TO TALK ABOUT HUMAN OBLIGATIONS

The initiative to draft a Universal Declaration of Human Responsibilities is timely. Although traditionally we have spoken of human rights, and indeed the world has come a long way in the international recognition and protection of rights since the adoption of the Universal Declaration of Human Rights by the United Nations in 1948, it is time now to initiate an equally important quest for the acceptance of human duties or obligations.

This new vision of human obligations is necessary for several reasons. Of course, this idea is new only to some regions of the world; many societies have traditionally conceived of human relations in terms of obligations rather than rights. This is true in general terms, for instance, for much of Eastern thought. While traditionally in the West the concepts of freedom and individuality have been emphasized, in the East the notions of responsibility and community have prevailed. The fact that a Universal Declaration of Human Rights was drafted instead of a Universal Declaration of Human Responsibilities undoubtedly reflects the philosophical and cultural background of the document's drafters who, as is known, represented the Western powers that emerged victorious from the Second World War.

This paper was presented at the InterAction Council High-Level Expert Group Meeting on "A Universal Declaration of Human Responsibilities," held April 20–22, 1997, in Vienna, Austria.

Bridging the Divide: Religious Dialogue and Universal Ethics, ed. T.S. Axworthy. Montreal and Kingston: McGill-Queen's University Press, Queen's Policy Studies Series.

Although human rights are recognized throughout most of the world as the minimum condition for a decent standard of living, the concept of *rights that pertain to humans solely by being human* is not wholly compatible with the traditional values of all cultures. This is particularly true for those societies where the notion of social acceptance—and the granting of rights—depend on the performance of or compliance with certain social duties. By focusing on the active aspect of human relations, the Universal Declaration of Human Responsibilities will balance rights with duties, which together constitute the basic fabric of all social relations, thus making the idea of human rights more accessible to those for whom it may otherwise be alien.

The concept of human obligations also serves to balance the notions of freedom and responsibility: while rights relate more to freedom, obligations are associated with responsibility. Despite this distinction, freedom and responsibility are interdependent. Responsibility, as a moral quality, serves as a natural, voluntary check for freedom. In any society, freedom can never be exercised without limits. Thus, the more freedom we enjoy, the greater the responsibility we bear toward others as well as ourselves. The more talents we possess, the bigger the responsibility we have to develop them to their fullest capacity.

The opposite is also true: as we develop our sense of responsibility, we increase our internal freedom by fortifying our moral character. When freedom presents us with different possibilities for action, including the choice to do right or wrong, a responsible moral character will ensure that the former will prevail.

Sadly, this relationship between freedom and responsibility has not always been clearly understood. Some ideologies have placed greater importance on the concept of individual freedom, while others have given priority to unquestioning commitment to the social group. Without a proper balance, unrestricted freedom is as dangerous as imposed social responsibility. Great social injustices have resulted from extreme economic freedom and capitalist greed, while at the same time cruel oppression of people's basic liberties has been justified in the name of communist ideals and society's interests.

Either extreme is undesirable. At present, with the disappearance of the East–West conflict and the end of the Cold War, with the failure of Marxist experiments and the gradual humanization of capitalism, humanity seems closer to the desired balance between freedom and responsibility. We have struggled for freedom and rights. It is now time to foster responsibility and human obligations.

The initiative to draft a Universal Declaration of Human Responsibilities is not only a way of balancing freedom with responsibility but also a means of reconciling ideologies and political views that were deemed antagonistic in the past. The basic premise, then, should be that humans deserve the greatest possible amount of freedom, but we should also develop our sense of responsibility to its fullest in order to correctly administer our freedom.

FROM RIGHTS TO RESPONSIBILITIES

Because rights and duties are inextricably linked, the idea of human rights makes sense only if we acknowledge the duty of others to respect those rights. Regardless of a particular society's values, human relations are universally based on the existence of both rights and duties.

The Universal Declaration of Human Rights describes a detailed set of conditions that, if present, are believed to be conducive to a good life. Among these are freedom, equality, economic and social security, and peace, aspirations that portray the main challenges that lie ahead of humanity.

Nevertheless, of the Declaration's thirty articles, only one—Article 29—refers to human duties. The only other reference to obligations is a brief section of Article 1, which states that "all human beings ... are endowed with reason and conscience, and should act towards another in a spirit of brotherhood." This spirit of brotherhood, or solidarity, is precisely what the world needs more of today: solidarity with our fellow humans, solidarity between nations, and solidarity toward our planet Earth.

The importance of the concept of responsibility should not be overlooked. After all, it is a sense of responsibility that makes people accountable for their actions. Indeed, we are all responsible for the problems humanity faces today: destruction of the environment, extreme poverty, and the persistence of armed conflict around the globe. These threats are nothing other than the result of human action—action driven in most cases by greed, selfishness, or just plain ignorance. Whatever the reasons, humanity clearly can no longer afford to endure such tragedies.

TOWARD A UNIVERSAL DECLARATION OF HUMAN RESPONSIBILITIES

Challenges such as environmental breakdown, global warming, depletion of the ozone layer, deforestation, pollution, overpopulation, and nuclear war affect all people without regard to nation, race, religion, sex, or status. Thus, each and every one of us has a direct interest in solving these problems. Most of all, since these problems were created by our direct or indirect actions, we are responsible for the solution.

Considering the previous reflections, there are at least three strong arguments for developing a code of human responsibilities:

- The problems humanity faces are entirely the result of human action.
- All of humanity has a direct interest in solving those problems.
- Since rights and duties are inextricably linked, human rights should also entail human duties.

Moreover, traditionally human rights have been conceived in terms of obligations of states vis-à-vis individuals. Solidarity demands that we also think of responsibilities between individuals. I propose, then, that a code of human responsibilities consider at least four dimensions of human action:

- obligations between persons,
- obligations between nations,
- obligations toward planet Earth, and
- obligations toward ourselves.

Obligations between Persons

His Holiness the Dalai Lama has expressed in simple but effective terms the principle that should guide human relations. He says that if we aim to be happy, we should acknowledge that others also desire to achieve happiness. If we believe we have a right to be happy, others should also have the same right. If we would like others to help us achieve happiness, we must be committed to helping others achieve their own happiness.

There is no need for a complex set of rules to guide human action. There is one ancient rule that, if truly followed, would ensure just human relations: the Golden Rule. In its negative form, the Golden Rule mandates that we not do to others what we do not wish be done to us. The positive form implies a more active role in building solidarity: Do unto others as you would have them do unto you.

Bearing in mind the Golden Rule, the Universal Declaration of Human Rights provides the ideal starting point from which to consider some of the main obligations between persons.

- If we have a right to life, then we have an obligation to respect life. Beyond the mere fact of existence, every human being should be entitled to a happy and healthy life; thus, we are committed to creating the conditions for others to enjoy such an existence.

- If we have a right to liberty, we have an obligation to respect other people's liberty as long as it does not cause harm to ourselves or to others.
- If we have a right to security—not just mere security from aggression but human security in its broadest sense: security from hunger, from disease, from ignorance—then we have an obligation not to hinder other people's same right. We have the obligation to help create the conditions for every human being to enjoy true human security.
- If we have a right to partake in our country's political process and elect our leaders, we have an obligation to participate and ensure that the best leaders are chosen. In particular, political leaders who run for office and ask their fellow citizens for their support acquire special responsibilities toward those constituents. We have the right to be governed by honest and capable leaders who are committed to the well-being of their people and their country. It is also our obligation to demand that commitment from them. When a government is mismanaged, political leaders may be held responsible, but the citizens who could have prevented the situation but did not should be held responsible as well.
- If we have a right to work under just and favourable conditions to provide a decent standard of living for ourselves and our families, we also have an obligation to perform to the best of our capacities. Public employees in particular have an obligation to provide the best possible service.
- If we have a right to freedom of thought, conscience, and religion, we also have an obligation to respect others' thoughts or religious principles. No single person or religion possesses the absolute truth, and each provides valuable contributions in humanity's quest to give meaning to life. Under no circumstances should religion be used as an excuse for violence or hate.
- If we have a right to be educated, we have an obligation to learn as much as our capabilities allow us and, where possible, share our knowledge and experience with others.

Obligations between Nations

At the beginning of the twenty-first century, humanity faces challenges never before experienced. While wars have been a constant in human history, the production, stockpiling, and proliferation of nuclear and other weapons of mass destruction pose an immediate risk to the entire planet. Furthermore, while the world's economy has expanded fivefold in the last four decades, extreme poverty grips one-fifth of humanity. Rapid population growth, more than ninety percent of it occurring in the Third World, swells the ranks of the destitute while critically impacting the environment.

Yet, we also possess greater capacities to face these challenges. Fortunately, the end of the Cold War has brought new opportunities for democratization, economic transformation, and peace. Globalization means that nations must assume collective responsibility for making this a better world.

While all nations share responsibility for safely managing the planet and improving living conditions for its population, wealthier countries bear a greater burden. Official development assistance from the industrialized nations to the Third World is a necessary condition in order to help the poorer countries advance their economies. Developed nations must strive to meet the internationally agreed, official development assistance target of 0.7 percent of the gross national product.

Despite the need for assistance from the North, developing nations bear the main responsibility for their own economic and social progress. Two billion people lack safe sanitation, one and a half billion do not have access to potable water, and one billion are illiterate, and yet developing countries spend billions of dollars each year on arms purchases and military expenses, depriving already poor people of basic needs and services. In most cases, these countries do not face real threats to their external security. Instead, many regimes take advantage of the arms trade to abuse their own people.

Efforts to reduce unnecessary military and arms spending would liberate enormous amounts of resources that can, and should, be invested in human development and environmental conservation. Four percent of the $150 billion dollars spent annually by the developing world on their military budget would help pay for programs that would increase literacy by fifty percent, provide universal primary education, and educate women to the same level as men. Eight percent of this budget could provide basic family planning packages to all willing couples and help stabilize world population by the year 2015. And the additional cost of providing universal primary health care, including immunization for all children, elimination of severe malnutrition, and provision of safe drinking water for everyone would represent only twelve percent of this same budget.

Although there has been a trend toward decreased global military spending since the end of the Cold War, there is also a clear arms surplus, which means that more weapons can be purchased at a lower cost. Light weapons, in particular, can easily be obtained through black markets and then smuggled to other countries, eventually finding their way to terrorists, organized crime rings, and drug dealers or common criminals.

These facts indicate that states share some *basic* obligations:

- To resolve international disputes peacefully, by using the methods indicated in the United Nations Charter or resorting to the International Court of Justice. War should never be a legitimate means of solving disputes among nations.
- To reduce military spending, including arms purchases and the size and budget of national armies, to its lowest possible level. We have already seen a reduction in global military expenditure from $995 billion in 1987 to $767 billion in 1994. An international agreement for each country to reduce its spending by three percent per year could bring global expenditures down even further.
- To ensure transparency in arms transfers by participating in the United Nations Register of Conventional Arms. The register is an instrument that contributes to the growth of trust between member states and can also serve to denounce unusual concentrations of weapons in certain countries or regions.
- To develop multilateral agreements to control the arms trade. For maximum effectiveness, an International Code of Conduct on the Arms Trade, approved by the United Nations and adopted by all arms-exporting nations, must be developed. The code would require recipient countries to endorse democracy in terms of free and fair elections, the rule of law, and civilian control over the military and security forces. Its government should not engage in gross violations of internationally recognized human rights or be engaged in armed aggression in violation of international law. The code would also require the purchasing country to participate fully in the United Nations Register of Conventional Arms.
- To end the production of nuclear, chemical, biological, and other weapons of mass destruction and progressively eliminate those already in existence.

Obligations toward Earth

In the Western cultural tradition, people were taught to see the Earth as a dead resource separate from its living beings and at the service of mankind, just as the rest of creation. Today, we are coming to understand that the Earth, together with all its life forms, behaves like one living organism, with humanity as just one of its components. For several million years, the Earth has maintained a temperature suitable for life even though the sun has been getting hotter and the surface properties and the atmosphere's conditions have varied. The balance of nitrogen and oxygen in the air we breathe is constantly regulated by various life forms working together. Rather than adapting to the atmospheric conditions, it seems Earth's life creates those conditions to sustain itself.

Sadly, the natural balance of the Earth's processes is being altered rapidly by human action. Between seventeen and twenty million hectares of tropical forests are destroyed each year, also resulting in the loss of countless species, some unknown to humankind. In the Antarctic, in the spring of 1994, the hole in the ozone layer measured ten million square kilometres. Growing quantities of chemicals, some extremely toxic, are dumped into the soil, air, and water, altering nature's biological systems. The emission of carbon dioxide and other gases is resulting in a gradual warming of the Earth, a phenomenon scientists are now taking seriously, as global warming could raise the temperature by four to nine degrees Fahrenheit, resulting in an increase in the sea level of between 25 to 140 centimetres.

As population levels increase, so will environmental hazards. In particular, world population is expected to double by the middle of the twenty-first century, and about ninety percent of the increase will happen in developing nations. In their struggle for survival, the poor are forced to consume whatever resources they have within their reach: they will cut down tropical forests, overcultivate farm land, and deplete their natural resources. When people are starving, they think only of their own survival and are forced to disregard environmental considerations. While industrialized nations may not experience the immediate effects of global population growth, they are never immune to the long-term consequences because of migrations and related environmental concerns.

Underdevelopment is not the only cause of environmental degradation. The overconsumption and waste of resources on the part of the industrialized nations is also a great problem. As is well known, the consumption rate of non-renewable resources and energy in industrialized nations is greatly disproportionate to that of the developing world.

Therefore, the minimum human obligations toward Earth should include

- protecting the remaining natural forests and initiating reforestation plans,
- ensuring that biological diversity is protected,
- shifting the consumption of non-renewable fossil fuels to other, cleaner sources of energy,
- stopping the production of gases responsible for the greenhouse effect and the depletion of the ozone layer, and
- ensuring that sustainable development principles are incorporated into every country's economical and social policies.

Obligations toward Ourselves

We must accept that today's problems were created by our thoughts and actions; peace, human development, and environmental sustainability must begin in our own minds and deeds. The world cannot change without a transformation in human consciousness, and that transformation can only happen if we each assume certain responsibilities:

- If we want to be at peace with our fellow humans, and if we seek peace among nations, then we must start by developing inner peace. Honesty, solidarity, generosity, fairness, and compassion are human characteristics that can foster inner peace. We must begin by being honest with ourselves, acknowledging our faults but also learning to forgive ourselves for our mistakes.

- If we want to enjoy sustainable human development, we must be prepared to adapt our lifestyles to sustainable patterns of living. We must seek peace with our bodies by realizing what our real physical needs are. We must discard those patterns of overconsumption or abusive indulgence that do not contribute to our health and well-being and also place unnecessary pressure on the Earth's resources.

- If we want to enjoy emotional security, we must remember that people should be valued based on who they are, not what they have. By resting our sense of emotional security in material possessions, we condemn ourselves to insecurity because material possessions can always be lost, destroyed, or taken away. Instead, real emotional security depends on our ability to give and receive love, a psychological disposition that will foster human relations based on compassion, generosity, and solidarity.

As humans we have an unlimited potential for self-fulfillment. Thus, we have the obligation to develop our physical, emotional, intellectual, and spiritual capacities to their fullest. This is an obligation we have to ourselves and to our Creator. By striving to do our best, we are certainly contributing to making this a better world for all.

HUMAN RIGHTS AND HUMAN RESPONSIBILITIES IN THE AGE OF TERRORISM

CHAIRMAN'S REPORT

Rt. Hon. Malcolm Fraser

Since Magna Carta, since the adoption of habeas corpus, there has been a long march toward the liberty of individual citizens. In the twentieth century, efforts have been focused on establishing basic rights and the rule of law throughout the wider international community. Fearing a clash of civilizations and seeking to reinforce moves toward a law-based world, the InterAction Council convened a meeting in Rome in 1987 where the world's major religions were represented at a high level. The purpose was to decide whether an ethical statement could be drafted that was acceptable to all religions and to all faiths.

Out of this discussion evolved a common view about what is needed for a peaceful, cohesive, and constructive society where discrimination and prejudice would be brushed aside. With the advice of philosophers and religious leaders, the InterAction Council drafted in 1997 a Universal Declaration of Human Responsibilities, which is a statement of ethical principles. It states the responsibilities and obligations of all persons and all states.

The Rt. Hon. Malcolm Fraser chaired the InterAction Council High-Level Expert Group Meeting on "Human Rights and Human Responsibilities in the Age of Terrorism" on April 1–2, 2005, at Santa Clara University, California.

It was and still is our view that if major states can be persuaded to accept such a statement, it will become an important companion declaration to the Universal Declaration of Human Rights. We believe that an acceptance of universal "responsibilities" would enhance the acceptance of human rights around the world.

The InterAction Council's Declaration was not initially accepted by the human rights community. Some argued that it was already extremely challenging to persuade nations to accept their obligations under the Universal Declaration of Human Rights and that a second declaration would confuse the issue and obstruct efforts to promote adherence to the declaration on human rights. Others argued that some states would use the draft statement on responsibilities in a repressive or even a reactionary fashion. Some believed that the Declaration on Responsibilities was a matter for individual and not governmental action; therefore, it would be wrong for governments to be prescriptive about what individuals should or should not do. Furthermore, many human rights advocates argued that existing international instruments already address the importance of responsibilities, such as in Article 29 of the Universal Declaration of Human Rights.

Since the war on terror began, many democratic states have diminished human rights in an effort to combat terrorism. This movement, which is substantial in some states, underlines the need to reinforce the human rights movement and to reverse this discouraging trend. A broader acceptance of responsibilities of a common ethic would assist greatly in this process.

Establishing a common ethic is a task long overdue.

This ethic calls for a responsible balancing of security and the rule of law. The speed with which governments in the West, after 9/11, turned their backs on due process and the rule of law, and embraced the methods and techniques of tyrants, greatly disturbs us. In particular, we believe that governments have gone too far in attempting to provide security by infringing upon the rights of the innocent, shifting the burden of proof, and removing due process. Too easily, some world leaders have accepted the idea that liberty cannot be defended by the principles of liberty.

These events demonstrate that a debate about responsibilities and ethics is an urgent necessity today for all countries, but in particular for Western democracies.

Human rights are the possession of all people, including future generations, and they are inalienable. But without leaders and governments making ethical decisions that allow citizens the opportunity to enjoy those rights, the goals of the Universal Declaration of Human Rights will not be achieved. The international community would do better in the war against terror if it could demonstrate that the war can be fought while respecting and implementing rights and responsibilities.

The concept of human responsibility is nothing new. For millennia, before the discussion of rights began, Western and Eastern philosophers have discussed responsibilities. They have taught about the necessity of inner transformation in order to discipline our human emotions. The issue of reviving responsibility is especially crucial today.

We are facing a crisis of responsibility. In field after field, individuals have failed to embrace a sense of ethics in their everyday lives. In recent headlines from every domain, there are examples of political leaders who have misled people deliberately or inadvertently, corporate leaders who have lied, auditors who have assisted in that lying, reporters who have fabricated stories, and church leaders who have failed to provide moral examples.

Responsibilities and rights are deeply intertwined. With rights, there are responsibilities for each of us. Our society would disappear without individuals paying their taxes; it would not function without individuals fulfilling their contracts. Society thrives on trust and personal conscience. The first defence of civilization is the internal ethics of each and every one of us. The second defence is the maintenance of the rule of law.

It is certainly the responsibility of states and political leaders to provide reasonable security and stability. Security is particularly crucial today in the age of terrorism; however, we all must remember how economic and social situations threaten security and lead to terrorism. We share a responsibility for the way in which that protection is achieved. Today, certain states practise and justify torture in the name of security. Conventions on international human rights must be strengthened because of that torture. Yet there is little outrage in response to this derogation of basic human rights.

What is required in the global architecture is a document that outlines core principles of moral responsibility—a code of ethics and responsibility that places a premium on truth, respect for every individual, and concern for the security and well-being of all. This code would engage the moral compass of our leaders. The problem with international machinery is not the law or the treaties, but the absence of political will. The failure of that political will underlines the need for a publicly stated code of ethics.

We remember that the United Nations' Declaration of Human Rights began as a series of principles, not law. In the same way, our document on responsibility also starts with principles. The two concepts of rights and responsibility are complementary. One is a precondition of the other. If human rights and decent societies are to be experienced and enjoyed, all individuals, institutions, corporations, and governments must behave responsibly. A code of ethics is essential to re-establishing the primacy of human rights.

In a time when we talk about the clash of civilizations, a Universal Declaration of Human Responsibilities is especially important because it was derived from the Golden Rule of all major religions—Buddhism, Christianity, Confucianism, Hinduism, Islam, Judaism, and Taoism. The Declaration offers an ethical orientation of everyday life that is as comprehensive as it is fundamental. The basic demand is the Golden Rule: "what you do not wish to be done to yourself, do not do to others" and "do unto others as you would have them do unto you." We have never needed it more.

A World Charter on Responsibility, adopted by the United Nations, would not have legal force. But like the Universal Declaration of Human Rights, it would be a light on the hill. It would be a beacon of hope for the wide acceptance of a common world ethic.

RECOMMENDATIONS

1. (a) Because it is essential to gain the support of the human rights community for an international code of ethics, and because of concerns expressed in the past regarding competition with the Universal Declaration of Human Rights, the name of the InterAction Council's document should be changed to the World Charter on Responsibility.

   (b) If the Council accepts a change in the title of the document, a small committee should be established to examine criticisms made since 1997 to see if alterations should be made to the statement.

2. Because of the reaction of many states in the war against terror, it is all the more necessary to advance the concept of human responsibilities. The InterAction Council should make a renewed commitment to propagate the Charter worldwide—in both the public and private sectors.

3. If our objective is to be achieved, it will be through a paradigm shift in attitude. We must ensure that those in positions of responsibility can regain the public trust essential to a new worldwide culture of ethical leadership.

LIST OF PARTICIPANTS

InterAction Council Members

H. E. Prime Minister Malcolm Fraser, Co-chair (Australia)
H. E. Prime Minister Abdul Salam Majali (Jordan)

High-Level Experts

Prof. Thomas Axworthy, Chair of the Asia Pacific Foundation of Canada
  (Canada)
Dr. Kai Chan, Centre for Conservation Biology, Department of Biological
  Sciences, Stanford University (USA)
Mr. Luis Alberto Cordero, Executive Director of the Arias Foundation (Costa Rica)
Mr. Jean-Dominique Giuliani, President, The Robert Schuman Foundation (France)
Prof. Kirk O. Hanson, Executive Director, Markkula Centre for Applied Ethics,
  Santa Clara University (USA)
Prof. Nagao Hyodo, Tokyo Keizai University (Japan)
Mr. Hiroshi Kawamura, Director, Policy Planning Division, Ministry of Foreign
  Affairs (Japan)
Prof. Hans Küng, Professor Emeritus, Tübingen University (Switzerland)
Prof. Paul Locatelli, S. J., President, Santa Clara University (USA)
Prof. Kathleen Mahoney, Professor of Law, University of Calgary (Canada)
Dr. Robert S. McNamara, Former Secretary of Defence, Former President of
  World Bank (USA)
Prof. Mitsuhei Murata, Tokai Gakuen University (Japan)
Dr. Bertrand Ramcharan, Former Acting High Commissioner for Human Rights,
  United Nations (Switzerland)
Air Commodore Jasjit Singh, Director, Centre for Strategic & International
  Studies (India)
Prof. Jiri Toman, School of Law, Santa Clara University (Czech Republic)

On a Politician's Ethics

Helmut Schmidt

First, I would like to thank you, dear Hans Küng. I was very pleased to accept this invitation, as I have followed the Global Ethic Project most positively since the start of the 1990s. The words *global ethic* may seem too ambitious to some, but the goal, the task to be solved is truly and, by necessity, very ambitious. Perhaps at this point I can mention that an array of former heads of state and government from all five continents have set themselves a common goal very similar to this one since 1987 as members of the InterAction Council; however, as of yet our work has had relatively little success. In contrast, the achievements of Hans Küng and his friends are outstanding.

I myself can thank a devout Muslim for first inspiring me to consider the moral laws common to the great religions. More than a quarter of a century has gone by since Anwar Al Sadat, then president of Egypt, explained the common roots of the three Abrahamic religions to me, as well as their many resemblances, and in particular their corresponding moral laws. He knew of their shared law on peace that is expressed, for example, in the psalms of the Hebrew Bible, in the Christian Sermon on the Mount, and in the fourth surah of the Muslim Qu'ran. If only the people were also aware of this convergence, if only the people's political leaders, at least, were aware of this ethic correspondence between their religions, then, he believed, long-lasting peace would be possible. He was firmly convinced of this.

This global ethic lecture was presented at the InterAction Council High-Level Expert Group Meeting on "World Religions as a Factor in World Politics," held May 7–8, 2007, in Tübingen, Germany.

Bridging the Divide: Religious Dialogue and Universal Ethics, ed. T.S. Axworthy.
Montreal and Kingston: McGill-Queen's University Press, Queen's Policy Studies Series.

Some years later, as president of Egypt, he took political steps to match his conviction and visited the capital and parliament of the State of Israel, which had previously been his enemy in four wars, to offer and conclude peace.

At my advanced age, I have experienced the deaths of my own parents, siblings, and many friends, but Sadat's assassination by religious fanatics shook me more severely than other losses. My friend Sadat was killed because he obeyed the law of peace.

I will return to the law of peace in a moment, but first a proviso: a single speech, especially one restricted in length to less than an hour, cannot come close to exhausting the topic of a politician's ethics. For this reason, I must concentrate on a few salient points: namely, the relationship between politics and religion, then the role of reason and conscience in politics, and finally the need to compromise, and the loss of stringency and consistency this inevitably entails.

~

Now let us return to the law on peace. The maxim of peace is an essential element of the ethics or morals that must be required of a politician. It applies equally to domestic and foreign policy. Along with this, there are other universal laws and maxims. This ethic naturally includes the Golden Rule taught and demanded in all world religions. Immanuel Kant merely reformulated it in his categorical imperative; it is popularly reduced to the phrase "Do as you would be done by." The Golden Rule applies to everyone. I do not believe that different basic moral rules apply to politicians than to anybody else.

However, at a level below the key rules of universal morality are many special adaptations for specific occupations or situations. Just think of the respected Hippocratic oath of doctors, for example, or the professional ethic of judges; or think of the special ethical rules required of businesspeople, moneylenders or bankers, employers, and soldiers at war.

As I am neither a philosopher nor a theologian, I will not attempt to present you with a compendium or codex for a specific political ethic and thus compete with Plato, Aristotle, or Confucius. For more than two and a half millennia, great writers have brought together all kinds of elements or components of the political ethic, sometimes with highly controversial results. In modern Europe this effort extends from Machiavelli and Carl Schmitt to Hugo Grotius, Max Weber, and Karl Popper. I, on the other hand, must restrict myself to presenting you with some of the insights I have gained during my life as a politician and political publicist—for the most part in my home country, and, for the rest, in dealing with neighbouring countries both nearby and farther away.

At this juncture I would also like to point to my experience that, whereas talk of God and Christianity has been relatively rare in German domestic affairs, the same is not true in discussions within other countries and negotiations with their politicians. Recently, when referendums were held in France and The Netherlands on the draft European Union constitution, for many people there the lack of reference to God in the text of the constitution was a decisive motive for rejecting it. A majority of politicians, however, had chosen to refrain from invoking God in the text of the constitution.

The German constitution or Basic Law, which was formulated by a majority of politicians in 1948–49, rests on the rule of reason. God does appear in the preamble: "Conscious of their responsibility before God"; and God is mentioned a second time in the wording of the oath of office in Article 56, which finishes "So help me God." However, immediately after that the Basic Law says, "The oath may also be taken without religious affirmation." In both places it is left up to individual citizens to decide whether they mean the God of the Catholics or the Protestants, the God of the Jews or the Muslims. In a democratic order, under the rule of law, politicians and their reason play the decisive role in formulating constitutional policy, rather than any specific religious confession or its scribes.

We recently experienced how the Holy See, after centuries had passed, finally reversed the verdict once rendered by power politics against Galileo and his use of reason. Today, we experience every day how religious and political forces in the Middle East are locked in bloody battles for power over people's souls—and how reason, the rationality we all possess, repeatedly falls by the wayside. When, in 2001, some religious zealots took their own lives and those of three thousand people in New York, convinced they were serving their God, Socrates' death sentence—for godlessness!—was already two and a half thousand years in the past. Obviously, the perennial conflict between religion and politics, religion and reason, is a lasting element of the human condition.

~

Perhaps I can add a personal experience here. I grew up during the Nazi period; at the start of 1933 I had only just turned fourteen. During my eight years of compulsory military service, I placed my hopes in the Christian churches to re-build society after the expected catastrophe. However, after 1945, I experienced how the churches were able neither to re-establish morality nor to re-establish democracy and a constitutional state. My own church was still struggling over Paul's epistle to the Romans: "Be subject unto the higher powers."

Instead, at first some experienced politicians from the Weimar period played a significant part in the new beginning: Adenauer, Schumacher, Heuss, and others. However, at the start of the Federal Republic it was less the old Weimarians and far more the incredible economic success of Ludwig Erhard and American Marshall aid that swung the Germans toward freedom and democracy and in favour of the constitutional state. There is no shame in this truth: after all, since Karl Marx we have known that economic reality influences political convictions. This conclusion may comprise only a half-truth, but the fact remains that every democracy is endangered if its governing authorities cannot keep industry and labour in adequate order.

As a result, I remained disappointed by the churches' sphere of influence, not only morally but also politically and economically. In the quarter of a century since I was chancellor, I have learned a lot of new things and have read a lot. In this process, I have learned a little more about other religions and a little more about philosophies that previously I was not familiar with. This enrichment has strengthened my religious tolerance; at the same time, it has put me at a greater distance from Christianity. Nonetheless, I call myself a Christian and remain in the church, as it counterbalances moral decline and offers many people support.

~

To this day, what continues to disturb me about references to the Christian God, both among some churchpeople and some politicians, is the tendency to exclude others that we come across in Christianity—and equally in other religious confessions, too: "You are wrong but I am enlightened; my convictions and aims are godly." It has long been clear to me that our different religions and ideologies must not be allowed to stop us from working for the good of all; after all, our moral values actually resemble one another's closely. Peace among us is possible, but we need to always recreate this peace and "establish" it, as Kant said.

It does not serve the aims of peace if a religion's believers and priests try to convert the believers of another religion and proselytize to them. For this reason, my attitude toward the basic idea behind missions of faith is one of deep skepticism. My knowledge of history plays a special role in this; I am referring to the fact that for centuries both Christianity and Islam were spread by the sword, by conquest and subjugation, not by commitment, conviction, and understanding. The politicians of the Middle Ages, that is, the dukes and kings, the caliphs and popes, appropriated religious missionary thoughts and turned them into an instrument to expand their might—and hundreds of thousands of believers willingly let themselves be used in this way.

In my eyes, for example, the Crusades in the name of Christ, where soldiers held their Bibles in their left hands and their swords in their right, were really wars of conquest. In the modern age, the Spanish and the Portuguese, the English, the Dutch, the French and, finally, also the Germans used violence to take over most of the Americas, Africa, and Asia. These foreign continents may have been colonized with a conviction of moral and religious superiority, but the establishment of the colonial empires had very little to do with Christianity. Instead, it was all about power and egocentric interest. Or take the *Reconquista* on the Iberian peninsula: it was not only about the victory of Christianity but, at its heart, concerned the power of the Catholic monarchs, Ferdinand and Isabella. When Hindus and Muslims fight today on Indian soil, or when Sunni and Shiite Muslims battle in the Middle East, time after time the crux of the matter is power and control. The religions and their priests are used to this end, as they can influence the masses.

It greatly concerns me that today, at the start of the twenty-first century, a real danger has developed of a worldwide "clash of civilizations" that is religiously motivated or in religious guise. In some parts of the modern world, motives of power, under the guise of religion, are mixed with righteous anger about poverty and with envy at others' prosperity. Religious missionary motives are mixed with excessive motives of power. In this context it is hard for the balanced, restrained voices of reason to gain attention. In ecstatic, excited crowds, an appeal to the individual's reason cannot be heard at all. The same is true today in places where Western ideologies and teachings on democracy and human rights, which are perfectly respectable in themselves, are forced with military might and almost religious fervour upon cultures that have developed in a totally different manner.

~

I myself have drawn a clear conclusion from all of these experiences: mistrust any politician, any head of government or state, who turns religion into an instrument in his or her quest for power. Stay clear of politicians who mingle their religion, oriented toward the next world, with their politics in this world.

This caution applies equally to politics at home and abroad. It applies equally to the citizens of a country and to its politicians. We must demand that politicians respect and tolerate believers from other religions. Anyone who is not capable of this as a political leader must be seen as a risk to peace—to peace within one's country as well as to peace with others.

It is a tragedy that, on all sides, the rabbis, the priests and pastors, the mullahs and ayatollahs have, to a great degree, kept all knowledge of other religions from us. Instead, they have variously taught us to think of other religions disapprovingly and even to look down upon them. However, anyone who wants peace among the religions should preach religious tolerance and respect. Respect toward others requires a minimum amount of knowledge about them. I have long been convinced that, in addition to the three Abrahamic religions, Hinduism, Buddhism, and Shintoism rightly demand equal respect and equal tolerance.

Because of this conviction, I welcomed the Chicago declaration *Towards a Global Ethic* by the Parliament of the World's Religions, seeing it not only as desirable but also as urgently necessary. Based on the same fundamental position, in 1997 the InterAction Council of former heads of state and government sent the Secretary-General of the United Nations a draft entitled "A Universal Declaration of Human Responsibilities," which we had developed on the initiative of Takeo Fukuda from Japan. Our text, written with help from representatives of all the great religions, contains the fundamental principles of humanity. At this point, I would particularly like to thank Hans Küng for his assistance. At the same time, I gratefully recall the contributions made by the late Franz Cardinal König of Vienna.

~

However, I have also come to understand that, two and a half thousand years ago, some of humanity's seminal teachers—Socrates, Aristotle, Confucius, and Mencius—had no need for religion, although they paid lip service to it on the margins of their work to satisfy people's expectations. Everything we know about them tells us that Socrates based his philosophy, and Confucius his ethics, on the application of reason alone; none of their teachings had religion as a basis. Yet both have come to lead the way, even today, for millions upon millions of people. Without Socrates there would have been no Plato—perhaps even no Immanuel Kant and no Karl Popper. Without Confucius and Confucianism, it is hard to imagine that the Chinese culture and the "Kingdom of Silk," whose lifespan and vitality are unique in world history, would have existed.

Here, one experience is important to me: Clearly, it is entirely possible to produce outstanding insights, scientific achievements, and thus also ethical and political teachings even if the originator does not consider himself bound to a God, to a prophet, to a holy scripture, or to a certain religion but feels bound only by reason. This experience applies equally to socioeconomic and political achievements. However, it cost the American and European Enlightenment many centuries of struggle and battle before it was possible for this experience to make its breakthrough in our part of the world.

The word *breakthrough* is justified with respect to science, technology, and industry. With respect to politics, on the other hand, the breakthrough of reason unfortunately applies to the Enlightenment only to a limited extent. Whether it is the example of Wilhelm II seeing himself as a monarch "by the grace of God," whether it is an American president invoking God, or politicians today invoking Christian values with their politics: they consider themselves bound religiously as Christians. Some plainly and clearly feel that they have a position of Christian religious responsibility; others perceive this responsibility only vaguely, just as most Germans probably do today. Many Germans have, after all, broken away from Christianity; many have left their church; some have also broken away from God—and yet are good people and good neighbours.

~

Today, the vast majority of Germans share some important, fundamental, binding political convictions. Above all, I mean they are bound to the principles of inalienable human rights and democracy. This inner commitment is evidently independent of their personal belief or lack of belief in God and the Christian religion, and it is also independent of the fact that neither principle is included in Christian teachings.

Not only Christianity, but also the other world religions and their holy books have mainly imposed laws and duties upon their believers, whereas the rights of the individual are hardly ever found in the holy books. On the other hand, the first twenty articles of our Basic Law speak almost entirely of the constitutional rights of individual citizens, whereas their responsibilities and duties are hardly mentioned. Our list of civil rights was a healthy reaction to the extreme suppression of the freedom of the individual under Nazi rule. These rights are built not upon Christian or other religious teachings but entirely upon the basic value expressed plainly and clearly in our constitution: "inviolable human dignity."

In the same breath, in the same Article 1, the legislature, the executive, and the judiciary are bound by the basic rights as directly applicable law; this provision also means that all politicians are bound, whether they are lawmakers, governing authorities, or administrators; whether in the federal government, in the *Länder*, or in the municipalities. At the same time, politicians have a wide scope for action, as the Basic Law allows good or successful politics just as it does poor or unsuccessful politics. For this reason, we need not only the lawmakers' and ruling parties' compliance with the constitution; not only, secondly, their regulation by the Constitutional Court; but also, thirdly and most importantly, the regulation of politics by the voters and public opinion.

Of course politicians succumb to error; of course they make mistakes. After all, they are subject to the same human weaknesses as any other citizen, the same weaknesses as public opinion. From time to time, politicians are forced to make spontaneous decisions; mostly, however, they have sufficient time and opportunity to get advice from several sources, and to weigh the available options and foreseeable consequences before coming to a decision. The more politicians allow themselves to be led by a fixed theory or ideology, by their party's interests in power, the less they will weigh all the discernible factors and consequences of their decision in each individual case—and the greater the danger of error, of mistakes and failure. This risk is particularly high when a decision has to be made spontaneously. In each case political leaders are responsible for the consequences, and more often than not this responsibility can be a real burden. In many cases politicians do not find any help in making their decisions in the constitution, in their religion, or in any philosophy or theory, but have to rely upon their reason and judgment alone.

This is why Max Weber was being rather too general when he spoke in his still-readable speech of 1919, "Politics as a Vocation," of a politician's "sense of proportion." He added that a politician must "give an account of the results of his action." In fact, I believe, not only the results in general but also specifically the unintended or tolerated side effects must be justified; the aims of a politician's actions must be morally justified, and the ways and means must, equally, be ethically justified. The "sense of proportion" must suffice for any unavoidable, necessary, spontaneous decision. Yet if there is enough time to weigh things up, there must be careful analysis and deliberation. This maxim does not only apply to decisions made in extreme, dramatic cases but also to normal, everyday legislation, such as tax or labour policy; it applies equally to decisions about new power stations or new motorways. It applies without constraint.

In other words, politicians cannot square their actions and the consequences of those actions with their conscience unless they have applied their reason. Good intentions or honourable convictions alone cannot relieve the burden of their responsibility. For this reason I have always seen Max Weber's words on the necessity of an ethic of responsibility, in contrast to an ethic of ultimate ends, as valid.

At the same time, however, we know that many people who enter politics are motivated by their convictions, not by reason. Equally, we must concede that some decisions, both on domestic and foreign affairs, are born of people's convictions—and not of rational deliberation. And hopefully we have no illusions about the fact that a large proportion of voters base their choices on who to vote for in politics principally on their convictions as stirred by the current mood.

Nonetheless, I have expressed the fundamental importance of the two elements of political decision making—reason and conscience—in my speech and writing for many decades.

~

I must add something, however: as simple and unambiguous as this conclusion sounds or reads, it is not that simple in democratic reality. In a democratic system of government, it is actually the exception if one person alone makes a political decision. Most often it is not an individual who decides but a majority of people. This is true for all legislation without exception.

In order to attain a legislative majority in parliament, several hundred people have to agree on a common text. A relatively unimportant matter can, at the same time, be complicated or hard to approach. In this kind of case, it is easy to rely upon the recognized experts or leaders in one's own parliamentary party. But there are many cases involving important matters in which some members of parliament start off with different, well-founded opinions on one or several points. To achieve a consensus, one has to accommodate them.

In other words, legislating and decision making by parliamentary majority mean that all these individuals must have the ability and the will to compromise! Without compromise, a majority consensus cannot be formed. Anyone who, as a matter of principle, cannot or does not want to compromise is of no use in the process of democratic legislation. Admittedly, compromise often goes hand in hand with a loss of stringency and consistency in political actions, but a democratic member of parliament must be willing to accept losses of this kind.

~

Likewise, compromises are always necessary in foreign policy to keep peace between countries. A national *sacro egoismo*, such as that currently cultivated by the government of the United States, cannot work peacefully in the long term.

It is true that across thousands of years—from Alexander and Caesar, from Genghis Khan, Pizarro, and Napoleon, all the way to Hitler and Stalin—the ideal of peace rarely played a decisive role in the implementation of foreign policy. It equally rarely played a role in theoretical governmental ethics or the integration of philosophy into politics. On the contrary, for thousands of years, from Machiavelli to Clausewitz, war was almost taken for granted as an element of politics.

It was not until the European Enlightenment that a small number of writers— such as the Dutchman Hugo Grotius and the German Immanuel Kant—elevated peace to its position as a desirable political ideal. Yet throughout the entire nineteenth century, for the major European states, war remained a continuation of politics by different means—and so it went on in the twentieth century. The people had long seen war as one of humanity's cardinal evils to be avoided; however, it was not until the appalling misery of the two World Wars that this view was adopted by leading politicians in the West and in the East. This shift can be seen in the attempt to create a League of Nations and later in the founding of the United

Nations, still in force today; it can also be seen in the arms limitation treaties aimed at achieving a balance between the United States and the Soviet Union, as well as in the establishment of European integration in the 1950s and the German *Ostpolitik* in the early 1970s.

Incidentally, Bonn's *Ostpolitik* toward Moscow, Warsaw, and Prague is a notable example of a crucial element of any peace policy: a head of state wanting to act in the interests of peace must speak to the head of state on the other side (that is, the potential enemy) and must listen! Speak, listen and, if possible, come to a compromise. Another example is the Final Act of the Conference on Security and Cooperation in Europe (Helsinki Declaration) in 1975, which was a compromise in the interests of peace. The Soviet Union gained the signatures of Western heads of state under a declaration of the inviolability of Eastern European frontiers, and the West gained the signatures of Communist heads of state under the point on human rights (which was later to become famous as Basket Three of the Accords). The collapse of the Soviet Union fifteen years later was, then, not the result of military force from outside—thank God!—but instead the internal implosion of a system that had far overstretched its power.

A converse, negative example is the wars and acts of violence perpetrated for decades between the State of Israel and its Palestine and Arabic neighbours. If neither side talks to the other, compromise and peace remain only an illusory hope.

Since 1945, international law in the shape of the United Nations Charter has forbidden any external interference in a state's affairs by means of force; only the Security Council may decide upon exceptions to this basic rule. It appears urgently necessary to me today to remind politicians of this basic rule. For example, the military intervention in Iraq—one based, moreover, on falsehoods—is unambiguously a violation of the principle of non-interference, a flagrant violation of the United Nations Charter. Politicians of many nations share the blame for this violation. Equally, politicians of many nations (including Germans) share the responsibility for interventions on seemingly humanitarian grounds that contradict international law. For example, for more than a decade, violent conflicts of interest in the Balkans have been disguised behind the cloak of humanitarianism on the part of the West (including the bombing of Belgrade).

~

However, I would like to leave this digression into foreign policy and return to parliamentary compromise. The mass media, which in our open society shapes public opinion to a great extent, sometimes speaks of political compromise as "horse trading" or "lazy" compromise; sometimes the media is incensed by supposedly immoral party discipline. Although it is good and useful for the media to critically examine the opinion-forming process, at the same time the theorem of the democratic necessity of compromise remains true. After all, a legislative body in which the individual members all stuck unyieldingly to their individual opinions would throw the state into chaos; the government would be unable to rule. Every governmental minister and every member of a parliamentary party knows this. All democratic politicians know they must compromise. Without the principle of compromise, there can be no principle of democracy.

In reality, however, there are also bad compromises made, for example, at the expense of third parties or of generations to come. There are inadequate compromises that do not solve the problem at hand but give only the impression of solving it. In this way, then, the necessary virtue of compromise faces the temptation of mere opportunism. The temptation of opportunistic compromise with public opinion, or elements of public opinion, recurs daily! For this reason, politicians who are willing to compromise must rely on their personal conscience.

A politician should not enter into compromises that go against his or her conscience. In this type of case, the only thing left open to a politician is to face public dissent; sometimes, all that remains is resignation or the loss of one's seat. Politicians who go against their conscience undermine their honour and morals—and others' trust in their personal integrity.

But then there is also the error of conscience. One's own reasoning can fail, and so can one's own conscience. In cases like this, moral reproach is not justified, yet terrible damage can be done. If, in cases like this, politicians later recognize their error, they face the question of whether they should admit the error and tell the truth. In this kind of situation, politicians usually act in only too human a manner: it is hard for any of us to admit our own errors of conscience and the truth about ourselves in public.

～

The question of truth can sometimes contrast with the passion Max Weber identified as one of the three pre-eminent qualities of a politician. The question of truth can also contrast with the required rhetorical ability, already seen as one of the most important arts two and a half thousand years earlier in democratic Athens—and which, if anything, has become even more important in today's television society. Those wanting to be elected have to present voters with their intentions, their manifesto. In doing so they are in danger of promising more than they can later fulfill, especially if they want to appeal to a television audience. Every campaigner is vulnerable to the temptation of exaggeration. The competition for prestige and, above all, the need to appeal to a television audience have further intensified this temptation compared with the old newspaper-reading society.

Our modern mass democracy is, rather like Winston Churchill once said, truly by far the best form of government for us—compared with all those other forms we have tried from time to time—but it is by no means ideal. It is inevitably afflicted with great temptations, with errors and deficiencies. What remains decisive is the positive fact that the electorate can change governments without violence or bloodshed, and that for this reason those elected and the parliamentary majority behind them must answer for their actions before the electorate.

~

As well as passion and a sense of proportion, Max Weber believed the third characteristic quality for a politician was a feeling of responsibility. The question remains, responsibility toward whom? For me, the electorate is not the final authority to whom a politician must answer; voters often make only very general, trend-following decisions based on their feelings and whims. Nonetheless, their majority decision must command the politician's obedience.

For me, the final authority remains my own conscience, although I realize that there are many theological and philosophical opinions about the conscience. The word was already in use in ancient Greece and Rome. Later, Paul and other theologians used it to mean our awareness of God and God's ordained order and, at the same time, our awareness that every violation of this order is a sin. Some Christians speak of the "voice of God in us." In the writings of my friend Richard Schröder, I have read that our understanding of the conscience emerged from Biblical thought coming into contact with the world of Hellenism. On the other hand, his whole life long, Immanuel Kant never gave thought to the basic values of his conscience without religion playing a role in it. Kant described the conscience as "the awareness of an inner court of justice in man."

Whether one believes that conscience comes from people's reason or from God, there is little doubt about the existence of the human conscience. Whether a person is a Christian, a Muslim, or a Jew, an agnostic or a free thinker, an adult human being has a conscience. I shall add, rather quietly, that all of us have gone against our own conscience more than once: we have all had to live with a guilty conscience. Of course, this all-too-human weakness is shared by politicians, too.

~

I have tried to describe to you a few insights gained during three decades of experience as a professional politician. Of course, these comments are very limited extracts from a multifaceted reality. One final, double insight is very important to me. Firstly, our open democratic society suffers from many imperfections and deficiencies, and all politicians still have all-too-human weaknesses. It would be a dangerous error to think of our real, existing democracy as a pure ideal. But, secondly, we Germans—due to our catastrophic history—nonetheless have every reason in the world to cling to democracy with all our might, constantly revitalizing it and constantly standing up bravely to its enemies. Only when we agree upon this will our national anthem, with its "Unity and Justice and Freedom," be justifiable.

Part Four

CONCLUSIONS OF THE INTERACTION COUNCIL

A s Helmut Schmidt writes in his foreword, the work of the InterAction Council on religion and politics has been cumulative. In 1987, the Rome Statement made the key point about the commonality of ethical norms, which has animated the Council discussions ever since. In 1996, the Council began to codify those norms, and in 1997, the Council endorsed a Universal Declaration of Human Responsibilities. This universal declaration has been taken by the Council to the United Nations and to many national governments for endorsement. The Council believes that it should become a companion document to the famous 1948 Universal Declaration of Human Rights.

ROME STATEMENT

*Consultative Meeting on the Interrelated Questions
of Peace, Development, Population, and Environment*

*March 9–10, 1987
La Civiltà Cattolica
Rome, Italy*

PREFACE TO THE ROME STATEMENT

*Takeo Fukuda
Honorary Chair, InterAction Council*

My greatest concern has been and continues to be the difficult situation the world faces. Whether one looks at the world politically, militarily, or economically, problems abound. The physical conditions surrounding our life, including population, development, and the environment, also present us with unprecedented crises. We simply will have no future if we fail in our responses to these precarious situations. Perseverance and determined effort is required on our part if we want to leave the world safe for posterity.

Starting with this awareness, I founded the InterAction Council in 1983 to bring together over two dozen former heads of state and government to consider how these problems could be solved and to act upon our convictions. While incumbent leaders are also concerned with these problems, they are preoccupied with daily

---

The InterAction Council wishes to express its sincere gratitude to the Jesuit Fathers who kindly made their headquarters available for this meeting.

events and are constrained by their respective national interests. I felt that former leaders with abundant experience, which provides a certain dimension of wisdom, should not be complacent. Between 1983 and 1987 the InterAction Council convened five plenary sessions and many special study group meetings. And we have had considerable impact on the world.

But I thought further: I have long felt that world peace and human welfare concern religious groups as much as political figures. Would it not be significant for political and religious leaders to gather together and discuss problems and issues of mutual concern? I felt that an understanding could be obtained from religious groups and that a certain common denominator might be found. After all, the importance of being human is universal.

Therefore, some of the InterAction Council members met with leaders of five major religions of the world in Rome in the spring of 1987. It was agreed that the world's situation is such that there will be no future for humanity if we fail to take up the challenges presented to us, and that a forum was needed for political and religious leaders to jointly contribute to solving some of these problems. It is enormously gratifying for me to confirm that broad agreement was reached on the fundamental difficulties of the world by representatives of groups conventionally considered to have such divergent and even confrontational views.

The agreement reached in Rome encourages us to continue our efforts. The meeting was an unprecedented effort in human history and a very valuable one. I know that continued efforts to seek the meeting of minds will bring about joint actions. I am grateful to have confirmed my belief with my own eyes, and I offer my profound appreciation to providence.

PREFACE TO THE ROME STATEMENT

Helmut Schmidt
Chair, InterAction Council

Since the deep impressions that my conversations with Anwar Al Sadat in the mid-seventies left on me—and especially after reflecting more about Sadat—my curiosity about the religious, philosophical, and ethical tangencies and correspondences among the cultural areas of the world has become ever greater. Without mutual understanding, it is difficult to serve peace.

But whether in Palestine or any other place in the world, it is difficult to imagine that the idea of an "eternal peace" (as propagated by Immanuel Kant) could become reality. Of course, most people accept the moral value of this goal. Nevertheless, it also seems deducible from history that there is a high probability of further conflicts that will also be solved by arms in the future—in spite of a League of Nations or the United Nations and the far-reaching cartel of world powers.

Yet, the fact remains true: the earlier and the more often conflicts are defused and transformed toward compromise, the greater the hope of evading wars. Conversely, the more people resort to religious, nationalistic, racial, or ideological radicalism and fundamentalism, the lesser will be their mutual understanding and the greater the probability of war and the use of force.

It was the wish for mutual listening that brought together religious and political leaders in Rome. We convened not only as Muslims, Jews, or Christians, as Hindus, Buddhists or free thinkers but also as democrats or communists, as conservatives or liberals; we came from utterly different dictatorships or utterly different democracies; we came from all five continents of the world; we were black, brown, yellow, or white. Despite these enormous differences, we did not only understand each other but even agreed on deadly important questions.

It may seem simple to agree upon the wish for peace. But it is difficult—and this applies equally to religious and political leaders—to tangibly serve peace in our daily actions and omissions. It may also be relatively simple to realize that the world's population explosion, which so far we been unable to slow down, will in a few generations mean great economic suffering for billions of people and a level of energy consumption that inevitably will change the chemical composition of the troposphere. The resulting greenhouse effect will have catastrophic consequences for an even greater number of people. Yet, in our daily actions and omissions, it is difficult to work toward a slowing down of the world's population growth and to make family planning a priority for billions of couples.

It was an important signal that priests of all religions as well as political leaders from all quarters of the world acknowledged the importance of family planning. Many other leaders must also be made aware.

Scarcities are not unilateral. To give is to have. At the end of the twentieth century, the threats to humanity can only be avoided by solidarity.

Statement on Global Issues

Introduction

For the first time in recent history, in March 1987 political and spiritual leaders from all continents and five major religions met in Rome at the invitation of the InterAction Council. For two days the participants engaged in a discussion on world peace, the global economy, and the interrelated areas of development, population, and environment.

The leaders agreed that humankind is confronted by the greatest set of crises in history, yet measures adequate to meet them have not been defined or devised. Unless there are effective and correct responses to the challenges presented by these crises, there will be no enduring future.

They further agreed that, in addressing these problems, there are many areas for cooperation between spiritual and political leaders in their shared devotion to moral values, peace, and human well-being.

This initial exchange of views resulted in a striking degree of commonality in the perception and evaluation of present dangers, and recognition of a need for action built on a widely shared ethical basis.

The leaders assembled in Rome agreed that such contacts involving political, intellectual, and scientific leaders must be continued by the InterAction Council and others at global and regional levels, and that these consultative meetings should influence, with the support of the media, political decision-making processes.

PEACE

Today, peace has lost its true meaning in a world that since World War II has not seen a single day without war, conflict, poverty, and large-scale human and environmental degradation. Ethical principles shared by all participants led them to conclude that genuine peace can be accomplished only through an ongoing process of dialogue and receptive understanding permeating all areas of society and international contacts.

All participants, therefore, welcomed efforts to bring about disarmament. The United States and Soviet Union should honour their treaty commitments to achieve cuts in strategic weapon levels and continue negotiations aimed at even further reductions. Policies of countries like the People's Republic of China and Argentina to cut their military budgets provide examples of progress.

Scientific and engineering resources and capabilities presently devoted to the arms race should be redirected toward the solution of global problems threatening human survival and welfare: the development of alternative energy resources and new transportation systems and technologies to mitigate the effects of impending climatic changes; the further exploration of the decay of the ozone layer; the prevention of a continued decline in the number of biological species; and measures to counter the threats to the biosphere.

World Economy

For moral, political, and economic reasons, humanity must strive toward a more equitable economic structure, reversing the appalling poverty that afflicts vast numbers of human beings throughout the world. Change can only be accomplished through dialogue and a series of decisions predicated on enlightened self-interest on the part of industrialized countries and mutually supportive policies on the part of developing countries.

The debt crisis with its ominous consequences must be resolved with a sense of urgency. Debt servicing cannot be met at the price of suffocating a country's economy, and no government can morally demand of its people privations incompatible with human dignity. All parties involved must make a tangible contribution and honour the moral principle of burden-sharing.

Emergency assistance programs are an indispensable part of ensuring the survival of many people and communities currently enduring abject poverty. There is a paramount need for fostering a sense of global solidarity for survival.

Development – Population – Environment

It was stressed that moral values for the family and recognition of the common responsibility of women and men are indispensable in dealing with these issues. Rapid population growth in many developing countries vitiates any advance in development. This situation fuels the vicious cycle of underdevelopment, population growth, and the erosion of human life-support systems. Responsible public policies require systematic projections of population, environmental, and economic trends with particular attention to their interaction.

Cognizant of the different approaches of religions toward family planning policies and methods, the leaders nonetheless agreed that present trends make the pursuit of effective family planning inevitable. The positive experience of several countries and religions should be shared, and scientific research into family planning should be accelerated.

PARTICIPANTS OF THE CONSULTATIVE MEETING WITH SPIRITUAL LEADERS

Members

Takeo Fukuda
> Former Prime Minister of Japan, Honorary Chair of the InterAction Council, and Chair of the Consultative Meeting in Rome

Helmut Schmidt
> Former Chancellor of the Federal Republic of Germany, Chair of the InterAction Council

Jenoe Fock
> Former Chair of the Council of Ministers of the Hungarian People's Republic

Malcolm Fraser
> Former Prime Minister of Australia

Olusegun Obasanjo
> Former Head of the Federal Military Government of Nigeria

Misael Pastrana Borrero
> Former President of Colombia

Maria de Lourdes Pintasilgo
> Former Prime Minister of Portugal

Bradford Morse
> Former Administrator of the United Nations Development Program, Honorary Member of the InterAction Council

Spiritual Leaders

Dr. A.T. Ariyaratne
> Buddhist, Founder and President of the Sarvodaya Shramadana Movement, Sri Lanka

Prof. K.H. Hasan Basri
> Muslim, General Chair of the Majelis Ulama (Council of Islamic Scholars), Indonesia

Rev. John B. Cobb
> Methodist, Visiting Professor at the Harvard Divinity School, United States

Franz Cardinal König

>   Roman Catholic, Archbishop Emeritus of Vienna, Former President of the
>   Pontifical, Secretariat for Non-Believers, Austria

Mr. Li Shou-Pao

>   Protestant, Vice-Chair, National Committee of the "Three-Self," and
>   General Secretary, National Committee of the Young Men's Christian
>   Association of China, People's Republic of China

Dr. Karan Singh

>   Hindu, President of the Virat Hindu Samaj, India

Prof. Elio Toaff

>   Jewish, Chief Rabbi in Rome and Member of the Italian Rabbinic
>   Council, Member of the Executive Committee of the European
>   Rabbinical Conference

Mr. Lester Brown

>   Expert representing the scientific community, President of the
>   Worldwatch Institute

IN SEARCH OF GLOBAL ETHICAL STANDARDS

*Report on the Conclusions and Recommendations
of a High-Level Expert Group*

*March 22–24, 1996
Vienna, Austria
Chaired by Helmut Schmidt*

INTRODUCTION

As human civilization advances into the twenty-first century, the world is entering a period of transformation at least as profound and far-reaching as that of the industrial revolution. Globalization of the world economy is matched by globalization of the world's problems—population, environment, development, unemployment, security, and moral and cultural decadence. Humankind is crying out both for justice and for meaning.

The physical changes in technology and the applied sciences have far outstripped the ability of our institutions to respond. The state is still the main instrument for translating the collective will into concrete action, but everywhere the concept of state sovereignty is under siege. To repeat the well-known phrase, the nation-state is too small for big problems and too big for local problems. Multinational corporations enjoy unprecedented opportunities as world trade and investment expand, but corporate leaders now face agonizing questions about corporate responsibility in unfamiliar areas like human rights. Religious institutions still command the loyalty of hundreds of millions of people, but secularization and consumerism command even more support. The world is also afflicted by religious extremism and violence preached and practised in the name of religion. The use of the word *fundamentalism* in this regard is a misnomer, because religious people everywhere believe deeply in the fundamentals of their faiths, but most religious people also reject violence and believe that force should never be used to advance their cause. So the world is in flux. Where do we turn?

CONCRETE RECOMMENDATIONS

1. To promote the dissemination of ethical norms, the InterAction Council recognizes that sovereign states are still the primary vehicles of change. Granted that sovereign states are the main target, we should also pay due attention to the role of electronic mass media and possibly of transnational organizations that are increasingly gaining power on the global scene.

2. To ensure some significant degree of success in promoting a global ethic, it is essential and perhaps crucial that religions of the world with divergent belief systems and regions of influence should cooperate closely in persuading the sovereign states and various relevant institutions to help realize this goal. This collaborative effort will serve at least two important functions. On the one hand, it will demonstrate that adherents of different religions can indeed meet with open minds to reach an agreement on the urgent problems facing humanity today and on the ethical standards and norms required to combat this world crisis. On the other, the mere fact that all the religions of the world have been able to work in concert to promote global ethical standards will ease the task of disseminating such norms throughout the world.

3. Meetings of the world religious leaders could facilitate the cause of global ethics. Specifically, religious leaders could use such meetings to urge sovereign states and their leaders, educational institutions, the mass media, as well as their own religious institutions to adopt and promote by every means possible a consensus on the global ethic. It should be stressed that such gatherings should represent all of the major world religions, making sure to include women. Existing global religious organizations could facilitate these meetings.

4. Recommendations by world religious leaders should be directed mainly toward the people in decision-making positions of government, education, mass media, non-governmental non-profit organizations, and religious organizations of each sovereign state. These groups have direct or indirect involvement with the propagation and inculcation of global ethical standards and with other basic information related to world religions.

5. If religious leaders accept the invitation of the InterAction Council to meet, the world will welcome a discussion of a concrete action plan to promote the dissemination of the global ethic. While not exclusive, such a plan could include the following elements:

   - A common code of ethics compiled in booklet form and disseminated across the globe.
   - Specific codes of ethics for the professions, business, political parties, mass media, and other critical interests. In addition to the general code of ethics, these specific codes would contribute to self-regulation.
   - Suggestions to the world's leaders that in 1998, the fiftieth anniversary of the Universal Declaration of Human Rights, the United Nations should convene a conference to consider a Universal Declaration of Human Responsibilities to complement the earlier, crucial work on rights.
   - Development of a global educational curriculum that would include the best contributions of the world's religions and philosophies. Such a curriculum should be available to every educational institution and accessible through the most current communications technologies.
   - To broaden understanding and to combine the intellectual resources necessary for the development of such a curriculum, the United Nations should consider establishing as part of the United Nations University system a World Interfaith Academy that would bring together scholars, students, and leaders of the world's faiths.

The Need for Global Ethical Standards

6. As Aristotle taught us, the human being is a social animal. Because we must live in society—because we must live with each other in harmony—human beings need rules and constraints. Ethics are the minimum standards that make a collective life possible. Without ethics and the self-restraint that results, humankind would revert to the jungle. In a world of unprecedented change, humankind has a desperate need for an ethical base on which to stand.

7. The world's religions constitute one of the great traditions of wisdom for humankind. This repository of wisdom, ancient in its origins, has never been needed more. Ethics should precede politics and the law, because political action is concerned with values and choice. Ethics, therefore, must inform and inspire our political leadership. Education at its best opens the

human potential for understanding and tolerance. Without ethics and the teaching of right and wrong, our schools become mere factories mass-producing labour soon to be obsolete. Mass communication is one of the most powerful mediums in influencing the mind and behaviours of human beings, but the violence, degradation, and triviality of much of the media pollutes the human spirit rather than elevate it.

8. To respond to this world of change, each of our institutions needs a rededication to ethical norms. We can find the sources of such a rededication in the world's religions and ethical traditions. They have the spiritual resources to give an ethical lead to the solution of our ethnic, national, social, economic, and religious tensions. The world's religions have different doctrines, but they all advocate a common ethic of basic standards. What unites the world's faiths is far greater than what divides them. They all advocate self-restraint, obligations, responsibilities, and sharing. They all advocate the virtues of humility, compassion, and justice. Each assesses the maze of life and in its own way discerns the patterns that give meaning to the whole. To solve our global problems, we must begin with a common ethical base.

The Core of a Global Ethic

9. Today, humanity possesses sufficient economic, cultural, and spiritual resources to introduce a better global order, but old and new ethnic, national, social, economic, and religious tensions threaten the peaceful building of a better world. In such a dramatic global situation, humanity needs a vision of peoples living peacefully together, of ethnic and ethical groupings and of religions sharing responsibility for the care of earth—a vision that rests on hopes, goals, ideals, and standards. We are therefore grateful that the Parliament of the World's Religions, which assembled in Chicago in 1993, proclaimed a Declaration Toward a Global Ethic that we support in principle.

10. There have been landmark advances to strengthen human rights in international law and justice beginning with the United Nations adopting the Universal Declaration of Human Rights, strengthened by the two human rights covenants on Civil and Political Rights and Economic, Social, and Cultural Rights, and elaborated by the Vienna Declaration on Human Rights and Program for Action. What the United Nations proclaimed on the level of rights, the Chicago Declaration confirmed and deepened from the perspective of obligations: the full realization of the intrinsic dignity of the

human person, the inalienable freedom and equality in principle of all humans, and the necessary solidarity and interdependence of all humans with each other, both as individuals and as communities. Also, we are convinced that a better global order cannot be created or enforced by laws, prescriptions, and conventions alone; that action in favour of rights and freedoms presumes a consciousness of responsibility and duty, and therefore both the minds and hearts of women and men must be addressed; that rights without obligations cannot long endure; and that there will be no better global order without a global ethic.

11. The global ethic is no substitute for the Torah, the Gospels, the Qur'an, the Bhagavad Gita, the Discourses of the Buddha, or the Teachings of Confucius and of others. A global ethic provides a necessary minimum of common values, standards, and basic attitudes. In other words, it provides a minimal, basic consensus relating to binding values, irrevocable standards, and moral attitudes that can be affirmed by all religions despite their dogmatic differences and can also be supported by non-believers.

12. In affirmation of the Chicago Declaration, which for the first time in the history of religions formulated this minimal basic consensus, we recommend two principles that are vital for every individual, social, and political ethic:

- Every human being must be treated humanely.
- Do unto others as you want others to do unto you. This Rule is part of every great religious tradition.

13. On the basis of these two principles there are four irrevocable commitments on which all religions agree and that we fully support:

- a commitment to a culture of non-violence and respect for life,
- a commitment to a culture of solidarity and a just economic order,
- a commitment to a culture of tolerance and a life of truthfulness, and
- a commitment to a culture of equal rights and partnership between men and women.

14. Cognizant of the different approaches of religions toward family planning policies and methods, it was nevertheless agreed that present population trends make the pursuit of effective family planning inevitable. The positive experience of several countries and religions should be shared, and scientific research into family planning should be accelerated.

15. Education, at all levels, has a crucial role to play in inculcating global ethical values in the minds of the younger generation. From the primary school to the university, curricula and syllabi should be restructured to include common global values and to promote understanding of religions other than one's own. Educational programs should inform values like "affirmative tolerance," and curricular materials should be produced accordingly. The development of the aspirations of youth should be a major emphasis. UNESCO, the United Nations University, and other international bodies should work together to achieve this objective. The electronic media should also be enlisted.

16. We note the ongoing participatory process, initiated by the Earth Council and Green Cross International, to develop an Earth Charter. We welcome this initiative as an example of an effort to involve the world's religions and other groups in defining the basic change in values, behaviour, and attitudes of government, the private sector, and civil society needed for a shift to sustainable development.

17. Because respect of life is a core ethical commitment, combatting the scourge of war and violence must be at the top of the world's priorities. Two issues in particular must receive immediate attention: the trade in small arms and semiautomatic weapons must be curbed, and the easy availability of such weapons must cease. And like small arms, landmines have destroyed a score of innocent lives. This problem is especially acute in Cambodia, in the former Yugoslavia, in Africa, and in Afghanistan. The systematic removal and dismantling of landmines is an urgent need.

List of Participants

InterAction Council Members

Helmut Schmidt, Chair
Andries van Agt
Pierre Elliott Trudeau
Miguel de la Madrid Hurtado

Experts

Mughram Al-Ghamdi, Dean, King Fahad Academy, London, United Kingdom
Michio Araki, Professor, University of Tsukuba, Japan
Shanti Aram, President, Shanti Ashram Coimbatore, India
Thomas Axworthy, Executive Director, CRB Foundation, Canada
Abdolijavad Falaturi, Director, Islamic Scientific Academy, and Professor,
    University of Cologne, Germany
Ananda Grero, former Judge of the Court of Appeal, Sri Lanka
Kim Kyong-Dong, Professor, Seoul National University, Korea
Cardinal Dr. Franz König, Vienna, Austria
Hans Küng, Professor, University of Tübingen, Germany
Peter Landesmann, Professor, University of Vienna, Austria
Liu Xiao-feng, Academy Director, Institute of Sino-Christian Studies, Hong Kong
L.M. Singhvi, High Commissioner for India, London, United Kingdom
Majorie Suchocki, Dean, School of Theology at Claremont, United States
Shizue Yamguchi, former Member of Parliament, Japan (observer)

Journalist

Flora Lewis, International Herald Tribune

A UNIVERSAL DECLARATION OF HUMAN RESPONSIBILITIES

Proposed by the InterAction Council

September 1, 1997

INTRODUCTORY COMMENT

It is time to talk about human responsibilities

Globalization of the world economy is matched by global problems, and global problems demand global solutions on the basis of ideas, values, and norms respected by all cultures and societies. Recognition of the equal and inalienable rights of all people requires a foundation of freedom, justice, and peace—but this also demands that rights and responsibilities be given equal importance to establish an ethical base so that all men and women can live peacefully together and fulfill their potential. A better social order both nationally and internationally cannot be achieved by laws, prescriptions, and conventions alone, but needs a global ethic. Human aspirations for progress can only be realized by agreed values and standards applying to all people and institutions at all times.

Next year will be the fiftieth anniversary of the Universal Declaration of Human Rights adopted by the United Nations. The anniversary would be an opportune time to adopt a Universal Declaration of Human Responsibilities, which would complement the Human Rights Declaration and strengthen it and help lead to a better world.

The following draft Declaration of Human Responsibilities seeks to bring freedom and responsibility into balance and to promote a move from the freedom of indifference to the freedom of involvement. If one person or government seeks to maximize freedom but does it at the expense of others, a larger number of people will suffer. If human beings maximize their freedom by plundering the natural resources of the earth, then future generations will suffer.

The initiative to draft a Universal Declaration of Human Responsibilities is not only a way of balancing freedom with responsibility but also a means of reconciling ideologies, beliefs, and political views that were deemed antagonistic in the past. The proposed declaration points out that an exclusive insistence on rights can lead to endless dispute and conflict, that religious groups in pressing for their own freedom have a duty to respect the freedom of others. The basic premise should be to aim at the greatest amount of freedom possible but also to develop the fullest sense of responsibility that will allow that freedom itself to grow.

The InterAction Council has been working to draft a set of human ethical standards since 1987. But its work builds on the wisdom of religious leaders and sages down the ages who have warned that freedom without acceptance of responsibility can destroy freedom itself, whereas when rights and responsibilities are balanced, then freedom is enhanced and a better world can be created.

The InterAction Council commends the following draft Declaration for your examination and support.

UNIVERSAL DECLARATION OF HUMAN RESPONSIBILITIES

Preamble

Whereas recognition of the inherent dignity and of the equal and inalienable rights of all members of the human family is the foundation of freedom, justice, and peace in the world and implies obligations or responsibilities,

whereas the exclusive insistence on rights can result in conflict, division, and endless dispute, and the neglect of human responsibilities can lead to lawlessness and chaos,

whereas the rule of law and the promotion of human rights depend on the readiness of men and women to act justly,

whereas global problems demand global solutions which can only be achieved through ideas, values, and norms respected by all cultures and societies,

whereas all people, to the best of their knowledge and ability, have a responsibility to foster a better social order, both at home and globally, a goal which cannot be achieved by laws, prescriptions, and conventions alone,

whereas human aspirations for progress and improvement can only be realized by agreed values and standards applying to all people and institutions at all times,

Now, therefore,

The General Assembly

proclaims this Universal Declaration of Human Responsibilities as a common standard for all peoples and all nations, to the end that every individual and every organ of society, keeping this Declaration constantly in mind, shall contribute to the advancement of communities and to the enlightenment of all their members. We, the peoples of the world, thus renew and reinforce commitments already proclaimed in the Universal Declaration of Human Rights: namely, the full acceptance of the dignity of all people, their inalienable freedom and equality, and their solidarity with one another. Awareness and acceptance of these responsibilities should be taught and promoted throughout the world.

FUNDAMENTAL PRINCIPLES FOR HUMANITY

Article 1

Every person, regardless of gender, ethnic origin, social status, political opinion, language, age, nationality, or religion, has a responsibility to treat all people in a humane way.

Article 2

No person should lend support to any form of inhumane behaviour, but all people have a responsibility to strive for the dignity and self-esteem of all others.

Article 3

No person, no group or organization, no state, no army or police stand above good and evil; all are subject to ethical standards. Everyone has a responsibility to promote good and to avoid evil in all things.

Article 4

All people, endowed with reason and conscience, must accept a responsibility to each and all, to families and communities, to races, nations, and religions in a spirit of solidarity: What you do not wish to be done to yourself, do not do to others.

NON-VIOLENCE AND RESPECT FOR LIFE

Article 5
Every person has a responsibility to respect life. No one has the right to injure, to torture, or to kill another human person. This does not exclude the right of justified self-defence of individuals or communities.

Article 6
Disputes between states, groups, or individuals should be resolved without violence. No government should tolerate or participate in acts of genocide or terrorism, nor should it abuse women, children, or any other civilians as instruments of war. Every citizen and public official has a responsibility to act in a peaceful, non-violent way.

Article 7
Every person is infinitely precious and must be protected unconditionally. The animals and the natural environment also demand protection. All people have a responsibility to protect the air, water, and soil of the earth for the sake of present inhabitants and future generations.

JUSTICE AND SOLIDARITY

Article 8
Every person has a responsibility to behave with integrity, honesty, and fairness. No person or group should rob or arbitrarily deprive any other person or group of their property.

Article 9
All people, given the necessary tools, have a responsibility to make serious efforts to overcome poverty, malnutrition, ignorance, and inequality. They should promote sustainable development all over the world in order to assure dignity, freedom, security, and justice for all people.

Article 10

All people have a responsibility to develop their talents through diligent endeavor; they should have equal access to education and to meaningful work. Everyone should lend support to the needy, the disadvantaged, the disabled, and to the victims of discrimination.

Article 11

All property and wealth must be used responsibly in accordance with justice and for the advancement of the human race. Economic and political power must not be handled as an instrument of domination, but in the service of economic justice and of the social order.

TRUTHFULNESS AND TOLERANCE

Article 12

Every person has a responsibility to speak and act truthfully. No one, however high or mighty, should speak lies. The right to privacy and to personal and professional confidentiality is to be respected. No one is obliged to tell all the truth to everyone all the time.

Article 13

No politicians, public servants, business leaders, scientists, writers, or artists are exempt from general ethical standards, nor are physicians, lawyers, and other professionals who have special duties to clients. Professional and other codes of ethics should reflect the priority of general standards such as those of truthfulness and fairness.

Article 14

The freedom of the media to inform the public and to criticize institutions of society and governmental actions, which is essential for a just society, must be used with responsibility and discretion. Freedom of the media carries a special responsibility for accurate and truthful reporting. Sensational reporting that degrades the human person or dignity must at all times be avoided.

Article 15

While religious freedom must be guaranteed, the representatives of religions have a special responsibility to avoid expressions of prejudice and acts of discrimination toward those of different beliefs. They should not incite or legitimize hatred, fanaticism, and religious wars but should foster tolerance and mutual respect between all people.

MUTUAL RESPECT AND PARTNERSHIP

Article 16

All men and all women have a responsibility to show respect to one another and understanding in their partnership. No one should subject another person to sexual exploitation or dependence. Rather, sexual partners should accept the responsibility of caring for each other's well-being.

Article 17

In all its cultural and religious varieties, marriage requires love, loyalty, and forgiveness and should aim at guaranteeing security and mutual support.

Article 18

Sensible family planning is the responsibility of every couple. The relationship between parents and children should reflect mutual love, respect, appreciation, and concern. No parents or other adults should exploit, abuse, or maltreat children.

CONCLUSION

Article 19

Nothing in this Declaration may be interpreted as implying for any state, group, or person any right to engage in any activity or to perform any act aimed at the destruction of any of the responsibilities, rights, and freedoms set forth in this Declaration and in the Universal Declaration of Human Rights of 1948.

ENDORSEMENT OF THE DECLARATION

The proposed Universal Declaration of Human Responsibilities has the endorsement of the following individuals:

InterAction Council Members

Helmut Schmidt (Honorary Chair)
>   Former Chancellor of the Federal Republic of Germany

Malcolm Fraser (Chair)
>   Former Prime Minister of Australia

Andries A. M. van Agt
>   Former Prime Minister of The Netherlands

Anand Panyarachun
>   Former Prime Minister of Thailand

Oscar Arias Sanchez
>   Former President of Costa Rica

Lord Callaghan of Cardiff
>   Former Prime Minister of the United Kingdom

Jimmy Carter
>   Former President of the United States

Miguel de la Madrid Hurtado
>   Former President of Mexico

Kurt Furgler
>   Former President of Switzerland

Valery Giscard d'Estaing
>   Former President of France

Felipe Gonzalez Marquez
>   Former Prime Minister of Spain

Mikhail S. Gorbachev
>   Chair of the Supreme Soviet and President of the Union of Soviet Socialist Republics

Selim Hoss
>   Former Prime Minister of Lebanon

Kenneth Kaunda
>   Former President of Zambia

Lee Kuan Yew
>   Former Prime Minister of Singapore

Kiichi Miyazawa
    Former Prime Minister of Japan
Misael Pastrana Borrero
    Former President of Colombia
Shimon Peres
    Former Prime Minister of Israel
Maria de Lourdes Pintasilgo
    Former Prime Minister of Portugal
Jose Sarney
    Former President of Brazil
Shin Hyon Hwak
    Former Prime Minister of the Republic of Korea
Kalevi Sorsa
    Former Prime Minister of Finland
Pierre Elliott Trudeau
    Former Prime Minister of Canada
Ola Ullsten
    Former Prime Minister of Sweden
George Vassiliou
    Former President of Cyprus
Franz Vranitzky
    Former President of Austria

Supporters

Ali Alatas, Minister for Foreign Affairs, Indonesia
Abdulaziz Al-Quraishi, former Chair of Saudi Arabian Monetary Agency (SAMA)
Lester Brown, President, Worldwatch Institute
Andre Chouraqui, Professor in Israel
John B. Cobb Jr., Claremont School of Theology, United States
Takako Doi, President, Japan Socialist Democratic Party
Kan Kato, President, Chiba University of Commerce, Japan
Henry A. Kissinger, former US Secretary of State
Teddy Kollek, Mayor of Jerusalem
William Laughlin, American entrepreneur
Chwasan Lee Kwang Jung, Head Dharma Master, Won Buddhism
Federico Mayor, Director-General, UNESCO
Robert S. McNamara, former President, World Bank

Rabbi Dr. J. Magonet, Principal, Leo Baeck College, London
Robert Muller, Rector, University for Peace, Costa Rica
Konrad Raiser, World Council of Churches
Jonathan Sacks, Chief Rabbi of the United Kingdom
Seijuro Shiokawa, former Minister of Home Affairs, Education, and
    Transportation of Japan
Rene Samuel Sirat, Grand Rabbi of France
Sir Sigmund Sternberg, International Council of Christians and Jews
Masayoshi Takemura, former Finance Minister of Japan
Gaston Thorn, former Prime Minister of Luxembourg
Paul Volcker, Chair, James D. Wolfensohn Inc.
Carl Friedrich v. Weizsäcker, Scientist
Richard v. Weizsäcker, former President of the Federal Republic of Germany
Mahmoud Zakzouk, Minister of Religion, Egypt

Participants and Special Guests

(Participants in preparatory meetings in Vienna, Austria, in March 1996 and April 1997, and special guests at the 15th Plenary Session in Noordwijk, The Netherlands, in June 1997)

Hans Küng, Tübingen University, Germany (academic advisor to the project)
Thomas Axworthy, CRB Foundation, Canada (academic advisor to the project)
Kim, Kyong-dong, Seoul National University, Korea (academic advisor to the
    project)
Cardinal Franz König, Vienna, Austria
Anna-Marie Aagaard, World Council of Churches
A.A. Mughram Al-Ghamdi, The King Fahad Academy, London, United
    Kingdom
M. Aram, World Conference on Religion & Peace
A.T. Ariyaratne, Sarvodaya Movement of Sri Lanka
Julia Ching, University of Toronto, Canada
Hassan Hanafi, University of Cairo, Egypt
Nagaharu Hayabusa, The Asahi Shimbun
Yersu Kim, Division of Philosophy and Ethics, UNESCO
Peter Landesmann, European Academy of Sciences
Lee, Seung-Yun, former Deputy Prime Minister and Minister of Economic
    Planning Board of the Republic of Korea

Flora Lewis, International Herald Tribune
Liu, Xiao-feng, Institute of Sino-Christian Studies
Teri McLuhan, Canadian author
Isamu Miyazaki, former State Minister, Economic Planning Agency of Japan
J. J. N. Rost Onnes, Executive Vice President, ABN AMRO Bank
James Ottley, Anglican observer at the United Nations
Richard Rorty, Stanford Humanities Centre, United States
L. M. Singhvi, High Commissioner for India
Marjorie Hewitt Suchocki, Claremont School of Theology, United States
Seiken Sugiura, House of Representatives of Japan
Koji Watanabe, former Japanese Ambassador to Russia
Woo, Seong-yong, Munhwa Ilbo
Wu Xuequian, Vice Chairman, Chinese People's Political Consultative
    Conference
Alexander Yakovlev, former Member, Presidential Council of the Soviet Union

Queen's Policy Studies
Recent Publications

The Queen's Policy Studies Series is dedicated to the exploration of major public policy issues that confront governments and society in Canada and other nations.

Our books are available from good bookstores everywhere, including the Queen's University bookstore (http://www.campusbookstore.com/). McGill-Queen's University Press is the exclusive world representative and distributor of books in the series. A full catalogue and ordering information may be found on their web site (http://mqup.mcgill.ca/).

School of Policy Studies

Immigration and Integration in Canada in the Twenty-first Century, John Biles, Meyer Burstein, and James Frideres (eds.), 2008
Paper ISBN 978-1-55339-216-3 Cloth ISBN 978-1-55339-217-0

Robert Stanfield's Canada, Richard Clippingdale, 2008   ISBN 978-1-55339-218-7

Exploring Social Insurance: Can a Dose of Europe Cure Canadian Health Care Finance?
Colleen Flood, Mark Stabile, and Carolyn Tuohy (eds.), 2008
Paper ISBN 978-1-55339-136-4 Cloth ISBN 978-1-55339-213-2

Canada in NORAD, 1957–2007: A History, Joseph T. Jockel, 2007
Paper ISBN 978-1-55339-134-0 Cloth ISBN 978-1-55339-135-7

Canadian Public-Sector Financial Management, Andrew Graham, 2007
Paper ISBN 978-1-55339-120-3 Cloth ISBN 978-1-55339-121-0

Emerging Approaches to Chronic Disease Management in Primary Health Care,
John Dorland and Mary Ann McColl (eds.), 2007
Paper ISBN 978-1-55339-130-2 Cloth ISBN 978-1-55339-131-9

Fulfilling Potential, Creating Success: Perspectives on Human Capital Development,
Garnett Picot, Ron Saunders and Arthur Sweetman (eds.), 2007
Paper ISBN 978-1-55339-127-2 Cloth ISBN 978-1-55339-128-9

Reinventing Canadian Defence Procurement: A View from the Inside, Alan S. Williams, 2006
Paper ISBN 0-9781693-0-1 (Published in association with Breakout Educational Network)

SARS in Context: Memory, History, Policy, Jacalyn Duffin and Arthur Sweetman (eds.), 2006
Paper ISBN 978-0-7735-3194-9 Cloth ISBN 978-0-7735-3193-2
(Published in association with McGill-Queen's University Press)

Dreamland: How Canada's Pretend Foreign Policy has Undermined Sovereignty, Roy Rempel, 2006
Paper ISBN 1-55339-118-7 Cloth ISBN 1-55339-119-5
(Published in association with Breakout Educational Network)

Canadian and Mexican Security in the New North America: Challenges and Prospects,
Jordi Díez (ed.), 2006   Paper ISBN 978-1-55339-123-4 Cloth ISBN 978-1-55339-122-7

Global Networks and Local Linkages: The Paradox of Cluster Development in an Open Economy, David A. Wolfe and Matthew Lucas (eds.), 2005
Paper ISBN 1-55339-047-4 Cloth ISBN 1-55339-048-2

Choice of Force: Special Operations for Canada, David Last and Bernd Horn (eds.), 2005
Paper ISBN 1-55339-044-X Cloth ISBN 1-55339-045-8

Force of Choice: Perspectives on Special Operations, Bernd Horn, J. Paul de B. Taillon, and
David Last (eds.), 2004   Paper ISBN 1-55339-042-3 Cloth 1-55339-043-1

New Missions, Old Problems, Douglas L. Bland, David Last, Franklin Pinch, and Alan Okros
(eds.), 2004   Paper ISBN 1-55339-034-2 Cloth 1-55339-035-0

*The North American Democratic Peace: Absence of War and Security Institution-Building in
Canada-US Relations, 1867-1958*, Stéphane Roussel, 2004
Paper ISBN 0-88911-937-6 Cloth 0-88911-932-2

Implementing Primary Care Reform: Barriers and Facilitators, Ruth Wilson, S.E.D. Shortt
and John Dorland (eds.), 2004   Paper ISBN 1-55339-040-7 Cloth 1-55339-041-5

Social and Cultural Change, David Last, Franklin Pinch, Douglas L. Bland, and
Alan Okros (eds.), 2004   Paper ISBN 1-55339-032-6 Cloth 1-55339-033-4

Clusters in a Cold Climate: Innovation Dynamics in a Diverse Economy, David A. Wolfe and
Matthew Lucas (eds.), 2004   Paper ISBN 1-55339-038-5 Cloth 1-55339-039-3

Canada Without Armed Forces? Douglas L. Bland (ed.), 2004
Paper ISBN 1-55339-036-9 Cloth 1-55339-037-7

Campaigns for International Security: Canada's Defence Policy at the Turn of the Century,
Douglas L. Bland and Sean M. Maloney, 2004
Paper ISBN 0-88911-962-7 Cloth 0-88911-964-3

Understanding Innovation in Canadian Industry, Fred Gault (ed.), 2003
Paper ISBN 1-55339-030-X Cloth 1-55339-031-8

Delicate Dances: Public Policy and the Nonprofit Sector, Kathy L. Brock (ed.), 2003
Paper ISBN 0-88911-953-8 Cloth 0-88911-955-4

Beyond the National Divide: Regional Dimensions of Industrial Relations, Mark Thompson,
Joseph B. Rose and Anthony E. Smith (eds.), 2003
Paper ISBN 0-88911-963-5 Cloth 0-88911-965-1

The Nonprofit Sector in Interesting Times: Case Studies in a Changing Sector,
Kathy L. Brock and Keith G. Banting (eds.), 2003
Paper ISBN 0-88911-941-4 Cloth 0-88911-943-0

Clusters Old and New: The Transition to a Knowledge Economy in Canada's Regions,
David A. Wolfe (ed.), 2003   Paper ISBN 0-88911-959-7 Cloth 0-88911-961-9

The e-Connected World: Risks and Opportunities, Stephen Coleman (ed.), 2003
Paper ISBN 0-88911-945-7 Cloth 0-88911-947-3

Knowledge Clusters and Regional Innovation: Economic Development in Canada,
J. Adam Holbrook and David A. Wolfe (eds.), 2002
Paper ISBN 0-88911-919-8 Cloth 0-88911-917-1

Lessons of Everyday Law/Le droit du quotidien, Roderick Alexander Macdonald, 2002
Paper ISBN 0-88911-915-5 Cloth 0-88911-913-9

*Improving Connections Between Governments and Nonprofit and Voluntary Organizations:
Public Policy and the Third Sector*, Kathy L. Brock (ed.), 2002
Paper ISBN 0-88911-899-X Cloth 0-88911-907-4

Governing Food: Science, Safety and Trade, Peter W.B. Phillips and Robert Wolfe (eds.), 2001
Paper ISBN 0-88911-897-3 Cloth 0-88911-903-1

The Nonprofit Sector and Government in a New Century, Kathy L. Brock and
Keith G. Banting (eds.), 2001   Paper ISBN 0-88911-901-5 Cloth 0-88911-905-8

The Dynamics of Decentralization: Canadian Federalism and British Devolution,
Trevor C. Salmon and Michael Keating (eds.), 2001   ISBN 0-88911-895-7

Institute of Intergovernmental Relations

Comparing Federal Systems, Third Edition, Ronald L. Watts, 2008 ISBN 978-1-55339-188-3

*Canada: The State of the Federation 2005: Quebec and Canada in the New Century – New
Dynamics, New Opportunities,* vol. 19, Michael Murphy (ed.), 2007
Paper ISBN 978-1-55339-018-3 Cloth ISBN 978-1-55339-017-6

Spheres of Governance: Comparative Studies of Cities in Multilevel Governance Systems,
Harvey Lazar and Christian Leuprecht (eds.), 2007
Paper ISBN 978-1-55339-019-0 Cloth ISBN 978-1-55339-129-6

Canada: The State of the Federation 2004, vol. 18, *Municipal-Federal-Provincial Relations
in Canada,* Robert Young and Christian Leuprecht (eds.), 2006
Paper ISBN 1-55339-015-6 Cloth ISBN 1-55339-016-4

Canadian Fiscal Arrangements: What Works, What Might Work Better, Harvey Lazar (ed.), 2005
Paper ISBN 1-55339-012-1 Cloth ISBN 1-55339-013-X

Canada: The State of the Federation 2003, vol. 17, *Reconfiguring Aboriginal-State Relations,*
Michael Murphy (ed.), 2005   Paper ISBN 1-55339-010-5 Cloth ISBN 1-55339-011-3

Canada: The State of the Federation 2002, vol. 16, *Reconsidering the Institutions of
Canadian Federalism,* J. Peter Meekison, Hamish Telford and Harvey Lazar (eds.), 2004
Paper ISBN 1-55339-009-1 Cloth ISBN 1-55339-008-3

*Federalism and Labour Market Policy: Comparing Different Governance and Employment
Strategies,* Alain Noël (ed.), 2004   Paper ISBN 1-55339-006-7 Cloth ISBN 1-55339-007-5

The Impact of Global and Regional Integration on Federal Systems: A Comparative Analysis,
Harvey Lazar, Hamish Telford and Ronald L. Watts (eds.), 2003
Paper ISBN 1-55339-002-4 Cloth ISBN 1-55339-003-2

Canada: The State of the Federation 2001, vol. 15, *Canadian Political Culture(s) in Transition,*
Hamish Telford and Harvey Lazar (eds.), 2002
Paper ISBN 0-88911-863-9 Cloth ISBN 0-88911-851-5

Federalism, Democracy and Disability Policy in Canada, Alan Puttee (ed.), 2002
Paper ISBN 0-88911-855-8 Cloth ISBN 1-55339-001-6, ISBN 0-88911-845-0 (set)

Comparaison des régimes fédéraux, 2ᵉ éd., Ronald L. Watts, 2002   ISBN 1-55339-005-9

Health Policy and Federalism: A Comparative Perspective on Multi-Level Governance,
Keith G. Banting and Stan Corbett (eds.), 2001
Paper ISBN 0-88911-859-0 Cloth ISBN 1-55339-000-8, ISBN 0-88911-845-0 (set)

Disability and Federalism: Comparing Different Approaches to Full Participation,
David Cameron and Fraser Valentine (eds.), 2001
Paper ISBN 0-88911-857-4 Cloth ISBN 0-88911-867-1, ISBN 0-88911-845-0 (set)

Federalism, Democracy and Health Policy in Canada, Duane Adams (ed.), 2001
Paper ISBN 0-88911-853-1 Cloth ISBN 0-88911-865-5, ISBN 0-88911-845-0 (set)

John Deutsch Institute for the Study of Economic Policy

The 2006 Federal Budget: Rethinking Fiscal Priorities, Charles M. Beach, Michael Smart and Thomas A. Wilson (eds.), 2007
Paper ISBN 978-1-55339-125-8 Cloth ISBN 978-1-55339-126-6

Health Services Restructuring in Canada: New Evidence and New Directions, Charles M. Beach, Richard P. Chaykowksi, Sam Shortt, France St-Hilaire and Arthur Sweetman (eds.), 2006 Paper ISBN 978-1-55339-076-3 Cloth ISBN 978-1-55339-075-6

A Challenge for Higher Education in Ontario, Charles M. Beach (ed.), 2005
Paper ISBN 1-55339-074-1 Cloth ISBN 1-55339-073-3

Current Directions in Financial Regulation, Frank Milne and Edwin H. Neave (eds.), Policy Forum Series no. 40, 2005 Paper ISBN 1-55339-072-5 Cloth ISBN 1-55339-071-7

Higher Education in Canada, Charles M. Beach, Robin W. Boadway and R. Marvin McInnis (eds.), 2005 Paper ISBN 1-55339-070-9 Cloth ISBN 1-55339-069-5

Financial Services and Public Policy, Christopher Waddell (ed.), 2004
Paper ISBN 1-55339-068-7 Cloth ISBN 1-55339-067-9

The 2003 Federal Budget: Conflicting Tensions, Charles M. Beach and Thomas A. Wilson (eds.), Policy Forum Series no. 39, 2004
Paper ISBN 0-88911-958-9 Cloth ISBN 0-88911-956-2

Canadian Immigration Policy for the 21st Century, Charles M. Beach, Alan G. Green and Jeffrey G. Reitz (eds.), 2003 Paper ISBN 0-88911-954-6 Cloth ISBN 0-88911-952-X

Framing Financial Structure in an Information Environment, Thomas J. Courchene and Edwin H. Neave (eds.), Policy Forum Series no. 38, 2003
Paper ISBN 0-88911-950-3 Cloth ISBN 0-88911-948-1

Towards Evidence-Based Policy for Canadian Education/Vers des politiques canadiennes d'éducation fondées sur la recherche, Patrice de Broucker and/et Arthur Sweetman (eds./ dirs.), 2002 Paper ISBN 0-88911-946-5 Cloth ISBN 0-88911-944-9

Money, Markets and Mobility: Celebrating the Ideas of Robert A. Mundell, Nobel Laureate in Economic Sciences, Thomas J. Courchene (ed.), 2002
Paper ISBN 0-88911-820-5 Cloth ISBN 0-88911-818-3

The State of Economics in Canada: Festschrift in Honour of David Slater, Patrick Grady and Andrew Sharpe (eds.), 2001 Paper ISBN 0-88911-942-2 Cloth ISBN 0-88911-940-6

The 2000 Federal Budget: Retrospect and Prospect, Paul A.R. Hobson and Thomas A. Wilson (eds.), 2001 Policy Forum Series no. 37, 2001
Paper ISBN 0-88911-816-7 Cloth ISBN 0-88911-814-0

Our publications may be purchased at leading bookstores, including the Queen's University Bookstore
(http://www.campusbookstore.com/), or can be ordered online from: McGill-Queen's University Press, at
http://mqup.mcgill.ca/ordering.php

For more information about new and backlist titles from Queen's Policy Studies, visit the McGill-Queen's
University Press web site at:
http://mqup.mcgill.ca/